LIBERAL DEMOCRACY, LAW AND THE CITIZEN SPEAKER

This book delivers an original, theoretically informed analysis of the legal regulation of online speech. Rejecting the narrow pluralism of elitist and deliberative accounts of the citizen's role in political discourse, the book defends a participatory account of speech in non-deliberative settings. The latter account of political pluralism best captures the republican democratic aspiration for popular, on-going authorship of the laws and the centrality of freedom to dissent in democratic theory. The legal and policy implications for governments and social media platforms of this inclusive envisioning of public discourse are then elaborated upon.

In the digital world, anyone with access to the internet can be a speaker. Speech on public platforms has become democratised. At the same time, aspects of online speech are plainly problematic. Concerns exist about disinformation, 'fake news', 'deep fakes', 'weaponised speech' and 'trolls'. Offensive speech and the polarising effects of robustly expressed political opinion are also troublesome. These assorted downsides of democratised speech are said to undermine the integrity of democratic processes and institutions. Public debate is distorted and coarsened and the electorate are misled. How ought the liberal democratic state respond to these challenges?

The discussion is intended to be read by academics and researchers with interests in democratic theory, digital communications and freedom of expression. It offers a stimulating and distinctive contribution to debates about online speech.

Liberal Democracy, Law and the Citizen Speaker

Regulating Online Speech

Ian Cram

•HART•

OXFORD • LONDON • NEW YORK • NEW DELHI • SYDNEY

HART PUBLISHING

Bloomsbury Publishing Plc

Kemp House, Chawley Park, Cumnor Hill, Oxford, OX2 9PH, UK

1385 Broadway, New York, NY 10018, USA

29 Earlsfort Terrace, Dublin 2, Ireland

HART PUBLISHING, the Hart/Stag logo, BLOOMSBURY and the Diana logo are trademarks of Bloomsbury Publishing Plc

First published in Great Britain 2022

A catalogue record for this book is available from the British Library.

A catalogue record for this book is available from the Library of Congress.

ISBN: HB: 978-1-50994-582-5
ePDF: 978-1-50994-584-9
ePub: 978-1-50994-583-2

Typeset by Compuscript Ltd, Shannon

CONTENTS

1

Damaging Democracy? 'Fake News' and Moral Panics

Introduction

How ought the state/social media platforms in a liberal democracy respond to the following instances of online expression?

> On Election Day the leader of the main opposition party claims on Twitter that party supporters are being prevented from voting at polling stations.
>
> A candidate for elected office alters her Wikipedia entry to make a false claim about her past military record in order to gain credibility with voters.
>
> In the midst of the global spread of a virus that can be fatal for persons with serious comorbidities but generally non-fatal for persons with reasonable health, a group of politicians, economists and scientists upload to YouTube a vlog that disputes some of the claims made by the government's scientific advisers. Specifically, the YouTube vlog disputes aspects of the scientific and human behavioural basis of the worst-case scenario predictions made by the government's advisers.
>
> During the same pandemic, an anti-vaccination group encourages its supporters to post on their social media accounts the reasons why they have refused to be vaccinated.
>
> A community group concerned about water quality in local rivers publishes a series of vlogs on YouTube in which it knowingly exaggerates the ill-health symptoms of a group of recent bathers in order to prompt the water company into action.
>
> An anti-government website publishes what it claims are leaked documents that purport to show how government ministers and party donors have profited personally from government contracts awarded to private suppliers of protective health-care equipment. The website contains inaccurate information and personally abusive language when describing the conduct of individual ministers and party donors.

How ought the modern liberal democratic state respond to the fact of many speakers with something to say about politics? In the past, technological advances in communication have been heralded by some as bringing forth an era of greater democratic scrutiny over the acts of elected office holders. John Stuart Mill for example saw the potential of newspapers as mass forms of communication to keep politicians responsive to the discussion of public affairs in his 1861 *Considerations on Representative Government*:

> where unbounded publicity, and an ever-present newspaper press, give the representative assurance that his every act will be immediately known, discussed, and judged by his constituents, and that he is always either gaining or losing ground in the estimation.[1]

More recently in the Web 2.0 epoch, the democratising possibilities of technological progress have been stressed. Yochai Benkler in *The Wealth of Networks* (2006) noted the expanded speaking opportunities for non-elites. Individuals would become more actively engaged as participators in public conversations and debates with others in the networked public sphere. This represented a democratisation of the public sphere when compared alongside the public sphere of much of the twentieth century where a relatively small number of mass media owners controlled what got published and when.[2] At the same time, Benkler noted the tendency for internet users to cluster around a few dominant sites and raised the possibility that search engines such as Google could become so dominant on the desktop that it would act as a supernode through which much internet traffic would be channelled. Such a bottleneck could present a 'serious theoretical and empirical challenge to the claim … (of a) meaningfully decentralize(d) democratic discourse'.[3] A diverse set of speakers might be newly empowered to communicate their ideas and opinions but could they be sure of connecting with their intended audiences?

Fast forward to the present day and the dominant narratives around digital expression are much less sanguine. Indeed, the tone of much discussion is suggestive of a twenty-first century moral panic. Take for example Bartlett's *The People Vs Tech – How the internet is killing democracy (and how we save it)* published in 2018, where the author argues that in the next generation, 'Either tech will destroy democracy and the social order as we know it, or politics will stamp its control over the digital revolution'.[4] Concerned by monopolistic tech companies' amassing of users' personal data and the customisation of online content encountered by users that pushes us ever more insistently towards similar sorts of content, Bartlett challenges his readers to become 'better versions' of themselves by a series of self-help moves.[5] Others more directly accuse internet platforms and online speakers

[1] JS Mill *Essay on Representative Government*, ch XI, Of the Duration of Parliaments.

[2] *The Wealth of Networks – How Social Production Transforms Markets and Freedom* (New Haven, Yale University Press, 2006) see especially ch 7.

[3] ibid at 241.

[4] London, Ebury Press, 2018, back cover.

[5] These include 'Smash Your Echo Chamber', 'Fight Distraction', 'Update Election Campaign Laws'.

of fomenting a range of activities that are harmful to both individuals and societal interests. The indictment sheet reads that online speech is responsible for encouraging terrorist activity, an increase in acts of hatred directed at ethnic minorities and a range of damaging addictive personal behaviours. A specific allegation is that the structure and content of online political expression poses serious risks to democratic systems of government on account of features such as 'fake news', targeted, untransparent advertising (sometimes from foreign governments and their agents) and the encouragement of echo chambers. In respect of 'fake news', the quality of public discourse and informed democratic scrutiny of office holders is undermined by torrents of misinformation and deliberate falsehoods. A fairly typical analysis of the resulting serious harms states:

> An always-on, real-time information *tsunami* creates the perfect environment for the spread of falsehoods, conspiracy theories, rumors, and 'leaks.' Unsubstantiated claims and narratives *go viral* while fact checking efforts struggle to keep up. Members of the public, including researchers and investigative journalists may not have the expertise, tools, or time to verify claims. By the time they do, the falsehoods may have already embedded themselves in the collective consciousness. Meanwhile, fresh scandals or outlandish claims are *continuously raining down* on users, mixing fact with fiction[6] [emphasis added].

Mueller remarks that it is in the nature of such analyses to direct moral outrage at a 'single, identifiable target when the real problems often have more complex roots'.[7] Proponents of the digital moral panic thesis take the overly simplistic view that 'the serpent of social media has driven us out of an Eden of rationality and moderation'.[8] As the quote above illustrates, moral panics tend not to produce measured discussion of the problem. Rather they make it more likely that policymakers will rush to implement a set of disproportionate responses.

Social media platforms stand accused of having facilitated the deformation of hitherto elite-curated, rational political discourses by an 'ugly populism'. This is apparent in various accounts of the crisis of 'fake news' that is said to threaten the very foundations of democracy. Written in 2017 Matthew D'Ancona's *Post-Truth – The New War on Truth and How to Fight Back* sees evidence of the triumph of an irrational, emotive, illiberal politics that has overseen the victories of Donald Trump in the US and the Leave campaign in the UK's EU Referendum. This is the Web 2.0 victory of the visceral and the deceptively straightforward speaker who peddles 'fake news' to voters, except for D'Ancona, no quote marks around the term are needed. For D'Ancona, truth in politics is always discernible. It is just that we have lost trust in those who speak the truth since about 2016. There is an urgent

[6] R Deibert, 'The Road to Digital Unfreedom: Three Painful Truths about Social Media' (2019) 30 *Jo. of Democracy* 25, 32.

[7] M Mueller, 'Challenging the Social Media Moral Panic' (2019) 876 *Policy Analysis* (Cato Institute) 23 July, drawing on Stanley Cohen's seminal work *Folk Devils and Moral Panics* (Abingdon, Routledge, 2011).

[8] Mueller ibid at 3.

need to reconnect to a form of politics in which charismatic leaders (for D'Ancona a modern-day Lincoln, Franklin Roosevelt, Churchill, Martin Luther King) will be able to give contemporary direction to the Enlightenment's command to pursue the truth via reason and civility.

Some understandably might cavil with the implicit assumption in *Post Truth* of an earlier, golden era of non-partisan management of entirely truthful news stories by political elites and their corporate, media-owning supporters and journalist employees. Are we meant to be looking at the twentieth century (Beaverbrook and Rothermere, Hearst and Pulitzer?), or cast our eyes further back in time into the nineteenth century to revisit this halcyon period? D'Ancona's diagnosis may be felt to have more to do with a personal opinion that no rational voter could have voted for Trump or to leave the EU. Nonetheless, the worry that democracy has been seriously damaged by a 'post-truth' form of highly emotive politics is a commonly articulated concern and raises vitally important questions about freedom of political expression and media policy in a mature liberal democracy such as our own.

Should the field of politics be left only to those who establish the truth of their claims? Should I be prevented from blogging or tweeting about what I claim is the government's mismanagement of the economy or the failure of global markets and capitalism if I am adjudged not to have foregrounded the truth of that claim? How would I go about doing this? And who sits in judgment on whether my blog has failed to reach that threshold? Is it a government agency or a fact checker working for a tech giant? Do I go to prison if I repeatedly fail this test? Or does it suffice merely to incentivise social media platforms via government regulatory policy to remove unproven claims/deliberate lies? Punishing speakers and their media outlets for having told untruths about the government in democratic societies ostensibly committed to freedom of expression ought to make supporters of the move pause for thought. It is the sort of response usually associated with totalitarian regimes.

Viewed in historical perspective, there is a fairly clear pattern of repressive official responses to the growth of literacy and technological advances in communications systems. In pre-Reformation England for example, the Catholic Church had exercised control over the printed word. This control passed into the hands of the state after the Reformation. In the late sixteenth century, ordinances and regulations forbade the printing of books and pamphlets outside London, Oxford and Cambridge.[9] This prohibition was intended to prevent the publication of criticism of the Anglican Church. After the English Civil War, as literacy spread and printing presses brought the written word to more and more people, Cromwell's *Stationers' Company* was charged with registering all printed works. The Government, army and private citizens of the Commonwealth were all involved in the suppression of immoral and dangerous literature.[10] Bradshaw's Press Act 1649 and the Printing

[9] J Walker, 'The Censorship of the Press during the Reign of Charles II' (1950) 35 *History* 219.

[10] J McElligott, *Royalism, Print and Censorship in Revolutionary England* (Woodbridge, Boybell Press, 2007).

and Printer's Ordinance 1655 imposed strict licensing systems to uphold Puritan morality and suppress pro-Royalist sentiment. Greater levels of literacy and readership among the population in the late eighteenth century made more urgent the state's need to clamp down on radical publications supporting the American colonists and French revolutionaries.[11] By the early part of the twentieth century regimes of radio and subsequently television broadcasting were much more regulated than their print counterparts. This can be explained on account primarily of the (then) scarcity of bandwidth available to a few broadcasters only, together with the idea that the spoken word and image enjoyed a 'uniquely pervasive'[12] communicative reach across the listening/viewing audience. The public interest in maintaining a wholesome environment required close supervision by the state in terms of the content and delivery of programming. Today, when the bandwidth scarcity argument no longer offers a technological reason for limiting the number of online speakers, arguments for greater regulation of the digital sphere rest on the types of claim adverted to above.

Issues of Principle – How Open Should the Channels of Political Communication be in a Liberal Democracy?

The responses that readers give to the series of hypothetical scenarios posed at the beginning of this chapter will, in all probability, divide along a number of axes. For example, those who place a high premium on a truthful public domain will instinctively be wary of extending speech protection to deliberate falsehoods and so happily endorse legal and extra-legal means of excluding such statements from the public sphere. Others who attach importance to political pluralism and to challenging government narratives will be inclined to be more relaxed about the public dissemination of falsehoods, doubtless pointing in the case of anti-government expression to the ample counterspeech opportunities afforded to ministers and officials.

Responses to each scenario will rest in turn upon deeper-level commitments to a particular version of liberal democracy and the role(s) of the citizen within that system of government.[13] In chapter two I describe three main kinds of liberal democratic state with quite distinct understandings of citizen participation in political decision-making. These are respectively elitist democracies, deliberative democracies and agonistic democracies. For present purposes, a brief sketch of the central components of each version of liberal democracy is offered.

[11] Thomas Paine was convicted of seditious libel in 1792 for declaring his support for the French Revolution in *Rights of Man – An Answer to Mr Burke's Attack on the French Revolution.*

[12] The phrase is taken from Justice Stevens' opinion in *FCC v Pacifica* 438 US 726 (1978) at para 58.

[13] CE Baker, *Media, Markets and Democracy* (New York, CUP, 2002) ch 6.

Edwin Baker identifies as elitist liberal democracies those in which the complexity of the modern world is said to demand a 'vanguard leadership of elites or skilled experts' who possess the technical abilities and skills to navigate wisely through difficult political problems. Ordinary citizens are called upon from time to time to assent or refuse their assent to rival sets of elites in a competition for electoral votes.[14] They are not required to be actively involved in overseeing the daily business of governing since they lack the necessary competences to fulfil this role. Neither are ordinary citizens expected to engage as regular participants in questions about the normative validity of existing constitutional structures. The framing of political choices is to be left to professional politicians and organised interests. It follows from this that, provided a free professional press is able to expose elite corruption or incompetence that enable voters to reach an overall judgment about incumbent office holders, their policies and whether their rivals possess greater integrity and offer better policies, no effort need be made by the state (or professional media) to promote greater and more meaningful levels of citizen participation in politics. On this account, the citizen is to all intents and purposes the passive recipient of the political expression of organised political parties and a professional media commentariat. The opportunity to vote (accompanied by a reasonable turnout on Election Day) is usually considered sufficient in elite accounts of democracy to enable the winning party to claim a sociological or descriptive (ie non-normative) form of legitimacy to rule where the ruled accept the claims of winners to hold office and make laws and policies.

Normative accounts of democratic legitimacy can be found in two republican variants of liberal democracy, namely deliberative democracy and agonist democracy. Each variant stresses the opportunities for citizens as political equals to participate meaningfully in political decision-making. Citizens must be the active and regular authors of the political structures and rules that govern their lives for those structures and rules to enjoy democratic legitimacy. Deliberative democrats seek a set of inclusive participatory procedures and public spaces alongside representative institutions that will enhance ordinary citizens' engagement in political decision-making and, over time moreover, improve the quality of their contributions. The political conversations that occur in these spaces among political equals are to be reasoned, reflective, empathetic and aim to settle at the end of the deliberative process around consensus positions that advance the common good. Though undoubtedly committed to the notion of the citizen as an active and regular author of the laws of their community, deliberative democrats also believe that there are right answers to contested policy questions and want to be able to rule out certain kinds of discursive outcomes as incompatible with the common good. They also want to exclude contributions that are not demonstrably couched in appeals to

[14] He associates this position principally with inter alia Joseph Schumpeter, *Capitalism, Socialism and Democracy* (New York, Harper & Row, 1942) and Walter Lippman, *Public Opinion* (New York, Free Press, 1922) see *Media, Markets and Democracy* at 130.

public reason, logic and evidence. It follows that speakers in deliberative democratic settings are subject to an accompanying set of duties and responsibilities. These constraints inevitably narrow the types (and tone) of contributions from citizens that deliberative democrats are prepared to extend protection to under a principled commitment to freedom of expression.

Agonist democrats for their part also value inclusive participatory structures of political decision-making. They differ crucially from deliberative democrats in that they do not see political discourse as primarily concerned with overcoming divergent outlooks between differently situated participants and ultimately yielding unforced consensus among them. They are sceptical of appeals to rationality and public reason which screen out/make less visible certain viewpoints. For agonist democrats, the essence of political discourse is conflict between plural perspectives and thus the state should not try to eliminate the expression of difference, nor should participatory procedures be designed with a view to surmounting of those differences. Disagreement and disharmony are ineliminable facts of political life. Compromise and stabilisations of conflict are likely only to offer temporary states of accord between combatants. For agonists, what makes the polity legitimate in normative terms is the ability of individuals and groups to find public spaces to articulate their diverse perspectives and challenge dominant understandings of the just society. The popular sovereignty component of agonistic accounts of democracy entails the radical claim that the central norms and institutions of liberal democracy lie within the revisionary powers of citizens.

Notwithstanding some recent experimentation with citizens' assemblies in person and online in some liberal democracies,[15] the dominance of hierarchical centrist political parties and their technocratic managerial programmes in advanced liberal democracies and supranational (eg EU) governance structures may be said to exemplify modern-day elitist or oligarchic forms of rule. Governance and decision-making are left to a narrow set of centrist political elites and a technocratic class of administrators to manage with intermittent renewals of voter endorsement at the ballot box. For republicans, these modes of governance limit drastically the possibilities for political participation and thus active political choice among citizens. In 1958, Arendt had noted in *The Human Condition* that the liberal technocratic state was increasingly one in which genuine politics among plural human beings was being eradicated as human existence was governed by the economic processes of production and consumption. The final stage of the technocratic labouring society 'demands of its members a sheer automatic functioning, as though individual life had actually been submerged in the over-all life process of the species'.[16]

[15] Referenda on aspects of constitutional reform (sometimes previously discussed in citizen assemblies) have also featured in some liberal democracies. Although often merely advisory rather than binding, these forms of direct participation in law reform are discussed further in ch 2.

[16] *The Human Condition* (Chicago, University of Chicago Press, 1998) 2nd edn at 322.

In the intervening years, the popular sovereignty component in liberal democracy has become more marginalised. By 2004 Colin Crouch's *Post Democracy* was describing a diminished role for nationally elected political institutions and loss of national sovereignty in relation to multinational corporate interests:

> The fundamental cause of democratic decline in contemporary politics is the major imbalance now developing between the role of corporate interests and those of virtually all other groups. Taken alongside the inevitable entropy of democracy, this is leading to politics once again becoming an affair of closed elites, as it was in pre-democratic times.[17]

Crouch's work was written before the global financial crash. In a later article published in 2016, he noted that the response of governments and international organisations was to march 'a good way further down that (post-democratic) road'.[18] The most extreme instance of this post-democratic phase of rule making for Crouch was experienced in the euro zone. Here a cobbled together group made up of the European Commission, the European Central Bank, the International Monetary Fund and representatives from the banking sector were able to dictate financial rescue terms to debtor states in southern Europe and Ireland. Democratic cover for these punitive packages was provided by acts of ratification in national legislatures. The only directly elected body of the European Union, the European Parliament, had no role.[19]

The deliberative democrats' valiant attempt to engage more of us in decision-making structures more often does challenge this type of remote rule making by political elites. However we need to question whether, if its promise of wider political participation is conditional upon participants' commitment to rational, reasonable and civil forms of discourse, whether, and if so to what extent, these side constraints impact on the plurality of political expression. Specifically, we might enquire whether a new class of online speakers lacking professional training and access to in-house editorial/legal services are expected to reach the standards of 'responsible' journalism before they are permitted to communicate with audiences. Does the deliberative democratic solution to elite-dominated political expression impose significant constraints of its own making on the preferred structures of participatory decision-making? What do deliberative democrats have to say about debates around 'fake news'? A desire to ensure better-quality exchanges in the public sphere might countenance a collaborative approach between the state and social media platforms to remove unhelpful and deforming contributions. Fact-checking organisations might be given scope to help purify the zone of public discussion. Are there any dangers to political pluralism and active citizen participation in an approach that allows existing office holders and corporations to determine what views are fit to be expressed?

[17] Cambridge, Polity, 2004, at 104.
[18] C Crouch, 'The March Towards Post-Democracy, Ten Years On' (2016) 87 *Pol. Quarterly* 71.
[19] ibid at 73.

Tensions between Liberalism and Democracy

A major aim of this book is to develop a clearer understanding both at the level of theory and in the application of legal norms how opportunities for digital political participation in the liberal democratic constitution are being closed off and to ask what this entails for meaningful self government. One possible underlying explanation, I suggest, may be located in our thinking about the core meaning of the liberal democratic constitution which we tend to understand to be largely satisfied by the precepts of liberalism, as opposed to the claims of democratic self-rule. The claims of institutional stability and overarching constructs such as the rule of law, separation of powers and protection of minority rights are to the fore, even if these are understood in divergent ways among proponents of liberal constitutionalism. The parts of liberal democratic constitutionalism that stress the popular (and disruptive) basis of legitimate rule making have receded. Formal constitutional settlements which expressly adopt abstracted conceptions of the rule of law and universal human rights claims since 1945 are to the fore signifying the pre-eminence of liberal Enlightenment commitments to progress towards the better society via rational enquiry and reasoned deliberation among consensus-seeking political equals.

From an admittedly personal and highly anecdotal perspective as a teacher of constitutional law in the UK, I am struck by the high levels of support among law students for liberal forms of juridified rule rather than rule by popularly authored, democratic systems of government. This is apparent for example in their relative enthusiasm for undemocratically (judicially) determined rights and, correlatively, their more distrustful attitudes towards majoritarian (political) systems of rule making. This may simply reflect their opinions about existing public office holders in the UK. Is it wholly misconceived however to read my students' support as endorsing a more general critique of popular forms of government per se as in Jean Bodin's 'refuge of all disorderly spirits, rebels, traitors, outcasts who encourage and help the lower orders to ruin the great'?[20] Probably so. Some doubtless would say that support for an enhanced judicial role in determining policy questions is just an early career manifestation of the sort of self-interested reasoning that professional lawyers are prone to. Others would point more concretely to the anti-Brexit stance of younger voters and make links to the *Miller 1* and *2* litigation where, from a Remain perspective, the senior judiciary was seen to stand up to the Executive's improper attempts to avoid parliamentary scrutiny. More generally, it might be thought that judicial interventions are seen as valuable in advancing progressive political agendas.

One could look for example at the evolving nature of judicially determined environmental protections under Article 8 of the European Convention on Human Rights. The expanded scope of Article 8 protection for environmental interests

[20] *Les six livres de la Republique* (Paris, Librairie Generale Francaise, 1993) at 529.

in court actions brought against the policies of democratically elected national governments would seem to lend credence to this view.[21] If correct, it would make my students' endorsement of court-based resolutions of political disputes contingent upon whether judicial outcomes are seen as more aligned with their preferred positions on 'social/environmental justice' concerns than policies emanating from the legislature. To imagine a different scenario where a popularly elected left of centre government wishes to impose higher taxes on the wealthiest sections of the community or remove the favourable tax regime enjoyed by the independent (non-state) school sector, what would happen to current levels of support for judicial intervention if the Supreme Court was somehow to declare the proposed tax laws to violate the right to private property? My guess is that current levels of ardour for courtroom resolutions among some of my more radical students might cool somewhat. What I suspect would not occur – and why I believe this book project to have been justified – is a more fundamental re-evaluation of the liberal constitution's thwarting of meaningful popular participation in constitution forming and reforming. Attention remains fixed upon liberalism's clarion call to resist the 'tyranny of the majority' supplemented by regular denouncements of 'populism'. In plain sight but somehow much less visible stand (i) the repeated failures of the minority elites holding public office in liberal democratic states to deliver majority preferences expressed at the ballot box; and (ii) elite-directed catastrophic public policy failures (such as the global financial crash of 2008, military interventions in Iraq, Syria and Libya in the last two decades) and (iii) instances of financial misconduct benefiting office holders and other elites.[22]

Popular Sovereignty in Liberal Constitutionalist Thinking

One of the signal successes of liberal constitutionalism since the epochal French and American revolutions in the late eighteenth century is to have virtually obliterated the idea of the constituent sovereign. As Kalyvas states, the notion is 'barely

[21] See thus R Ekins and G Gee, 'Putting Judicial Power in its Place' (2017) 36 *University of Queensland Law Journal* 375.

[22] To take financial misconduct overseen by and benefiting elites, in the case of the UK, see the damaging MPs and Peers expenses scandal of 2009. In respect of the 2009 scandal, Flinders and Anderson write that Parliament was still operating 'under the shadow of the expenses scandal' in 2021, see M Flinders and A Anderson, 'MPs' expenses: the legacy of a scandal 10 years on' (2021) Br. Polit. at https://doi.org/10.1057/s41293-021-00173-9. One could add countless 'revolving door' instances where, shortly after leaving public office, ex ministers have joined the boards of private companies seeking public contracts. See for a recent example former Prime Minister David Cameron's lobbying of the Chancellor of the Exchequer for Greensill Capital in order to gain contracts under the Government's COVID-19 support scheme. Mr Cameron made repeated efforts to contact ministers in the Johnson Government. For a damning report see House of Commons Treasury Select Committee Report *Lessons from Greensill Capital* at https://publications.parliament.uk/pa/cm5802/cmselect/cmtreasy/151/15102.htm (published 20 July 2021).

mentioned in contemporary constitutional theory and when it is mentioned, it is quickly denounced and rejected'.[23] The negative connotations attaching to popular sovereignty are a leitmotif of leading US and European constitutional theorists, even among those who would consider themselves to be sympathetic to republican political theory. Consider for example as standard bearers in this field the outputs of Bruce Ackerman and Jurgen Habermas. Ackerman regards acts of the constituent power as something that is best avoided as it implies where 'law ends … (and) pure politics (or war begins)'.[24] Habermas for his part also looks on concernedly when he refers to popular constituent power as entailing 'an organic substantive, ethnic homogeneity to bind a community together … (which) … can lean towards a militant ethno-nationalism'.[25]

Present thus in liberal constitutional theory lies a set of anxieties about popular sovereignty that require the latter's subordination to constituted institutions and norms of the liberal state.

The *Introduction* to a recently edited collection *Radical Republicanism – Recovering the Tradition's Popular Heritage* picks up on this level of apprehension about popular sovereignty when it comments that:

> contemporary political theorists share a distinct conception of republicanism, associated with understandings where 'the people' is viewed with suspicion or even something to be guarded against; where courts and expert committees are empowered to counteract possible tyranny by the majority; and where representative government, the rule of law, and the separation of powers are seen as the ultimate guarantors of liberty. Republicanism's rich and diverse intellectual tradition has, in other words, become largely associated with concepts locating it within contemporary liberalism.[26]

Some have argued that the institutions and norms encapsulated in liberal constitutions have become so closely connected to the idea of democracy as to have become wholly constitutive of it.[27] To save the people from themselves and from damaging the careful, incrementally elaborated configuration of perfected citizen–state relations in liberal democracies, the institutions and norms must be thought of as having attained a degree of permanency and be placed beyond the amendatory reach of the people. The ability to authoritatively settle the meaning of the constitution must either be the sole preserve of the judiciary, or, at the very least, made considerably more difficult to alter by way of supermajority requirements in legislatures/national referenda. So installed, the liberal democratic constitution

[23] A Kalyvas, 'Popular Sovereignty, Democracy and the Constituent Power' (2005) 12 *Constellations* 223, 225.

[24] B Ackerman, *We the People II. Transformations* (Massachusetts, Harvard University Press, 1998) at 11.

[25] J Habermas, *The Inclusion of the Other: Studies in Political Theory* (eds C Cronin and P De Greiff) (Massachusetts, MIT Press, 1998) at 148.

[26] B Leipold, K Nabulsi and S White *Introduction* in (eds B Leipold, K Nabulsi and S White), *Radical Republicanism: Recovering the Tradition's Popular Heritage* (Oxford, OUP, 2020) at 1.

[27] J Colon-Rios, *Weak Constitutionalism – Democratic Legitimacy and the Question of Constituent Power* (Abingdon, Routledge, 2012) at 21–23.

can be assured of a degree of protection from transient political majorities, the general population and their ill-judged, impassioned responses to the latest policy crisis.

Liberals defend the entrenchment of political rights to expression and association to the extent necessary for establishing the preconditions for rational debate and the peaceful resolution of conflicting opinions.[28] Clearly free speech and freedom of association are both necessary for citizens to be able to engage successfully in political arguments. The freedom to speak and act politically with others allows for thoughtful reflection upon and revision of constitutional norms.[29] This is attractive for reasons of democratic practice. However, as Colón-Ríos contends, it is not clear that this entirely avoids problems of democracy legitimacy that attach in particular to entrenched political rights.[30] As he points out, the institutions entrusted with the safe keeping of the rights (legislatures and/or courts) might choose to interpret the right to free political expression in ways that allow corporations to skew the nature and content of political debates in self-serving ways.[31] Why should this patently non-isonomic account of the right to freedom of expression enjoy immunity from revision by popular majorities? The same general objection could be made to preferred legislative/judicial accounts of the right to liberty or hold property. Why should the meaning of a constitutionally enshrined right to private property be fixed by courts and legislatures (the constituted authorities), when such meanings impact on the ability of all citizens (the constituent power) to participate in politics? What if, more fundamentally, sections of the people dispute the validity of the liberal constitution's ultimate objective – the perfected harmonious society and the elimination of meaningful political conflict in accordance with rational progress towards the universal and abstract goals of Enlightenment thinking? Am I to be excluded from the fora of public deliberation because my commitment to politics as on-going, ineliminable disagreement on the basic principles of justice marks me out as 'irrational' (Rawls), or because I dispute the foundational constitutional insights of my forebears and contest the view that my political life is concerned with elaborating in a progressive temporality the overall project of perfecting my forebears' unimpeachable constitutional insights (Habermas)?

The success of liberal constitutionalism's endeavours is made most plain in the diminishing awareness of the idea of constituent power to the point where the latter

[28] It is clear too that other rights typically recognised in liberal constitutions, such as privacy, play a background role in securing meaningful participation in politics.

[29] This draws on the idea of constitutional pre-commitments articulated by Stephen Holmes, 'Precommitment and the Paradox of Democracy' in (ed J Elster and R Slagstad) *Constitutionalism and Democracy* (Cambridge, CUP, 2018).

[30] J Colón-Ríos, *Weak Constitutionalism – Democratic Legitimacy and the Question of Constituent Power* at 25.

[31] The classic instance being the US Supreme Court's ruling in *Citizens United v Federal Election Commission* 558 US 310 (2010) where corporately funded political expression was deemed to be protected under the First Amendment.

is rendered invisible and no longer invoked in our daily political vocabulary.[32] In this vein, Kalyvas points out that we have lost sight of the human origins of constitutional settlements. The centuries-old reverence shown in western liberal constitutional thinking towards the 'Glorious Revolution'/Bill of Rights or the Declaration of Independence/US Constitution (and accompanying Bill of Rights) makes it harder to recall that such settlements were not in fact handed down to us by an omnicompetent or eternal lawgiver. We can sometimes fail to remember that they were the intellectual products of an elite class of landed gentlemen who were appalled at the radical idea that the unpropertied, ordinary citizen should have any say in the government of the nation. The liberal notion that enlightened constitutional construction by elites is intended to endure (and therefore resist re-constitution) is evident in the words attributed to Benjamin Franklin on leaving Independence Hall in Philadelphia at the conclusion of the Constitutional Convention of 1787. Asked by Elizabeth Willing Powel who was waiting outside the hall about whether the Convention members had given the people a monarchy or a republic, Franklin pithily replied 'A republic if you can keep it'.[33] The work of the Convention was, in other words, intended for present *and* future generations. The carefully designed and delicately balanced constituted powers were to be venerated thereafter. In a striking contrast with Jefferson's radical idea of finite constitutions, the notion that the constituent people *had* the power and might want, at some point in the future, to start over the process of constitutional design *ab initio* or to revise the fundamental features of the Convention's work was evidently entirely outside Franklin's contemplation.[34]

The Popular Sovereignty Challenge to Liberal Constitutionalism and Two Anxieties

> the constituent power can do everything in relationship to constitutional making. It is not subordinated to a previous constitution. The nation that exercises the greatest, the most important of its powers, must be, while carrying this function, free from all constraints, from any form, except the one that it deems better to adopt.
>
> Sieyès, 'Reconnaissance et exposition raisonnée des droits de l'homme et du citoyen' *Orateurs de la Révolution française. Les Constituants*, Vol I, ed. François Furet and Ran Halévie (1989, Pléiade, Paris), at 1013.

To recap, liberals have been extremely successful in attempts to portray constitutional settlements as the enlightened product of an earlier generation of

[32] A Kalyvas, 'Popular Sovereignty, Democracy and the Constituent Power' (2005) 12 *Constellations* 223, 230 where Kalyvas calls the absence 'scandalous'.

[33] Attributed to Franklin by James McHenry a Maryland delegate to the Convention in his journal.

[34] Sunstein judges this remark correctly in my view in *#Republic* (New Jersey, Princeton University Press, 2018) as requiring citizens to act in ways that maintain the republic, at 261.

inspired and rational creators. It can be a struggle to pierce the Podsnappian veil of veneration.[35] Consequently, we can lose sight of the fact that each and every constitutional settlement must inevitably be the flawed human product of a particular moment in time and in the context of a particular conjunction of societal forces to organise the political life and institutions of a bounded territory. Such settlements must inevitably reflect the response of dominant forces to a political crisis that the previous constitutional institutions and norms arrangements were unable to accommodate. Yet how many constitutional law programmes in the western liberal democratic world direct students' minds to the idea of constituent power as a serious theoretical rival to the juridified or parliamentary state? Today in the UK for example, accounts of the ultimate source of legitimate authority focus almost exclusively on the doctrine of parliamentary sovereignty. Students are directed to look at the emergence of the parliamentary state in 1689 Bill of Rights and the triumph of the legislature over the Crown by way of explaining the orthodox account of sovereignty. The only serious rival account that students might be exposed to is common law constitutionalism where the courts rather than Parliament determine whether the legislature or executive is acting lawfully.[36] For common law constitutionalists, these foundational principles are 'discovered' by the judges themselves after a careful and objective perusal of the law books. These judge-discovered norms invariably empower the self-same judges to have the final say on what is constitutional and what is not. And, of late, in cases such as *Miller 1* and *Miller 2* UK judges have proved themselves to be quite creative in finding innovative legal routes to interfere with or entirely circumvent actions and controls in the political part of the constitution.

Were the idea of constituent power more visible in our constitutional theory, we should expect the literature to contain serious contestations of the ideas of parliamentary or judicial supremacy. To paraphrase Kalyvas here, 'the notion of the constituent sovereign discredits any sovereign ambitions that the legislative or judicial branch may entertain'.[37] The idea of the constituent sovereign renders parliamentary or judicial sovereignty an impossibility. In the case of parliamentary sovereignty, this is 'exposed as a usurpation of the constituent power by a constituted power, which reduces popular sovereignty to parliamentary representation and to the powers of elected officials'.[38] In so exposing, space opens up for spontaneous and extra-institutional forms of political discourse. The liberal constitutionalist focus on technical issues about what is legally permitted under

[35] Mr Podsnap is the character in Dickens' *Our Mutual Friend* who states to a visiting foreign guest, 'We Englishmen are Very Proud of our Constitution, Sir. It was Bestowed Upon Us By Providence. No Other Country is so Favoured as This Country'.

[36] Advanced programmes of study might look at ideas of dialogic constitutionalism where the legislature and courts work as common partners charged with working out jointly authoritative constitutional meanings.

[37] In Kalyvas' original quote the words 'or judicial' are not used, A Kalyvas, 'Popular Sovereignty, Democracy and the Constituent Power' (2005) 12 *Constellations* 223, at 229.

[38] ibid.

and within the constitution is discarded and attention switches to the question of the relationship between constitutions and their creators/addressees. Such a switch points up the exciting possibilities of digital expression for democratic republicans.

Unlike their liberal constitutionalist counterparts, democratic republican accounts of the constituent power are comfortable with the fact (indeed expect) that the demos will at times exceed the boundaries set down in the constituted order. Through such ruptures with the established legal order that may take the form of inter alia instances of civil disobedience, more direct acts of *a*constitutional conduct can be seen to have the positive effect of expanding the horizons of political participation. I take this to have occurred over and over again in the moves to mass universal suffrage in the nineteenth and early twentieth centuries when groups of non-enfranchised persons exceeded the lawful bounds of public protest to press their claims to full citizenship. For a much earlier example of *a*constitutional action that is thought to have brought about an expanded form of political participation we can turn to chapters III and IV of Machiavelli's *Discourses on Livy*. Here Machiavelli refers to the creation of the tribunate with veto powers over policies favoured by the nobles in the senate. This innovation to the Roman Constitution was instituted to pacify the plebs who had been provoked to a state of unlawful uproar and tumult by the actions of the nobles. The latter had moved to consolidate their powers when the Tarquin monarchs had been expelled from the city. Here the popular disorder that followed the ending of monarchical rule had the positive result of instituting a new form of popular participation in law making. Machiavelli concludes:

> And if the popular tumults led the creation of the tribunes, they merit all praise; since these magistrates not only gave its due influence to the popular voice in the government, but also acted as the guardians of Roman freedom.[39]

Separately, in respect of corrupt republics, Machiavelli defends the extra-legal elimination of venal elites by praising the Greek tyrants Hiero of Syracuse and Clearchus of Heraclea who after crushing the nobility, redistributed their wealth among ordinary people and instituted republican reform.[40]

One way of thinking about the idea of the constituent power and distinguishing it from what often passes as the fullest extent of democratic participation in liberal democracies is suggested by Colón-Ríos in *Weak Constitutionalism*. He identifies two traditional approaches that are deployed to answer the question whether a constitution is democratic.[41] Both, he argues, are deficient by virtue

[39] *Discourses on Livy* ch IV. That the Dissensions between the Senate and Commons of Rome made Rome free and powerful.

[40] *The Prince* ch VIII, 'Those who become rulers through wicked means' and see for commentary J McCormick, 'Of Tribunes and Tyrants: Machiavelli's Legal and Extra-Legal Modes for Controlling Elites' (2015) 28 *Ratio Juris* 252, 259–65.

[41] J Colón-Ríos, *Weak Constitutionalism – Democratic Legitimacy and the Question of Constituent Power* see esp chs 2 and 3.

of their respective neglect of the critical question of constituent power. The first 'substantive' account asks whether the constitution guarantees certain fundamental rights of participation in everyday decision-making to every citizen as political equals.[42] The second or 'procedural' approach is much less concerned with the contents of the rights possessed by citizens and focuses instead upon whether the laws and institutions are the products of a democratic process involving a freely elected legislature that regularly submits itself for re-election to the electors.[43] Each offers a means of assessing the daily practice of rule making in terms of their democratic credentials. They both omit however to consider the vital question of how, if at all, citizens are empowered to re-constitute the governing order. This is critical if we are to say something about the democratic legitimacy of the polity.[44] The act of reconstituting might take the form of a revolution or complete rupture from the old order. Here the old order, its norms and institutions are thrown over as occurred in Europe in the transformation from absolute monarchy to the liberal state. Alternatively, a reconstituting might take the form of re-imagining of the forms and institutions of the current state that is faithful to the original underpinning or foundational values but recognises that these values are no longer served well by current institutions and procedures.

In the UK and some Commonwealth countries such as New Zealand, the doctrine of parliamentary sovereignty makes no formal distinction between ordinary law and constitutional law. Although qualitative differences across types of law making are suggestive of a distinction, this is not signalled clearly in terms of a distinctive parliamentary procedure. The Dangerous Dogs Act 1991 passed through the same stages of deliberation in the UK Commons and Lords as did the Human Rights Act 1998. The formal lumping together of major constitutional reforms and non-constitution altering laws under the same non-hierarchical doctrine of parliamentary sovereignty is valuable for liberal constitutionalists. The absence of a formal binary divide between constitutional and non-constitutional statutes requiring distinct legislative procedures makes it harder for popular sovereigntists to cut through with their claim that, when the governing order is being reconstituted (as in the case of the Human Rights Act when the judiciary were given increased powers to interpret domestic law to ensure conformity with Convention rights), the people as the constituent power ought to be centre stage in authorising the constitutional change.[45] The unwritten constitution is invariably

[42] The substantive view is associated with Ronald Dworkin in inter alia *Law's Empire* (Massachusetts, Harvard University Press, 1986) and *A Bill of Rights for Britain* (London, Chatto & Windus, 1990).

[43] The procedural view is associated with Jeremy Waldron in inter alia *Law and Disagreement* (New York, OUP, 1999) and 'The Core of the Case Against Judicial Review' (2006) 115 *Yale LJ* 1346.

[44] See Colón-Ríos *Weak Constitutionalism* at ch 6.

[45] That is not to say that the constituted authorities never acknowledge even in abstract terms the idea of sovereignty resting in the people. Much was made of this in the UK by the winning Leave side in the aftermath of the EU referendum in June 2016. The UK Parliament had not however committed itself in law to giving effect to the referendum outcome. This did not stop the victorious Leave campaign referring to the binding moral force of the result. Of course, any attempt to bind its successors to honour the

the evolution of a set of understandings and consensual practices among elite political actors over an extended period of time, some of which find their way into legal form via statute or judicial pronouncement.[46] The most perhaps that can be said for the parliamentary system is that citizens are able to participate indirectly in constitution-building activity by voting, registering views with MPs, using e-petitions, responding to select committee calls for evidence etc. Not even the staunchest defenders of parliamentary sovereignty are able to deny, however, that current practices do anything other than as a matter of regular course privilege corporate and other organised groups' interests in terms of access to reform processes. The idea that our system comes remotely close to treating the political preferences of all citizens with equal respect is frankly risible.

On those occasions when the citizens have been consulted about constitutional change via a national referendum (change of the parliamentary voting system 2011; membership of the EEC 1975; membership of the EU 2016; devolution in Scotland and Wales (1979, 1997); independence for Scotland (2014); Northern Ireland (i) on staying in the UK 1973; (ii) Good Friday Agreement (1998); it would be misleading to characterise these exercises as instances of constituent power. The citizens determined neither the nature of the binary options on the referendum vote, nor their respective wording or the timing of the vote. Each of these matters was decided by MPs and unelected peers. Moreover in 1975 and 2016 the UK Parliament did not formally commit itself in law to implementing the majority verdict. In 2011 a commitment in law was made in the event of a majority vote to change the parliamentary voting system but, under the doctrine of parliamentary sovereignty, this obligation could have been removed by a later Parliament.

What is it precisely that makes defenders of the liberal constitution (both in 'written' and 'unwritten' forms) anxious about majoritarian forms of government and popularly authorised forms of rule? To propose that the citizens are the constituent authority is to make an unsettling claim on two interconnected counts. The first count concerns the lawless, arbitrary nature of the claimed power. Arendt observes that when the people combine together to throw off an existing government and constitute themselves in a new order they act in an unconstitutional manner. They have completely ruptured the old constitutional settlement. A show of brute force has factually ended the old regime. 'It is', she remarks, 'in the very nature of a beginning to carry with itself a measure of complete arbitrariness … The beginning has nothing to hold on to; it is as though it came out of nowhere'.[47] The second, anxiety-inducing feature of constituent power is its inherent lack

result would have been legally meaningless under the conventional view of parliamentary sovereignty. Incidentally, I am not endorsing the idea here that referendums as they have occurred here in the UK in 2011 (alternative voting system) and 2016 (EU membership) adequately secure popular participation in re-constituting the state.

[46] In the case of written constitutions, it is common to find an express judicial power to review the primary acts of the legislature for compliance with the constitution. These systems of judicial supremacy mean that the people 'participate' even less fully than citizens in parliamentary systems.

[47] H Arendt, *On Revolution* at 198.

of stability. If the constituent power creates a new order *ex nihilo* out of a legal void, how can it be anything other than transient and vulnerable to subsequent replacement by a future act of the constituent power. And what is there to prevent the constituent power from engaging in ceaseless reiterations of the state? Again Arendt puts it crisply: '... nothing threatens the very achievements of revolution more dangerously and more acutely than the spirit which has brought them about'.[48] Although the new regime may try to appeal to a sense of reconnection to a more ancient one (see in this regard how the US Founders and other key players in the American Revolution appealed back to Ancient Rome and even took the name of heroes of the Roman republic when publishing pseudonymously),[49] the decisive break with the previous constitutional order understandably makes the defenders of the new one anxious lest the constituent power once more wishes to flex its muscles. How might these disquieting claims be responded to?

Kalyvas provides an important answer to the problem of the lawless and arbitrary nature of the acts of the constituent power. He argues that this characterisation ignores the teleological purpose behind the constituent power which is to create a new legal order. The constituent power realises its own constitutional norms in that new order.[50] Arendt herself considered that the constituent power could avoid the charge of arbitrariness in terms of the content of the new laws if these were informed by principles that prompted the very act of reconstitution.[51] This required quality of immanence may be more elusive than Arendt lets on however. Although she refers to ideas of glory, honour and equality, there remain questions about how we know these to be the immanent principles and what their content is. Is there a means of discovering their centrality to the acts of re-constituting? And there are other questions too. For example, when a new constitutional settlement comes about after a combination of public acts by the constituent people some of which are violent in nature, how can we be sure that violence to secure the expression of the popular will has not become an immanent principle? On what criterion can it be ruled out?

One possible response to the problem of lawlessness and arbitrariness is to think about how the constituent power connects to the democratic ideal. The act of constituting or reconstituting is a collective enterprise in democratic self-government. It is always a joint activity that we engage in with our fellow citizens.

[48] ibid at 224.

[49] Walter Benjamin noted how the Jacobin revolutionaries also identified with the ancient glories of Rome. The 'French Revolution viewed itself as Rome reincarnate. It evoked ancient Rome the way fashion evokes costumes of the past.' W Benjamin 'Theses on the Philosophy of History' in *Illuminations: Essays and Reflections Theses on the Philosophy of History* (Boston, Mariner Books, 2019) at 205.

[50] A Kalyvas, 'Popular Sovereignty, Democracy and the Constituent Power' (2005) 12 *Constellations* 223, 233.

[51] *On Revolution* at 205, 'What saves the act of beginning from its own arbitrariness is that it carries its own principle, within itself ... The way the beginner starts whatever he intends to do lays down the law of action for those who have joined him in order to partake in the enterprise and to bring about its accomplishment.' This rejects the view that consistency is to be found in transcendental norms or rational universal precepts.

It has a definite aim, as Kalyvas remarked, of creating a new regime in which the people are both the authors and addressees of the new constitution. Crucially, the defining ideas of popular participation and democratic openness put a necessary limit on the constituent power. Where it is proposed that the constituent power be invoked to create a dictatorship or a form of government in which some citizens are excluded from future political participation or where the substance of the new laws will be beyond repeal or amendment, then such a regime would lack democratic legitimacy. These proposed laws cannot be legitimate exercises of the constituent power, since they directly limit future exercises of the constituent power. Following Colón-Ríos, it can be stated that the criterion of democratic legitimacy can only be satisfied where, after each exercise of the constituent power, 'the rights and institutions necessary to facilitate future constituent activities' remain in place.[52]

The second anxiety surrounding ideas of constituent power refers to the idea of permanent instability. Whatever is constituted today may be undone tomorrow. A helpful way of thinking about this issue involves seeing two distinct forms or modalities of the constituent power namely revolution and augmentation and their qualitative differences. In its revolutionary mode, the constituent power is used to create a new world and absolute beginning that fractures utterly the previous set of constituted bodies and norms. For Arendt, this was when an 'abyss of nothingness opens up before any deed that cannot be accounted for by any reliable chain of cause and event'.[53] Such a moment coheres with the agonistic emphasis upon tragedy and conflict.[54] Walter Benjamin wrote of the instant when the revolutionary classes 'are about to make the continuum of history explode … The great revolution introduce(s) a new calendar'.[55] A self-conscious way in which the revolutionary actors may signal their epoch-shattering powers is, Benjamin reminds us, nothing less than the resetting of time itself. The clock is put back to the beginning and the start of the revolution declared to be 'Year Zero'. It is mistaken however to see the revolutionary mode as exhausting the range of political action that the constituent power is capable of. By contrast, in its augmentative mode, the constituent power stresses the idea of innovation but, unlike the revolutionary mode, links this back to the terms of original founding, rather than initiating rupture This re-founding 'simultaneously expands and preserves an existing system of authority'.[56] It seeks to re-imagine the existing constitutional settlement in novel ways that, in the case of a liberal democracy, might recast the existing balance

[52] J Colón-Ríos, *Weak Constitutionalism – Democratic Legitimacy and the Question of Constituent Power* at 111.

[53] H Arendt, *The Life of the Mind* (Boston, Harcourt, 1978) at 207.

[54] M Wenman *Agonistic Democracy – Constituent Power in the Era of Globalisation* (Cambridge, CUP, 2013) at 10.

[55] W Benjamin 'Theses on the Philosophy of History' in *Illuminations: Essays and Reflections Theses on the Philosophy of History* at 206.

[56] M Wenman, *Agonistic Democracy* at 9.

between liberty and equality whilst stressing the continued centrality of both norms to the state. In the augmentative mode, the constituent power reworks the values prevailing at the time of the current constitution's founding in ways that track and align with what has gone before. Republican accounts of constituent political action can accommodate both absolute beginnings and new iterations of revolutionary settlement that remain faithful to the latter.

The complementarity of revolution and augmentation in republican accounts of freedom is nowhere better instanced than in Machiavelli's *The Prince* and *Discourses on Titus Livy*. The founding and retention of a new state (through acts of violence if necessary) occupies key sections of *The Prince*.[57] Since the odds of creating a new state were highly unfavourable at the outset, Machiavelli argues that where this unlikely outcome is achieved the new ruler will be held in great respect and hold office securely as head of state.[58] As well as this absolute beginning, Machiavelli developed an account in *Discourses* of how the ancient Roman state was able to innovate in terms of new forms of political structures that preserved or revitalised the state of liberty that was a foundational value of the Republic. The free city state is the one that is governed according to the will of all its members. The people are the keepers of their own liberties.[59] From time to time, they are required to preserve the state of individual liberty by innovative acts that augment this foundational commitment.

Mapping Liberalism's Ochlophobia – Current Restrictions on Freedom of Political Expression and a Republican Argument for Keeping the Channels of Political Change Open

Earlier in this Introduction I referred to a recent edited collection, *Radical Republicanism*, whose authors aim to liberate republican ideas from the distortion they undergo when located within liberal political thought. One of the central objectives of the authors is to reposition the idea of popular sovereignty

[57] See *Discourses* Book 1 Ch VI. 'New principalities acquired by one's own arms and ability' where he remarks 'If Moses, Cyrus, Theseus and Romulus had been unarmed, the new order which each of them established would not have been obeyed for very long'.

[58] ibid. Arendt argues that, notwithstanding Machiavelli's appeal to the glory of ancient Rome in *Discourses* to revive the failing city states of fifteenth and sixteenth century, he never abandoned the revolutionary idea of an united Italian national state, see *On Revolution* (2006, Penguin Books, London) at 29–30.

[59] *Discourses* Book 1 Ch 5 Whether the Guardianship May Be More Securely Lodged in the People or in the Upper Classes. See further Q Skinner, *Liberty before Liberalism* (CUP, Canto Classics, 2012) at 26 in 'The neo-roman theory of free states', and J McCormick, 'Of Tribunes and Tyrants: Machiavelli's Legal and Extra-Legal Modes for Controlling Elites' (2015) 28 *Ratio Juris* 252.

at the centre of republican thought.[60] To be of practical significance however, any renewal of democratic republican thinking must also devote considerable attention to the institutional reforms needed to secure ongoing popular participation in the republican constitution. For example, an evaluation of the merits of public office selection via sortition whereby citizens are chosen randomly to hold public office for short term periods is legitimately the subject of detailed academic enquiry.[61] Separately, class-specific legislative fora – the modern-day equivalent of the Roman tribunate – might be considered to institutionalise ordinary citizen representation with veto powers over the policy proposals of socio-economic elites.[62]

This book engages in two prior and more limited fronts; namely (i) mapping out the various ways in which citizens' participation in online-speech platforms are constrained and (ii) exploring liberal rationales for limits placed by the constituted authorities on political participation. To do this, the following chapters analyse some current restrictions upon digital political expression in the UK and Europe and the explicit/implicit reasoning that limits popular engagement in public discourse. It is intended to throw light on the anti-pluralism at the heart of liberal constitutional practice and the extent to which this serves the interests of socio-economic and political elites. My analysis shows that, both at the level of daily governance and more fundamentally at the level of re-constituting the basic norms and institutions of the legal order, clashes between rival world views are closed down. This is to say that liberal constitutionalism curtails forms of contestation (and thus revision) of the basic political and juridical arrangements with a view to protecting the existing version of liberal capitalist democracy from its more radical sets of challengers. The *post*-politics era of liberal democracy (the only 'rational' option on the anti-populist menu) endorses a narrow range of technocratic policies intended to shore up the values and constraints of finance capitalism. Once you are convinced of the case for rentier capitalism (the exploitation of scarce assets that allow arbitrary prices to be charged to captive consumers), globalised markets and labour flexibility, you may not think there is much value in allowing dissenting voices any sort of platform. At the very least, the ability of your non-mainstream opponents to challenge your narrative should be made more difficult.

The challenge for defenders of active, popular self government is to consider how the state and privately owned digital platforms may be made to facilitate ongoing forms of political contestation that challenge public office holders and

[60] B Leipold, K Nabulsi and S White *Introduction* in (eds B Leipold, K Nabulsi and S White), *Radical Republicanism: Recovering the Tradition's Popular Heritage* (Oxford, OUP, 2020).

[61] See existing treatments of the topic in inter alia O Dowlen, 'Sorting out Sortition: A Perspective on the Random Selection of Political Officers' (2009) 57 *Pol. Sts.* 298; Y Sintomer, 'From Deliberative to Radical Democracy? Sortition and politics in the twenty-first century' (2018) 46 *Pol. & Soc.* 337; H Buchstein, 'Countering the "Democracy Thesis" – Sortition in Ancient Greek Political Theory' (2015) 18 *Redescriptions* 126; A Barnett and P Carty, *The Athenian Option – Radical Reform for the House of Lords* (London, Demos, 1998).

[62] J McCormick, *Machiavellian Democracy* (New York, CUP, 2011).

render the exercise of political power amenable to popular oversight and control. Whether, as some have suggested, a republican belief in active self-rule requires/can accommodate a role for courts in policing restrictions on political discourse promulgated by politicians and/or social media platforms is addressed in the final chapter. For now, what can be said with some degree of certainty is that the democratic legitimacy of judicial interventions in this context can be judged according to the extent to which they safeguard the range of political freedoms that are needed to maintain the regularity of ordinary citizens' participation in framing constitutional meaning.

2

Closing Off the Agon: Legal Norms, Deliberative Democracy and 'Improved' European Public Discourse

Introduction

This chapter has two main objectives. The first is to show the dominance in European legal/constitutional norms for rational, reason-giving and civilised/responsible political expression. In textual terms, this commitment can be traced to ideas in Article 10 ECHR jurisprudence of a qualified entitlement to speak and receive information and ideas. A newly invigorated notion of the 'duties and responsibilities' element of Article 10(2) is being pressed into service to discipline digital speakers and the platforms they rely on for dissemination. I will argue that these correspond to ideas of socially responsible expression and attempt to promote consensual outcomes of the sort associated with deliberative accounts of democratic decision-making. The second, more analytical section of materials sets out to enquire whether and to what extent these preconditions 'slow down' politics by excluding contributions to public discourse from 'unreasoning' and 'unreasonable' non-elites. It sets down the distinct understandings of citizens' political participation in liberal elitist, deliberative and, finally, agonist accounts of democracy. Specific questions here include whether deliberative democracy perceives more radical forms of pluralism as a threat to enlightened self-rule as some have claimed?[1] Notwithstanding its republican heritage, does deliberative democracy effectively consign us to a 'post-democracy' form of politics in which political pluralism is substantially narrowed and citizen participation heavily constrained?

By way of framing rival overarching accounts of the citizens' role in political discourse, an early section of materials lays out the constitutive tension at the heart of liberal democracies between liberalism and democracy. The former's distrust and consequent disparagement of unmediated popular opinion naturally inclines to mechanisms and devices that constrain opportunities for democratic self-rule

[1] See thus N Fenton, *Digital, Political and Radical* (Cambridge, Polity Press, 2016).

and the exercise of constituent power. Citizens in this account are conceived of in largely passive terms, the very occasional visitors to the table of political debate who are tasked primarily with endorsing one or other sets of the rival parties' policy positions. The democratic account on the other hand stresses majoritarian and active forms of popular participation in the contested arena of political decision-making.

In the academic literature, 'social responsibility' theory suggests that the speakers have a range of functions including: 'servicing the political system by providing information, discussion and debate on public affairs; ... and enlightening the public so as to make it capable of self-government'.[2] Premised upon a view of humankind being prone to lethargy, social responsibility theory enlists the 'more alert' members of the community including journalists to goad the citizenry into exercising their powers of reasoning to secure enlightened self government.[3] Its core ideas are generally traced back to the work of the 1947 Hutchins' Commission on the Freedom of the Press.[4] The duties of the press according to Hutchins included offering a

> truthful, comprehensive and intelligent account of the day's events in a context which gives them meaning; ..., projecting the opinions and attitudes of the groups in society to one another ... (and) presenting and clarifying the goals and values of the society.[5]

The Commission was concerned that US citizens were largely ignorant of just how their press had fallen 'short of the requirements of a free society in the world today'.[6] The deficiencies of the US press in the 1940s were identified to include inaccurate reporting, partisan and profit-driven journalism. Hutchins asked how these might be ameliorated. The analysis of several Commission members was premised on a lowly opinion of members of the public, sub-groups of whom banded

[2] See, for example, S Gunaratne and M Safar Hasim, 'Social Responsibility Theory Revisited a Comparative Study of Public Journalism and Developmental Journalism' (2014) 3 *Javnost: The Public Journal of the European Institute for Communication and Culture* 97, 102; and see further P Coe, '(Re)embracing Social Responsibility Theory as a Basis for Media Speech: Shifting the Normal Paradigm for a Modern Media' (2018) 69 *NILQ* 403.

[3] Gunaratne & Hasim ibid at 105.

[4] *A Free and Responsible Press, A General Report on Mass Communication: Newspapers, Radio, Motion Pictures, Magazines and Books* (Chicago, University of Chicago Press, 1947). The label 'social responsibility' was first attached by Fred Siebert, 'The Role of Mass Communication in American Society' in (ed N Henry) *The Fifty-Third Yearbook of the National Society for Study of Education* (Chicago, National Society for the Study of Education, 1954).

[5] ibid at 20–21.

[6] ibid at 96–97. For a useful analysis of the Commission's work and the internal debates between its various members see S Bates, *An Aristocracy of Critics – Luce, Hutchins, Niebuhr and the Committee that Redefined Freedom of the Press* (New Haven, Yale University Press 2020). Bates' summary (at 202) of the different stances of the Commission members is worth reproducing here, as it demonstrates how the Commission's proposals were inevitably a messy compromise between competing ideals and values: 'Archibald MacLeish embraced individualism; Reihold Niebuhr and William Ernest Hocking decried it. Some members favored additional regulatory steps – not always the same ones – while Zechariah Chafee opposed them. In general MacLeish focused on speakers without audiences, Hocking on citizens without information, and Chafee on regulators without scruples.'

together in 'social islands' according to 'ideology, race, nationality or economic interests'.[7] Such socially fragmented citizens invariably lacked a commitment to reasoned deliberation in pursuit of the common good. They rejected information that did not conform to their world view. The partisan press fed these imperfect understandings of the world by supplying one-sided commentaries that tapped into and affirmed existing opinions, thereby growing sales revenue for newspaper owners. Polarised positions would also be exploited by non-mainstream politicians to advance factional interests. Citizens who came to believe that the system no longer served them might be tempted down the line to support more authoritarian ideas and leaders.

The solution Hutchins recommended centred upon improving the quality of press reporting so that mistaken perceptions might be corrected. Ethically informed good journalism served to clarify societal debates and analyse them in terms of the goals and values of society.[8] In turn, the citizen audience would become more cohesive as accurate and objective accounts of societal matters produced by professional journalists percolated into the general consciousness. What was needed was a *New York Times* for every major city.[9] Levels of trust in democracy itself and its governing institutions and practices would be moved in the right direction. Today, organisations like the *Knight Foundation* in the US continue the work of Hutchins in seeking via quality journalism to 'foster informed and engaged communities (that) … are essential for a healthy democracy'.[10]

This mission statement from the Knight Foundation would indicate that remnants of an older, more elitist account of political expression have survived into the digital era in which citizens continue to be conceived of in passive terms as the recipients of elite (often professionally accredited) speakers' ideas. At the same time – and in tension with this non-active account of citizenship – it is also fair to claim that citizens in western liberal democracies live in less deferential societies as compared to the United States of the 1940s. Politicians today would wish to be thought of as more knowledgeable about, and responsive to, the views of the electorate than previous sets of elected office holders. There is greater acceptance of the idea of two-way political communication between power holders and citizens. One possible mechanism for the channelling of non-elites' political expression is the citizens' assembly. National Governments in Europe and elsewhere have for some time now shown interest in the idea of advisory and randomly selected

[7] S Bates, *An Aristocracy of Critics – Luce, Hutchins, Niebuhr and the Committee that Redefined Freedom of the Press* ibid at 216.

[8] T Gleason, 'Saving Journalism from Itself (and From Us): The Hutchins Commission was Right Then, so What about Now?' (1998) 3 *Comm. L & Poly.* 409 at 412 lamenting how subsequent First Amendment jurisprudence did not follow Hutchins.

[9] S Bates, *An Aristocracy of Critics*, at 220.

[10] See https://knightfoundation.org/about/. The core beliefs of the Knight Foundation are (i) freedom of expression and the values of the First Amendment; (ii) an informed citizenry and (iii) engaged, equitable and inclusive communities. See the Strategy Statement at https://knightfoundation.org/statement-of-strategy/.

deliberative assemblies of citizens to frame constitutional reform options that are put to their fellow citizens in referenda. How well do such initiatives accommodate and permit the expression of diverse perspectives among the population? Where, as seems plausible, such assemblies or 'mini-publics' continue to find official favour as an element of the policy-formation fora, might they render other forms of participatory expression less necessary (and hence more easily regulated by the state or social media platforms)? What happens to dissenting opinion when the deliberative assembly has coalesced around a particular policy position? To what extent do these deliberative processes acknowledge the revisability and re-contestation of positions reached in the assembly? I argue below that the tendency of deliberative forms of democratic decision-making to conclude debates after rational enquiry is exacerbated in epistemic versions of deliberative democracy that insist upon the search for truth and 'correct' outcomes guided by experts. These features of deliberation ultimately cut against the core republican idea of the political equality of all citizens and the democratic legitimacy of permanently revisable policymaking by an active citizenry.

The Liberal and the Democratic Polity[11]

There is a constitutive tension at the heart of liberal democratic polities between the liberal tradition which has at its core commitments to the rule of law, separation of powers and individual rights on the one hand and the democratic tradition whose central animating precepts comprise the equal status of all citizens and the claim that ultimate political authority vests in the people on the other. Grounded in a 'long established tradition of elite suspicion of the masses' the liberal tradition stands for rule-based 'checks and balances' upon the constitutive powers of the people. The tendency towards unruliness and disorder in the polis is required to be 'slowed down' – a demand that is facilitated by constitutional controls such as the rule of law and individual rights (including rights to property and to enter contractual relations) adjudicated upon by independent courts and operating alongside the supplementary institutional checks offered by a representative assembly. These checks are needed to ensure the survival of the liberal democratic polity.[12] It is even claimed that allowing market forces to operate beyond the reach of 'predatory' and 'transient' elected political majorities determined to implement 'disruptive redistributive goals' is crucial to the survival of modern democratic states.[13] Famously, within this tradition is Madison's denunciation of what he

[11] An earlier version of this section of materials appeared previously in I Cram, 'Keeping the Demos out of Liberal Democracy? Participatory Politics, 'Fake News' and the Online Speaker' (2019) 11 *Journal of Media Law* 113.

[12] P Mair, *Ruling the Void: The Hollowing of Western Democracy* (London, Verso, 2013), Introduction.

[13] The phrases are taken from M Everson, 'Beyond the Bundesverfassungsgericht: On the Necessary Cunning of Constitutional Reasoning' in (eds. Z Bankowski and A Scott) *The European Union and its Order: The Legal Theory of European Integration* (Oxford, Blackwell, 2000) at 106.

labelled 'pure democracies' in Federalist Paper No 10. These, he declared, were 'ever spectacles of turbulence and contention; … incompatible with personal security, or the right of property …' His defence of representative forms of democracy invokes the idea of institutional mediation of the crudeness and short-termism/narrowness of popular opinion. The true public good could best be ascertained by the election of educated and disinterested persons capable of reflective and civilised debate in a representative assembly. This essentially elitist account of liberal pluralism emphasises the primary role of political parties and organised interests in framing policy debates. It posits a minimal role for the citizen in political decision-making that does not extend beyond receiving the speech of political elites and voting periodically at election time. Elitist accounts are grounded upon negative assessments of voter attentiveness and understanding of political issues and were developed in the early part of the twentieth century. Classic analyses by Joseph Schumpeter in *Capitalism, Socialism and Democracy* (1942) and Walter Lippmann in *The Phantom Public* (1925) defended the dominant role of organised political elites. Fears of Bolshevism and the mass rallies of the Nazis in the 1930s plainly influenced this lowly estimation of participatory politics. For Schumpeter, most citizens were not directly interested in most political questions, nor capable of enquiring into, let alone discerning a shared interest with their fellow citizens.[14] They were thus to be limited to having an opportunity of choosing at periodic intervals between competing sets of political leaders who would frame the terms of electoral contests.[15] Lippmann had a similarly dim view of the reasoning capacities of ordinary citizens. The private citizen was likened to a 'deaf spectator in the back row … He lives in a world he cannot see, does not understand and is unable to direct.'[16] Policymaking should be left to insiders working in government and legislatures. More recently Jonathan Sumption, in his *Reith Lectures*, defended the mediating role of political parties in the face of fissiparous popular opinion.[17] Referenda and other direct forms of expression of public opinion remain in his view unsuited to determining nuanced questions of public policy.

The democratic tradition speaks on the other hand for the ongoing right of all the people as the constituent power to redesign their laws and institutions. The liberal component of constitutionalism is faulted for limiting the people to occasional 'moments' of constitutional action. For the most part liberalism closes off opportunities for active and contestatory popular participation in the determination of laws and policies. In some constitutions closure is achieved via the mechanism of judicial review of primary legislation. In the political sphere it occurs through representative forms of government which allow merely periodic forms of unmediated political decision-making by the people such as occurs at referendums (rarely) and general elections. Individuals and groups remain free,

[14] *Capitalism, Socialism and Democracy* (New York, Harper & Row, 1942) at 262–63.

[15] The susceptibility of voters to manipulation by political parties is stressed by Schumpeter, ibid.

[16] *The Phantom Public* (New York, Harcourt, Brace and Co., 1925) at 47.

[17] J Sumption, *Trials of the State – Law and the Decline of Politics* (London, Profile Books, 2019).

of course, to raise political grievances and organise offline as well on social media to the extent permitted by the law and the 'acceptable use' policies of social media platforms.

Scholars whose normative position locates them more squarely within the democratic tradition criticise the liberal constitution's limited set of opportunities for popular expressions of political will. Wolin, for example, notes that an emphasis upon the settled laws and institutions of liberal democracy tames the creative power of the demos to refashion the polity. It reduces democracy to various representations of democracy; episodic contests among representative political parties for votes; to e-petitions; opinion polls; and public debates between leaders. In short, the liberal constitution closely regulates the amount and form of political contestation that is 'let in'. The democratic tradition by contrast insists upon the political primacy of citizens who enjoy equal status and from whom all authority to govern flows. It is an emancipatory republican project that draws on the potential of citizens to be the active and regular authors of the political structures and rules that govern their lives. A dramatic exposition is found in Thomas Jefferson's idea of finite constitutions that endure for one generation only. Jefferson considered it self-evident 'that the earth belongs in usufruct to the living; that the dead have neither powers nor rights over it'. More commonly, the democratic element of liberal democracy maintains that questions of constitutional meaning must ultimately be determined by the people directly or, at the very least, by their elected representatives, rather than the courts. Heavily implicated in this view of the primacy of political openness among equal citizens is the idea of maximum liberty of political expression. Without an extensive measure of freedom to engage in political discourse, ordinary citizens are inhibited from participating fully in the political life of their communities.

Situated within the democratic tradition, the 'deliberative turn' in political theory was a response to the challenge of voter apathy evident across a number of liberal democracies. It signalled a shift away from the limited, vote-centric accounts of citizen participation in politics found in Schumpeter and Lippmann. Deliberative theory wants the many to be at the centre of political decision-making. It sets out to institutionalise enhanced levels of citizen participation in political decision-making. Whilst not dismissing the role played by representative institutions of government, it draws upon accounts of participatory political decision-making in the 1960s and 1970s to make the case for popular involvement in framing societal laws and policies beyond periodic turnouts at the ballot box. A central function is assigned to 'the discussing of reasons' among citizens who, as political equals, become the authors of the laws under which they live. Whether in citizen assemblies or other fora (including online discussion spaces), deliberative democracy tasks participants with different world views to give reasons for their preferred policies in ways that are comprehensible and acceptable to others. They are encouraged to reflect upon and revise if necessary their earlier positions in the face of 'better' arguments put forward by others. The perfectionist component to deliberative democratic accounts stresses the improving effect on the quality of citizens' reason giving and interlocution in public affairs. The deliberative citizen can expect to be cured of his/her short-term and self-interested outlook on politics and be re-oriented towards the common good via the use of public and evidence-based reason. Discursive qualities of empathy, mutual respect and reciprocity are to be fostered among the participants. For participation to be productive the speaker must be responsible and responsive, seek common ground with others and develop thoughtful, cooperative strategies to realise shared goals. Inclusivity without the side restraints of public reason, civility and commonality results only in a 'cacophony of special pleadings'. The presence of side constraints means that short sighted, mob-rule incarnations of popular participation can be avoided. The republican credentials of deliberative democracy are evident in the stress upon decision-making structures of non-domination. Differences of status, education and wealth are required to be 'bracketed off' so that speakers interact as social peers.

The emphasis upon rational policymaking in deliberative democratic approaches is accentuated yet further in the epistemic variant of deliberative democracy. Endorsing the idea that large groups of people make smarter policy choices, the primacy of truth-seeking and outcome reliability in epistemic accounts over and above inclusive participatory procedures mean that political equality among citizens in policymaking will be sacrificed where inequality leads to more rational decision-making. To the epistemic democrat, expert-informed and led decision-making is preferable to more inclusive but error-prone mechanisms. Democratic legitimacy is happily traded away for quality outcomes. Significantly, the claims of patently 'irrational' and 'unevidenced' assertions and arguments to constitutional protection under a freedom of expression guarantee would not appear especially compelling.

Agonistic theories of democracy offer an alternative republican account of political pluralism, one based in the idea of unavoidable, ineradicable contestation among differently situated individuals and groups. Like deliberative accounts, agonist theories criticise two related features in liberal elitist accounts namely their (i) cynicism about levels of political apathy among citizens and (ii) lack of concern about the exclusion of poorly organised/articulated interests from decision-making fora. Similarly, the elitist model's conceptualisation of persons' values and norms as being formed and fixed in pre-political settings is at odds with agonist and deliberative democratic accounts who each point to the development and transformation of persons in the political sphere. At the same time, the perfectionist strand of deliberative democratic thinking is absent in agonist versions. The latter are not concerned to improve the quality of citizens' reasoning and encouraging their empathetic, other-regarding characteristics. Drawing on Greek antiquity, agonists hold out a tragic view of human life where conflict and suffering are unalterable features of an individual's existence. The deliberative democratic idea that political differences among citizens are surmountable and reconcilable given the right communicative framework is rejected. Agonists claim that differences are not capable of being progressively overcome by transcendent principles of rationality (public reason) deployed in institutional settings characterised by mutually respectful exchanges. Conflict between persons holding different worldviews is an ontological given. Deliberative democrats' emphasis upon commonality and shared interests is insufficiently attentive to the particular interests of differently situated individuals and groups. Human life for agonists is marked by struggle and disharmony. Any moments of accord and consensus in politics are mere contingent stabilisations which must sooner or later revert back to disharmony and conflict.

Privileging 'Responsible' Media – The Council of Europe's Narrowed Conception of Political Pluralism

The following section considers how the Council of Europe, in various institutional forms such as prominent advisory bodies (the Venice Commission for Democracy through Law and the European Audiovisual Observatory) and most importantly through the Strasbourg Court, has long advanced narrowed conceptions of political pluralism under Article 10 European Convention on Human Rights.[18] The narrowed conceptions correspond with ideas of socially responsible expression where care is taken to verify factual assertions, to evidence and corroborate claims and provide criticised parties with an opportunity to respond. Specifically, they are aligned to a model of journalism usually associated with professional media organisations. Legal protection for freedom of expression is made conditional on meeting professional codes of media practice. The seriously adverse implications of this conception of acceptable journalism for ordinary citizens' participation in political discourse require a greater degree of illumination than has hitherto been afforded in most Article 10 ECHR commentaries. The likely impacts of disfavouring non-professionally produced content are to consolidate existing elites' ability to shape the contours of public debate and further to marginalise disruptive, non-consensus seeking contributions As such, popular participation in public discourse is limited and political pluralism narrowed. An equivalent analysis of the processes by which UK domestic law and policy narrows political discourse is set out in chapter six.

[18] I do not discuss in detail complementary norms in EU law that place constraints on acceptable political expression. For a largely, though not wholly supportive, account of EU regulation of disinformation at odds with the critical stance taken in this book, see M Monti, 'The EU Code of Practice on Disinformation and the Risk of the Privatisation of Censorship' in S Giusti and E Piras *Democracy and Fake News* (London, Routledge, 2020). At the time of writing a new Digital Services Act package is proposed by the European Commission to tackle inter alia disinformation online. See also more generally J Oster, *European and International Media Law* (Cambridge, CUP, 2016).

The Venice Commission for Democracy through Law

The Venice Commission is comprised of constitutional judges, university professors of public and international law, MPs and civil servants nominated by its 62 strong member states.[19] The Commission acts as an advisory body and reports to the Council of Europe on 'issues of constitutional law including the functioning of democratic institutions and fundamental rights, electoral law and constitutional justice'. In 2016, the Commission published a compilation of opinions and reports concerning freedom of expression and media.[20] This stated:

> 1.4 LIMITATIONS ON THE FREEDOM OF EXPRESSION AND THE MARGIN OF APPRECIATION OF THE STATE
>
> (T)he Venice Commission does not support absolute liberalism. While there is no doubt that in a democracy all ideas, even though shocking or disturbing, should in principle be protected …, it is equally true that not all ideas deserve to be circulated. Since the exercise of freedom of expression carries duties and responsibilities, it is legitimate to expect from every member of a democratic society to avoid as far as possible expressions that express scorn or are gratuitously offensive to others and infringe their rights.[21]

Taking the meaning of 'gratuitous' to comprise 'unnecessary' and 'without cause or reason' the Venice Commission's understanding of protected expression under Article 10 of the Convention can be restated. Speakers should limit themselves to the non-scornful expression of ideas that *deserve* to be circulated. In respect of such ideas, their articulation must not offend others in ways that are unjustified or lacking in reason. As will be shown in the section on Convention jurisprudence below, the 'as far as possible' check on permissible speech limits does not significantly extend the range of permitted viewpoints or modes of expression. The angry speaker for example is expected to tone down his/her invective. The 'unreasonable' poster of online comments may still expect to have the post removed by a host platform. It is not too much of a stretch to say here that the Commission's view is that domestic authorities enjoy a broad leeway to close down forms of political expression that local majorities find offensive either on account of the tone or the content of the expression.

This reading of Article 10 offers a constitutional means for office holders and mainstream political parties to shut down their critics. As such, it might have merited particularly close scrutiny. Instead, it is the absence of reproving commentary concerning the Venice Commission's controversial reading of the outer

[19] There are 62 member states including 47 Council of Europe member states and 15 other countries including Algeria, Brazil, Kazakhstan, Kyrgyzstan, Morocco, Peru and the United States.

[20] European Commission for Democracy through Law: Compilation of Venice Commission Opinions and Reports concerning Freedom of Expression and Media (2016) available electronically at www.venice.coe.int/webforms/documents/?pdf=CDL-PI(2016)011-e (accessed January 2022).

[21] ibid at 8.

boundaries of political expression that is telling. The sanitised and safe public sphere that the constitutional judges and other legal experts on the Commission elaborated here bodes ill for an open and robust system of political contestation in which the technocratic, centrist policies of office holders are challenged by non-incumbents. When the representatives of a majority in a state say of a minority view that the opinion in question does not *deserve* to be circulated freely, that state's very commitment to an open democracy in which incumbent politicians are required to justify their actions and appeal to the ongoing support of the citizens must be in doubt.

The European Audiovisual Observatory and a Case of the Emperor's New Clothes

The *European Audiovisual Observatory* likewise operates under the aegis of the Council of Europe and provides 'a comparative European overview of the audio-visual industry in 41 different countries as well as detailed analysis of national and even regional industries'.[22] It has a Department of Legal Information that 'analyses key legal issues linked to the audiovisual sector and reports on major legal developments and ground breaking cases which affect media legislation in Europe'.[23]

In a 2017 report the *Observatory* stated that the proper function of journalism is neutral (ie non-partisan) observation and laying before the public 'new and correct information.[24] This is contrasted with 'partisan' or 'opinion journalism' 'which is asserted to bear its share of responsibility for 'the failure of the Weimar Republic and dominated until the end of National Socialism'.[25] The same section of materials is curiously nostalgic of developments in US print journalism at the end of the nineteenth century when the new business models of newspaper proprietors moved away from what the report labels 'opinion journalism' and party affiliation. Gaining mass markets through street sales and accompanying advertising revenues, the US media magnate Joseph Pulitzer is somewhat uncritically credited as an example of a proprietor who instituted a form of journalism that served no one political party 'but the people … (and was) the organ of truth'.[26] The Report proceeds to claim that 'this new information-based journalism determines modern journalism's self image'.[27]

[22] See www.obs.coe.int/en/web/observatoire/what-we-do (last accessed September 2019).

[23] ibid.

[24] K Renner 'The Historical Development of Norms of Journalism' in *Journalism and Media Privilege* IRIS *Special* European Audiovisual Observatory (Council of Europe) Strasbourg 2017, 4 available electronically at www.coe.int/en/web/freedom-expression/-/new-report-on-journalism-and-media-privilege-by-the-european-audiovisual-observatory- (last accessed July 2021).

[25] ibid.

[26] ibid.

[27] ibid at 5.

Leaving aside the highly questionable claim that the presses of media magnates such as Joseph Pulitzer[28] and William Randolph Hearst ever operated as the 'organs of truth' and promoted informed democratic government,[29] it is the broader construction and endorsement of journalism as non-partisan observation that truly stands out in the *Observatory* report. The idea that journalism has only ever been legitimately practised when it conveys factual information in a neutral way does not withstand any serious scrutiny. What is at issue here is the conceptual impossibility of neutrality and non-partisanship. The mere selection and ordering of new stories that are covered in the first place itself reveals value judgements about which current developments are important, less important and wholly unimportant in the eyes of journalists, editors and proprietors. Then, with respect to covered stories, the particular account that is rendered will give especial prominence to certain facts, less prominence to others and ignore others deemed irrelevant or wholly peripheral. Sources will be cited that themselves wish to advance particular partisan positions. The printed press across liberal democracies all tend to adopt and become known for their individual political leanings and places on the political spectrum. Broadly speaking, *El Pais* in Spain is considered centre left as is *La Repubblica* in Italy, whilst the *Frankfurter Allgemeine* in Germany is perceived as liberal-conservative as is *Le Figaro* in France. All this seems quite unremarkable and widely appreciated by readers. After all, there are no legal duties on print media to be fair and balanced to all political opinions when covering current affairs. The titles cited above are all examples of partisan journalism that, operating optimally, can only convey a partial and non-neutral account of public affairs.[30]

That said, a sceptical reader of the *Observatory's* Report is left with a sense of unease. Given its obvious detachment from realities of many current and previous emanations of the professional practice of journalism, what purpose is being served by the attempted perpetuation of a false and idealised notion of objective, non-partisan, truth-seeking journalists, editors and owners? Might it be possible that this version of the emperor's new clothes is being deployed to judge newer (non-traditional) digital speakers and outlets and find that the latter fall short of

[28] Pulitzer justified the sensationalism he deployed on his newspapers' front pages as Fuller writes, 'to lure people into the heart of the paper – especially the editorial page – where they would be educated', J Fuller, *What is Happening to News* (Chicago, University of Chicago Press, 2010) at 171. The luring was intended to bring readers round to the Joseph Pulitzer view of the world.

[29] William Randolph Hearst (like his father from whom he inherited several news titles) blatantly used his newspaper empire to advance his own political career. See further D Nasaw, *The Chief: The Life of William Randolph Hearst – The Rise and Fall of the Real Citizen Kane* (London, Gibson Square Books, 2003).

[30] In contrast, the broadcast sector in Europe is typically bound to observe duties of accurate reporting, impartiality and balance in its coverage of politics and current affairs. Now somewhat out of date Eric Barendt's *Broadcasting Law – A Comparative Study* (Oxford, Clarendon Press, 1995) nonetheless offers a useful survey of broadcasting regimes in Europe and the US. Of course, as for the same reasons that apply to the print media, the idea of a neutral broadcaster is an impossibility and thus lacks credibility.

the standards ('duties and responsibilities' in Article 10(2) ECHR) of their seemingly illustrious pre-digital professional counterparts? And might this falling short not unreasonably lead to the imposition of sanctions on these less professional speakers and, more importantly, the digital platforms that enable others to read/view the 'inferior and partisan' journalism that is being produced?

The European Court of Human Rights and Democratised Speech

> The danger that upper middle class judges and commentators will find middle class values fundamental is obviously present irrespective of methodology. I think it is exacerbated when 'reason' is the supposed value source, however, partly because the values we have mentioned are those of the 'reasoning class', and partly because 'reason' being an inherently empty source, may lend itself unusually well to being filled by the values of one's own kind.
>
> J Hart-Ely *Democracy and Distrust* (Massachusetts, Harvard University Press, 1980) 59 footnote **

Confronted in recent times with legal disputes arising from online expression, the Strasbourg Court has articulated a set of themes worthy of close attention. After paying lip service to the democracy-enhancing possibilities of digital speech, the Court has fallen back on a more fear-laden account of popular political expression. Policing the outer boundaries of Article 10 freedom of expression, the Court has fulfilled Hart-Ely's prediction by applying standards associated with professional journalism to content from non-professional speakers and found this democratised content to fall outside the protective ambit of Article 10. By granting national authorities a wide margin of appreciation to impose sanctions on content deemed irresponsible, the Court has positioned itself as the upholder of rational and civilised interchanges on matters of public interest as it doggedly resists the threats to an informed and decent democracy from such unwanted (though loosely defined) phenomena such as 'fake news' or 'hate speech'. The Court's stance in summary form seems to align with social responsibility theory, that is in favour of political expression framed by existing professional elites where the citizen features not (and cannot be trusted to act) as an active participant in political debates but almost exclusively as a member of the audience who is occasionally asked to select from a menu of political options laid before him/her by professional opinion formers. This under-inclusive account of political participation is manifested in several features of the jurisprudence detailed below. Ultimately it serves the liberal goal of holding popular sovereignty in check as judicial and political elites set the terms on which entry as a participant into the public sphere is conditioned. What is at risk however in this narrowed version of pluralist political debate is the democratic legitimacy of decision-making in Europe. Where political majorities in states and multi-national corporations are able to impose loosely crafted prohibitions on citizens' contributions to the public sphere, there is a palpable loss to the democratic legitimacy of processes and outcomes. The Strasbourg Court has played handmaiden to this loss of democratic legitimacy.

At the outset, we should note that lip service has been paid to the idea of a more participatory public arena in the digital era. In *Ahmet Yildirim v Turkey*[31] the blocking of Google sites hosting content not shown to be unlawful was found to have been in violation of Article 10, whilst in *Cengiz and others v Turkey*, the value of platform such as YouTube to citizen journalism was recognised in facilitating access to political materials often ignored by mainstream media.[32]

One of the important means by which the Court has narrowed political discourse is by requiring online, non-professional speech to be produced in accordance with ethical codes developed by professional news organisations. The Grand Chamber in *Stoll v Switzerland* for example advanced a conditional notion of journalistic freedom that requires speakers act in good faith and on an accurate factual basis and provide 'reliable and precise information'.[33] When the individual is 'confronted with vast quantities of information' from multiple sources including the electronic media, 'monitoring compliance with journalistic ethics takes on added importance'.[34] Aside from the Court's rather narrow conception of the citizen as merely the recipient of others' speech, it is apparent that professional codes' emphasis upon the verification and corroboration of published claims (and accompanying editorial processes) will usually be beyond the practical capacities of many bloggers and non-professional speakers.

In the case of user-generated content hosted on professional commercial news media sites on matters of undoubted public interest, the Court's fixing of legal duties and responsibilities on commercially run news portals in cases such as *Delfi As v Estonia* and *MTE & Index HU.ZRT v Hungary* is intended to avoid the contamination of public discourse.[35] In *MTE* 'heated discussions' and 'vulgar' comments from members of the public about the quality of estate agents' services from were adjudged to make no worthwhile contribution to an informed public sphere.[36] Placing the obligation on host sites to censor the intemperate and uncivil opinions expressed in online comments, naturally invites commercially run platforms to prioritise shareholder interests in avoiding any legal penalties.[37] Eight months previously, the Grand Chamber in *Delfi As v Estonia* had declined to find

[31] App No 3111/10 (Judgment 18 December 2012).

[32] App Nos 48226/10 and 14027/11 (Judgment 1 December 2015) and see for commentary D Voorhoof, 'Same Standards, Different Tools: The ECtHR and the protection and limitations of freedom of expression in the digital environment' in (eds N Bratza et al) *Human Rights Challenges in the Digital Age: Judicial Perspectives* (2020, Strasbourg, European Court of Human Rights & Council of Europe).

[33] App No 69698/01 (Judgment 10 December 2007) at para 103.

[34] ibid at para 104.

[35] *MTE & Index HU.ZRT v Hungary* (2016) App No 22947/13 (Judgment 2 February).

[36] ibid at para 72 (concurring judgment of Judge Kuris).

[37] At the same time the Court did note the limited adverse impact upon the criticised estate agents that followed from the fact that the comments were expressed online. See at para 77 'For the Court, the expressions used in the comments, albeit belonging to a low register of style, are common in communication on many Internet portals – a consideration that reduces the impact that can be attributed to those expressions.'

a violation of a commercial news portal's Article 10 rights.[38] The national courts had earlier held that a series of anonymous posts from members of the public in the comments section of the news portal's website were threatening, abusive and/or defamatory and had violated the personality rights of L, a board member of the ferry company. These posts had been made in response to a story published by *Delfi* about damage to ice bridges caused by a ferry company. The posts had not been caught by a software filter used by *Delfi* despite the fact that the posts complained of were in breach of *Delfi's* own rules that did not permit threatening/abusive/obscene or otherwise illegal posts. The offending statements were only removed after a number of weeks. By a majority of 15–2 the Grand Chamber found that fines imposed by the national courts did not breach Article 10. *Delfi* as an active publisher ought to have removed each post the moment it was uploaded, regardless of whether it had actual knowledge of the posts. The latitude given to national authorities by the Grand Chamber to regulate non-professional, invective-laden speech is striking. The Court was unwilling to revisit the questionable classification by national authorities of problematic 'hate' and 'abusive' speech forms, even when they referred to user comments on a matter of undoubted public interest. This can be particularly concerning where, as in *Delfi*, it occurs via a prior restraint in national law.[39]

These various assertions about the functions and duties of journalists and freedom of expression appear more attuned to an earlier, pre-digital era when just a few broadcast media outlets existed in each of the signatory states and controlled the dissemination of news and opinion about public affairs.[40] Even then as was argued above, print outlets across Europe have never been subject to the impartial and balanced coverage requirements typically imposed on the broadcast news/current affairs sector. The proprietors of print media and the journalists working for them have been free to advocate political viewpoints without facing legal liability for partisan coverage. Today those who receive content from online sources are aware that sources of news stories sent to their smartphones and tablets is partly a product of personal digital profiles created through past web usage.

The account of 'responsible journalism' offered by the Court in *MTE* and *Delfi* can also be considered in its normative dimension. Rather than seeing the emancipatory and democratising possibilities for digital speech in which channels of political participation and change are opened up to non-elite viewpoints, the citizen as 'speaker' is conceived largely as a threat to democracy, especially if he/she communicates intemperately. If he/she must speak at all, the various readings of Article 10 by the Venice Commission, the European Audiovisual

[38] App No 64569/09 (Judgment 16 June 2015).

[39] See additionally the strong condemnation of anonymised/pseudonymised speech in *Delfi* in Judge Zupancic's remarks. His stance overlooks the positive value of anonymous speech in certain situations for unpopular viewpoints in the workplace, neighbourhood or community, especially on matters of public interest, see further E Barendt, *Anonymous Speech* (Oxford, Hart, 2016).

[40] J Rowbottom, 'To Rant, Vent and Converse: Protecting Low Level Digital Speech' (2012) 71 CLJ 355.

Observatory and the Court cohere around the view that the speech of citizens must be deserving of dissemination and meet (or approximate closely to) professional journalist production values and etiquette. Crudely produced, highly-partisan comment on the other hand must be discouraged, since it hinders responsible and informed self-government. Whilst the desire for impartial, fact-driven, carefully edited journalism is understandable, it is not (as was noted previously) a standard that is required of professional print journalists. More fundamentally, it can be asked whether these standards ought to be applied in the first place if the *sine qua non* of an informed democracy is diversity of political viewpoint. The denial of constitutional protection under a free speech principle to those who fall short of these standards (via the imposition of civil/criminal liability upon the online platforms through which non-professionally produced political content is disseminated) is likely to discourage content from non-professional speakers who are less frequently and less widely heard than their professional counterparts. Even if such speakers are prepared to risk legal liability, they may well find that the hosting platform is not. As a consequence, the diversity of political viewpoint is diminished and challenges to mainstream and dominant opinion is made less visible.

Germany – Network Enforcement Act 2017

Across Europe, national laws are now imposing professional obligations on non-traditional speakers (objectivity, expertise, close approximation to practices associated with traditional journalism) or directly on social media platforms themselves to filter out certain types of content. Consider Germany's Network Enforcement Act 2017 (or NetzDG as it is sometimes referred to) which was widely heralded as the Federal Government's response to the problems of online 'hate speech' and 'fake news'.[41] The Act applies to social networks with more than 2 million registered users in Germany[42] and is intended to prompt platforms to respond more quickly and effectively to unlawful online content. Statutory deadlines for blocking such content are imposed. Thus 'manifestly unlawful' content must be blocked or taken down within 24 hours of a complaint being received. In respect of other unlawful content, the material must generally be blocked within a week of receiving a complaint. Platforms are also under an obligation to report and publish the outcomes of complaints cases where in excess of 100 complaints about unlawful content are made in the course of 12 months. Management systems to ensure compliance and the effective handling of complaints must be instituted.

[41] S Schwiddessen et al 'Germany's Network Enforcement Act – Closing the Net on Fake News?' (2018) 40 *European Intellectual Property Review* 539.

[42] At the time of its passing, the Act's 2 million user threshold was thought to catch some ten platform providers. The Act does not apply to platforms whose content is exclusively provided by professional journalists/editors or to one-to-one communications such as emails and messenger services such as WhatsApp.

Sanctions for systemic non-compliance[43] are primarily financial with a maximum penalty of 5 million euros for natural persons and 50 million euros for legal persons.[44]

The breadth of the restrictions upon 'unlawful content' is indicated by the list of prohibited forms of expression as set out in the *Strafgesetzbuch* (StGB or German Criminal Code). These include but are not limited to: dissemination of propaganda material or symbols of banned political parties;[45] public incitement to criminal activity;[46] dissemination of depictions of violence;[47] approving the commission of criminal offences;[48] insulting expression;[49] defamatory expression;[50] disturbing the exercise of religion.[51]

The 2017 Act is lauded in some quarters for incentivising the removal of material that is damaging to the formation of public opinion in democracies and making it more likely that rational discourse will prevail.[52] Criticism of the entrusting of censorship to democratically unaccountable private for-profit media platforms has been made by some, including David Kaye, the UN Special Rapporteur on Freedom of Opinion and Expression.[53] He concluded that the 2017 law would likely lead social networks to 'over-regulate expression – in particular to delete legitimate expression … as a precaution to avoid penalties'.[54] The short deadlines under which moderators were required to work would encourage blocking and removal of material, rather than a more considered approach to which material fell foul of the new law.[55] Significantly, the reach of the Act itself was criticised by the legal, science and research department of the *Bundesstag* as intruding into constitutionally protected expression.[56] One lawyer Joachim Steinhöfel has been active in representing clients banned by Facebook and Twitter for posts and tweets that were variously critical of Islam and German politicians.[57] He has been critical

[43] One safeguard for platforms is that fines can only be imposed in cases of systemic failure. In other words, one-off failures to block/remove will not be penalised.

[44] See www.taylorwessing.com/download/article-germany-nfa-impact-social.html.

[45] StGB s 86.

[46] StGB s 111.

[47] StGB s 131.

[48] StGB s 140.

[49] StGB s 185.

[50] StGB s 186.

[51] StGB s 166.

[52] See thus B Holznagel and M Hemmert-Halswick, 'Securing Rational Discourse Surrounding Referenda in Germany' in (eds S Baume, V Boillet and V Martenet) *Misinformation in Referenda* (Abingdon, Routledge, 2021).

[53] See www.ohchr.org/Documents/Issues/Opinion/Legislation/OL-DEU-1-2017.pdf (accessed in January 2022).

[54] ibid at 4.

[55] See www.taylorwessing.com/download/article-germany-nfa-impact-social.html.

[56] See www.bundestag.de/resource/blob/510514/eefb7cf92dee88ec74ce8e796e9bc25c/wd-10-037-17-pdf-data.pdf. For commentary on this and other criticism, see S Schwiddessen et al, 'Germany's Network Enforcement Act – Closing the Net on Fake News?' (2018) 40 *European Intellectual Property Review* 539, 542–44.

[57] See https://second.wiki/wiki/joachim_steinhc3b6fel#cite_note-jpost-581924-20.

of the social media platforms' role as the arbiters of permitted/censored expression. He created a NetzDG 'wall of shame' which he argued listed legal content suppressed under the 2017 Act.[58] Mueller reports that where right-wing nationalists in Germany were the early targets of takedowns, these groups then invoked the same provisions to have posts that were critical of the nationalist groups removed from the public sphere.[59] Other commentators have noted the tendency of laws such as NetzDG to incentivise excessive removal of material from platforms as they take a risk-averse response to new statutory regulations.[60]

Threats to Political Pluralism from Liberal Elitist, Deliberative (Civic Republican), Epistemic Accounts of Democracy

An earlier section of this chapter noted that liberal elitist accounts of democracy distrust direct and ongoing forms of popular participation in law and policymaking. Social responsibility theory, for example, is deeply troubled by the prospect of unmediated popular expression. The mainstream national political parties and a professional media commentariat function to guide political discussion away from non-elite outlooks and positions. Those who currently propose social responsibility theory as a cure to the ills of digital expression look back nostalgically to a Schumpertarian ideal of minimalist democracy – patrician office holders drawn from socio-political elites and a cadre of professional journalists and editors who frame and simplify public debates in terms that rarely deviate from the narratives of the mainstream political parties. Social responsibility proponents expect citizens to appreciate their own failings (apathy and ignorance in matters of politics) and then understand that these deficiencies mandate their minimal and irregular participation in the formulation of law and policy. Voters are to understand that the production and dissemination of news and opinion is the terrain of professional people and that popular participation and approval is required on an intermittent basis only to confer democratic legitimacy upon the policy positions devised by rival sets of party elites. In the Article 10 jurisprudence of European Court of Human Rights, the pre-digital era notion of the citizen as a passive listener/viewer, one who is transiently attentive to the choices presented to him/her by professional opinion formers persists into the digital epoch.

Contrastingly the deliberative turn in political theory associated with civic republicanism in the US literature (including by Cass Sunstein) and Jurgen

[58] See https://facebook-sperre.steinhoefel.de/.

[59] M Mueller, 'Challenging the Social Media Moral Panic' (2019) 876 *Policy Analysis* (Cato Institute) 23 July.

[60] D Keller 'Internet Platforms: Observations on Speech, Danger and Money' (2018) Hoover Institution Aegis Paper Series at https://papers.ssrn.com/sol3/papers.cfm?abstract_id=3262936 (accessed January 2022). I am grateful to Dr Eliza Bechtold for pointing out this source.

Habermas in works such as *Between Facts and Norms*[61] stresses the democratic legitimacy gains at a systemic level and the moral benefits at an individual citizen level of discursive justification and decision-making by autonomous politically equal citizens. The citizen is here an active author of law and policy who comes together in deliberative structures with other citizens. He/she is fair and reason-giving. He/she is also reflective and open to revise his/her original starting positions on account of better (more rational and reasonable) arguments from others about the public good. Sunstein's account of civic republicanism stresses four organising principles.[62] These are deliberation in politics; equality of political actors; universalism and citizenship.

The deliberative sphere favoured by Sunstein is characterised by considered reflection and debate. Its mediating institutions are designed to rule out immediate responses which he equates to impassioned, spontaneous contributions.[63] The principle of universalism posits that, through a well-functioning process of rational discussion and dialogue, 'substantively correct outcomes' on questions of the common good can be arrived at.[64] Amy Guttman, an advocate of deliberative structures, emphasises that the views and positions that participants bring to public deliberation must be 'reasonable'. Expression in favour of 'the routine murder of innocents, arbitrary arrests, systematic deception …' falls outside of the bounds of what counts as reasonable, thereby disqualifying the speaker from participation in public discourse.[65]

The implications of the deliberativists' emphasis upon rationality and reasonableness on the processes of democratic will formation are worth pausing to consider. Wenman comments that the overriding value attached to rationality and reasonableness in bringing the 'better' argument to the fore means that the

> constituent power is governed normatively from the start by transcendental principles of inclusion and reciprocity or locked into a dialectical process whereby interlocutors progressively learn these virtues as they move towards an unconstrained consensus.[66]

Honig for her part points out how in this model genuine moments of democratic innovation are 'assessed not in terms of the new worlds they may bring into being but rather in terms of their appositeness to … models already in place: incomplete

[61] Cambridge, MIT Press 1996.

[62] 'Beyond the Republican Tradition' (1988) 97 *Yale LJ* 1539.

[63] In *#Republic* (New Jersey, Princeton University Press, 2017), Sunstein argues against *all* direct forms of democratic decision-making. 'I have emphasised throughout that a republic is not a direct democracy, and that a good democratic system contains institutions designed to ensure a measure of reflection and debate – not immediate responses to whatever the people happen, at any particular moment in time, to say that they want' (at 258). Sunstein rules out, it will be noted, the possibility that a spontaneous, unmediated response may be both authentic and justified.

[64] 'Beyond the Republican Tradition' (1988) 97 *Yale LJ* 1539 at 1554.

[65] 'The Challenge of Multiculturalism in Political Ethics' (1993) 22 *Philosophy and Public Affairs* 171.

[66] M Wenman, *Agonistic Democracy – Constituent Power in the Era of Globalisation* (Cambridge, CUP, 2013) at 84.

but definitive in their contours'.[67] Conflict between values and worldviews is thus conceived of as a transient phenomenon and conquerable once a sense of a political community with shared objectives emerges. Citizens develop as autonomous reasoning agents able to evaluate for themselves the claims and counter-claims they encounter in the public sphere.[68]

For Mouffe, like Honig, even when presented in these terms, deliberation still presents 'a rationalist constraint on the democratic constituent power'.[69] The deliberative principles of fairness and reciprocity may, as Schaap observes, be said to 'predetermine what counts as legitimate political participation'.[70] Sanders for her part objects that deliberative democrats' insistence upon talk that is 'rational, contained and oriented towards a shared problem … implicitly excludes talk that is passionate … and the product of particular interests'.[71] She thus criticises some democrats for adopting and perpetuating the exclusionary standards of anti-democratic thinkers such as Joseph Schumpeter that appeal to notions of expertise, rationality and moderation. Sanders argues that these standards ensure the absence of ordinary citizens from public debate. Deliberative democrats are thus criticised for paying insufficient attention to how moral disagreements in politics are contoured by inequalities of power.[72] Others have doubted whether the promised nirvana of deliberative democracy – unforced consensual outcomes – do in fact emerge out of well designed structures. Shapiro for example has raised the disquieting (for deliberativists) possibility that deliberation might bring disagreements to the surface from a largely sub-conscious origin and into sharper focus, with the result that conflicts become exacerbated. He maintains that 'there is no particular reason to think that deliberation will bring people together, even if they (the deliberativists) hope it will and want to'.[73]

The precise implications of Sunstein's civic republicanism for the constitutional protection of free speech rest upon an understanding of the role played by objectively determined (ie universally valid) correct outcomes. How would Sunstein view the imposition by popularly elected representative legislatures of limitations on political expression? What of statutes banning (i) the advocacy

[67] 'Another Cosmopolitanism? Law and Politics in the New Europe' in R Post (ed) *Another Cosmopolitanism* (New York, OUP, 2006).

[68] There is a good critical summary of themes in deliberative democracy scholarship by Lynn Sanders, 'Against Deliberation' (1997) 25 *Pol. Theory* 347.

[69] C Mouffe, 'Democracy, Power and the "Political"' in (ed S Benhabib) *Democracy and Difference: Contesting the Boundaries of the Political* (New Jersey, Princeton University Press, 1996) at 138.

[70] See A Schaap, 'Agonism in Divided Societies' (2006) 32 *Phil. & Soc. Crit.* 255, 257 cited in M Wenman, *Agonistic Democracy: Constituent Power in the Era of Globalisation* at 85.

[71] 'Against Deliberation' (1997) 25 *Pol. Theory* 347, 360.

[72] A point also made by I Shapiro, 'Enough of Deliberation: Politics is about Interests and Power' in (ed. S Macedo, *Deliberative Politics: Essays on Democracy and Disagreement* (1999, OUP, New York) at 29.

[73] Shapiro ibid at 31. See also O'Leary who notes that deliberative democracy is 'bland and "considered" at a time when political life is passionate and adversarial', at K O'Leary, 'Machiavellian Democracy: An Engine for Reform' (2011) *The Good Society* 141, 152.

of abortion or (ii) the burning of the national flag? Redish and Lippman argue that Sunstein would not approve these sorts of limitations on popular expression since they are at odds with his own preferred moral standpoint.[74] On the other hand, statutory prohibitions on (i) mandating pupils to salute the national flag in state schools or (ii) speech that advocates the closure of abortion clinics are required on Sunstein's view to be treated with greater respect. The reason that saluting the flag/advocacy of abortion clinic closure may be barred on the civic republican account is that both repudiate the nation's ideals or the aspiration to be a political community.[75] Put another way, Sunstein is saying that the ideas targeted by the statute comprise viewpoints that are not worthy of being heard.[76] As Redish and Lippman point out, civic republicanism endorses viewpoint discrimination by the state and the consequent skewing of public discourse in favour of the 'correct' outcomes. This fatally compromises the ability of citizens to govern themselves. Civic republicans can thus be said to deny the 'intellectual integrity of the individual' and reject 'a pervasive moral scepticism about – and fear of – the possibility of a governmental ascertainment of universal moral truth'.[77] And if there are 'right' answers on political/moral questions that are knowable from the start, then why bother holding a deliberation exercise at all? At bottom, Sunstein's prescriptions about the terms on how citizens ought to participate in public forums should recall John Hart Ely's warning in *Democracy and Distrust* quoted earlier where he cautioned against an uncritical reliance upon the concept of 'reason'. This, he argued, was 'an inherently empty source' and lent itself 'unusually well to being filled by the values of one's own kind'.[78] Sunstein and other deliberative democracy scholars in the republican tradition depart entirely from ideas of popularly authored constitutions in favour of a liberal Enlightenment project that gives primacy and permanency to the constituted norms and institutions of the liberal state that are reflective of the use of public reason. The converse notion that political life might be characterised at an ontological level by ultimately irresolvable disputes engaged in by passionate and heated disputants who wish to start the world again in mutually irreconcilable ways is wholly absent from the bland and confected imaginings of the liberal mind that seeks the overcoming of political difference.

[74] M Redish and G Lippman, 'Freedom of Expression and the Civic Republican Revival in Constitutional Theory – The Ominous Implications' (1991) 79 *Cal. L. Rev.* 267, 290.

[75] See, for an argument along these lines, F Michelman, 'Saving Old Glory; On Constitutional Iconography' (1990) 42 *Stan. L. Rev.* 1337, 1362.

[76] Echoing Meiklejohn's preferred description of First Amendment freedoms as extending to the point where everything that was worth saying be said, as opposed to giving everyone the freedom to speak. See A Meiklejohn, *Political Freedom: The Constitutional Powers of the People* (New York, Harper, 1960) at 26.

[77] M Redish and G Lippman, 'Freedom of Expression and the Civic Republican Revival in Constitutional Theory – The Ominous Implications' (1991) 79 *Cal. L. Rev.* 267, 272.

[78] J Hart-Ely *Democracy and Distrust* (Massachusetts, Harvard University Press, 1980) 59 fn **.

Operationalising Deliberative (Not Popular) Democracy – The Citizens' Assembly

Citizens' assemblies have flourished in Ireland, Iceland and some Brazilian municipalities in recent years with unpaid members of the public being asked to give up weekends over a period of months to reflect on possible reforms to domestic laws on abortion, gay marriage, voting reform, budgetary matters and climate change.[79] Although academic commentaries have been favourable in the main, these should be viewed with a degree of scepticism. Some of the more sanguine accounts have been authored by the same academics who were instrumental in the advocacy of the assemblies in the first place and later helped in their operationalisation.[80] As mechanisms to promote popular participation in political discussion, however, the various 'mini-publics' such as citizens' assemblies promulgated by deliberative democrats are structured in ways that constrain the articulation of diverse, plural perspectives.

Citizens' assemblies may be brought into being by legislatures to deliberate upon a topic that has been pre-selected by the legislature. They may be tasked with sending recommendations back to the legislature for further consideration that might at some point culminate in a national referendum. Those favouring a truly participatory form of politics could be forgiven for having serious misgivings about this particular form of apparently active self rule.[81] After all, neither the selection of the topic under deliberation nor the decision to hold a national plebiscite nor the precise formulation or constitutional status of the plebiscite question are in the gift of the citizen deliberators. These matters remain at all times the preserve of the 'designing engineers', namely the professional politicians. To this we can add the role of the academic/professional expert in scoping possible reform options. This is clearly significant in terms of how citizens' assemblies identify the pressing issues at hand, the values that inform their resolution and the conclusions they are likely to endorse at the end of the process. It does not seem implausible

[79] For a positive overview see H Landemore, *Open Democracy – Reinventing Popular Rule in the Twenty-First Century* (New Jersey, Princeton University Press, 2020).

[80] See, for example, the sanguine accounts of D Farrell in inter alia, '"Systematizing" Constitutional Deliberation: the 2016–18 Citizens' Assembly in Ireland' (2018) 34 *Irish Pol. Sts.* 113 (with J Suiter and C Harris); and J Suiter, D Farrell and C Harris, 'The Irish Constitutional Convention: A Case of "High Legitimacy"?' in (eds) M Reuchamps and J Suiter, *Constitutional Deliberative Democracy in Europe* (2016, ECPR, Colchester) at 33–51.

[81] S White, 'Citizens' Assemblies and Republican Democracy' in (ed B Leipold, K Nabulsi and S White) *Radical Republicanism – Recovering the Tradition's Popular Heritage* (Oxford, OUP, 2020) at 92. He is more sanguine about the democratic republican credentials of the Petition-Assembly-Referendum model (PAR) in which ordinary citizens petition for a citizens' assembly on a topic of their choosing. When the number of petitioners crosses a specified threshold, the Citizens' Assembly is established and, on reaching its conclusions, is able directly to put its preferred position to the electorate in a referendum. Where the proposed reform is backed by a majority/special majority of voters, the legislators are then bound to enact an implementing law.

to say the briefing papers authored by such experts and circulated in advance to assembly members have an important steering role in identifying possible reform options and ruling out others. The executive's choice of the briefing academic/professional expert/politician alone would inevitably shape the identification of pertinent issues, the articulation of implicated values and the range of possible solutions likely to be recommended by the assembly. The risk of elite manipulation of the process must also be addressed. In the Irish Constitutional Convention set up in 2012 one-third of the 99 members were politicians (29 drawn from the Oireachtas and 4 members representing the main political parties). In a noticeably more critical analysis of the Convention's work, Carolan highlighted the risks of manipulation by elite actors. As he notes, the fact 'that those elites may have been liberal, charitable or voluntary in character does not make their involvement unobjectionable'.[82] The unequal access to and influence exerted over the agenda of the Convention is rightly faulted by Carolan as 'substantially weaken(ing) its descriptive and deliberative legitimacy'.[83]

Nor does it seem that lay members of deliberative assemblies are always randomly selected. In the case of the Irish Constitutional Convention the 'random' selection managed to pick a husband and wife, as well as two next-door neighbours.[84] The demands of regular weekend deliberations would have screened out those with clashing family/work responsibilities. In one 99-member assembly, only 61 members attended the concluding session whilst a mere 28 members managed to attend every single meeting.[85] Proponents of citizen assemblies concede that assembly meetings tend to be peopled by the 'usual suspects' who already constitute the keenest participants in local and national elections.[86] In an otherwise positive evaluation of the Icelandic Constitutional Process 2010–13, Landemore concedes that the directly elected 25 member *Constitutional Council* tasked with producing a draft constitution to be put to the electorate in a non-binding referendum was 'elitist'.[87] She records the fact that the academic community were overrepresented, as were citizens drawn from the capital city Reykjavik as opposed to outlying rural areas. In class terms, only one trade unionist was on the committee. Wealthier individuals were more likely to engage with the process than their less wealthy counterparts. Even the act by Council members of posting drafts of proposed constitutional reforms online for all to see highlighted, Landemore concedes, the

[82] E Carolan, 'Ireland's Constitutional Convention: Behind the Hype about Citizen-led Constitutional Change' (2015) 13 *Int. Jo. Const. Law* 733, 744–45.

[83] ibid. McCormick's otherwise admirable defence of popular decision-making, *Machiavellian Democracy* (Cambridge, CUP, 2013), omits to consider the potential for elite domination in citizen assemblies, see 182–83.

[84] See www.politico.eu/article/the-myth-of-the-citizens-assembly-democracy/.

[85] See www.politico.eu/article/the-myth-of-the-citizens-assembly-democracy/.

[86] ibid, citing the concerns of Professor Will Jennings, a proponent and designer of citizen assemblies in the UK.

[87] H Landemore, *Open Democracy – Reinventing Popular Rule for the Twentieth First Century* 160 fn 14.

'demographically skewed' nature of the online respondents.[88] She reveals them to be 'mostly older, educated, white males'. Wealthy individuals from outside Iceland also participated in the exercise. One respondent, a wealthy American who owned property in Iceland wrote on the Council's Facebook page that she hoped the interest of foreign property owners would be properly considered.

The Epistemic Democratic Turn

A development to come out of the deliberative turn in political philosophy is epistemic democracy which is committed to procedures of citizen decision-making assisted by 'expert' briefings from selected academics and other professionals. For some epistemic democrats, there is a clear benefit to scaled-up versions of citizen deliberation in even larger 'mini-publics'. The greater the number of citizens that are involved in the deliberative exercise – giving public reasons for their policy preferences and reflecting on the views of others – the greater the likelihood that they will become more competent interlocutors thereby increasing the likelihood that correct/truthful outcomes will be generated.[89] For the epistemic democrat, there need to be independent criteria for ascertaining which procedures best advance the search for the truth and just outcomes. Epistemic democrats emphasise that meaningful self-government is hindered by the inclusion of claims in public discourse that lack truthful content. The screening out of falsehoods is vital if there is to be progress towards ever more 'enlightened' and 'rational' forms of self-government.

Schwartzberg notes how much epistemic democracy scholarship is anchored to justifications about outcome reliability. Although seemingly supportive of the 'wisdom of crowds'[90] epistemic accounts of democracy ultimately prioritise the generation of truthful outcomes over the deliberativists' more procedural emphasis upon inclusive and mutually respectful interlocutions. Schwartzberg pertinently questions the appeal 'to comprehensive doctrines, or … the truth-aptness of most questions confronting modern democracies'.[91] Is there a 'correct' answer to whether corporation tax should be at 10 per cent, 25 per cent or 60 per cent? Is it true that public spending on schools and hospitals should be increased year on year regardless of the overall state of GDP? What is the right level of immigration

[88] ibid at 162. Unsurprisingly, Landemore reveals them to be 'mostly older, educated, white males'. One respondent, a wealthy American who owned property in Iceland wrote on the Council's Facebook page that she hoped that the interests of foreign property owners would be properly considered.

[89] But see Sunstein in *Republic.com* on the problems of (i) pressure to conform in group discussions and (ii) information cascades whereby some the judgments of some sub groups are persuasive by other sub groups who fail separately to exercise their own judgment, at 83–92.

[90] See thus H Landemore, 'Deliberation, Cognitive Diversity, and Democratic Inclusiveness: An Epistemic Argument for the Random Selection of Representatives' (2013) 190 *Synthese* 1209 and by the same author *Open Democracy – Reinventing Popular Rule in the Twenty-First Century*.

[91] M Schwartzberg, 'Epistemic Democracy and its Challenges' (2015) 18 *Am. Rev. Pol. Sci.* 187 at 188.

for a society such as the UK?[92] That an epistemic democrat would claim to know the 'correct' answer to such questions begs a more fundamental question about why any degree of citizen participation in political decision-making is valued at all. If outcome reliability is the critical marker of the well-functioning or otherwise of a decision-making process, then there is no reason why the degree of citizen participation in this process is relevant.

Urbinati in *Democracy Disfigured* rightly criticises the foundational nature of outcome reliability in epistemic democracy accounts. She contends that the legitimacy of democracy properly understood rests upon ideas of *doxa*, that is freely formed common opinion and the revisability of decisions, as opposed to the ability of democratic systems of government to generate correct decisions. Although 'good outcomes are what candidates promise and citizens expect',[93] the failure to generate such outcomes does not for Urbinati render democracy weak. The success or otherwise of a democratic polity is whether an open and free competition between different views and ideas is permitted. The epistemic democrats seek to quieten the clamour and disputatious public realm by depoliticising democracy.[94] As Urbinati states, '(o)nce it is made the terrain of truth, politics becomes inhospitable to contestation and liberty'.[95] Epistemic democrats' primary insistence upon the pursuit of truth over the expression of opinion 'deform(s) democracy's distinctive cacophony and imprecise character which is essential to the enjoyment of political freedom'.[96]

Moreover, once the search for truthful outcomes is prioritised, the idea of political equality and its fundamental connection to self-government is liable to be questioned because intellectual understanding of political issues is not possessed to the same degree across the citizenry. From this premise, one can justify the substitution (as has occurred recently in some European states) of elected governments by technocratic ones on the grounds that the latter are far better equipped to identify and implement supposedly rational policy decisions in economic and financial matters.[97] In chapter six which deals with the regulation of disinformation in the UK with reference to the coronavirus pandemic, the epistemic democratic goal of having experts determine the contours of the collective decision-making processes is shown to inform current governmental thinking. Ensuring that the people reject

[92] As Schwartzberg states, '(t)he most obvious challenge is whether we should believe that most questions posed to democracy have right answers', ibid at 193.

[93] N Urbinati, *Democracy Disfigured: Opinion, Truth and the People* (Massachusetts, Harvard University Press, 2014) at 98.

[94] ibid at 96.

[95] ibid at 99.

[96] ibid at 6.

[97] N Urbinati, *Democracy Disfigured* at 83. For a recent attempt to justify a role for 'expert' inputs to democratic decision-making on epistemic grounds see C Holst and A Molander, 'Epistemic Democracy and the Role of Experts' (2019) 18 *Contemp. Pol. Theory* 541. As stated earlier, such arguments do however rely on the foundational (and highly questionable) claim that there can be 'truth' about political decisions and that some expert-led/assisted procedures are better at tracking these truthful outcomes than their non-expert equivalents.

bad/incorrect opinions and policies and endorse instead good/correct alternatives lies at the heart of recent developments such as the UK Government's Coronavirus Disinformation Unit and the regulatory strategy of OFCOM (the UK's communications regulator) on COVID-19 dis/misinformation. Working alongside social media platforms, these emanations of the state aim to stamp out purported falsehoods about the coronavirus and its mutations. A group of experts and officials appointed/employed by the executive work to ensure the removal/non-appearance of problematic claims in online spaces. Regrettably at the time of writing, there would seem to be little or no appetite on the part of the UK legislature to engage in democratic oversight of the work of these agencies.

Of course, even if we could confidently identify 'correct' policy decisions in areas where science and politics conjoin,[98] an irritating question would remain about what is to happen to dissenting opinion once it is revealed to be 'wrong'. Does epistemic democracy require that such opinion be silenced or, less dramatically, merely made less visible via a search algorithm that demotes ('shadow bans') the erroneous material away from the top search results on the topic? Faced with a choice between an expert elite that is capable of identifying 'wise' policy positions and a more broadly participative and democratic set of procedures for determining policy outcomes, the epistemic democrat will always lean away from intellectually deficient collective decision-making in favour of epistocratic forms of rule.[99]

In summary, both the epistemic and deliberative accounts of democracy seek the exclusion of what each considers to be unreasoned contributions from public discourse. They share the view that majoritarian decision-making procedures whether direct (elections and referenda) or indirect (as via elected assemblies/legislatures) are prone to democracy's inherent failing, namely a lack of rationality. The agon must be closed off to those who cannot or will not commit to reasoned discourse.

Containing Majoritarian Passions – Pettit's Aristocratic Republic of Reason and Critics

The role played by deliberative reason in republican political thought is perhaps most fully brought out in the work of Phillip Pettit. His distrust of the impassioned

[98] This must remain doubtful for a number of reasons, not the least of which is the fact that what science can reveal about anything at any one time is, at best, falsifiable and open to be doubted by others in subsequent replicated studies. The provisional nature of scientific understanding is sometimes called 'Popperian' after Karl Popper's work on the non-conclusive nature of affirmatory positive results in scientific experimentation and explanation. See also in this regard Richard Feynman's work *The Pleasure of Finding Things Out* (New York, Basic Books, 1999), in which the central role played by doubt in advancing human knowledge is stressed. 'A scientist is never certain. We all know that. We know all our statements are approximate statements with different degrees of certainty' at 111.

[99] D Estlund and H Landemore, 'The Epistemic Value of Democratic Deliberation' in (eds. A Bachtiger et al) *The Oxford Handbook of Deliberative Democracy* (Oxford, OUP, 2018) at ch 7.

nature of ordinary citizen participation in political decision-making locates his body of work most firmly in the category of aristocratic republicanism.[100] Pettit's republican account of liberty not only draws upon a Madisonian-type aversion to the 'pure' democracy associated with fifth century BC Athens, it also doubts the capacity of representative forms of majoritarian democracy to avoid arbitrary exercises of power over the lives of citizens. These features of Pettit's work are examined in more detail in chapter four.[101] For the time being we can note several anti-popular features of his deliberative republican state. The 'republic of reason' he constructs is designed to protect the individual from the passions and will (tyranny) of the majority. Popularly reached decisions are tainted by an endemic lack of rationality. Here everyday passions, aspirational morality and sectional interests combine to derail the pursuit of rational policies derived from reasoned argument. Governments will, he fears, naturally tend to adopt policies that track the interests of the majority to the neglect of minorities.

The major role in framing political choices has to be entrusted elsewhere. For Pettit, the task of framing is best left to institutions where rational thought can be trusted to prevail. It is to deliberative fora, expert advisory committees and judicial review that we should turn to generate policy positions. The role of popularly elected assemblies in Pettit's republic is limited to the affirmation or rejection of policy proposals. The initiation and deliberation functions that we associate with executives and legislatures today are thus stripped away. Parliament needs to be removed from the policy initiation and deliberation stages of law and policymaking on account of the fact that it reflects the passions and the incompetencies of the demos. A question that arises for Pettit here is how can he be sure that these flaws do not infect the legislature's affirmatory processes too?

Pettit's depoliticisation strategy advocates 'contestatory practices' where citizens can monitor and challenge the outcomes of decision-making bodies away from 'tumult of popular discussion and away even, from the theater of parliamentary debate'.[102] Unsurprisingly, Pettit does not think that referenda can be a safe way of contesting or editing the decisions of legislatures since they give direct expression to people's incompetence and passions, thereby facilitating irrational outcomes. As will be seen in chapter four, the 'editorial' role Pettit advocates for citizens via contestation of the affirmatory decisions of legislatures turns out on closer inspection to be far removed from ideas of popular oversight or veto over the outputs of elected bodies. Pettit's focus on the threat of arbitrary interference in minority lives posed by impassioned majoritarian politics leads him to endorse elite mechanisms of oversight such as expert commissions and, to a significant degree, courts and judges. The underlying assumption that such commissions and courts will avoid simply endorsing/reproducing outcomes favourable to another

[100] J McCormick, *Machiavellian Democracy* (Cambridge, CUP, 2012) at ch 6.
[101] P Pettit, *Republicanism: A Theory of Freedom and Government* (Oxford, OUP, 2001) at 176.
[102] ibid at 196. See also P Pettit, 'Depoliticizing Democracy' (2004) 17 *Ratio Juris* 52.

minority – existing socio-economic elites – remains unproven. It is difficult, however, to dismiss entirely the plebeian concern that the senior judiciary and other panels of the 'great and good' selected by existing office holders will 'edit' laws in ways favourable to such elites. Pettit could thus fairly be said to disregard the patent and oft-repeated failure of elite office holders to track majoritarian interests. As Hirschl comments in his comparative analysis of the juridification of rights, when policy choices are taken out of democratic politics, this move is often implicitly endorsed or even actively prompted by hegemonic elites and powerful vested interests on the basis that it will likely maintain the existing distribution of wealth and power.[103] Pettit's faith in the ability of judges to protect vulnerable minorities' interests is particularly concerning when one considers in addition just how unequal access to courts and legal proceedings is for many citizens. In the final analysis, Pettit's prescriptions disclose an absence of concern for isonomia. He is unperturbed by the unequal opportunity for differently placed citizens to shape the laws. Indeed, in Pettit's republic of reason, it is rather the institutions and laws of the republic that are required to be protected from the citizens.

A more clearly delineated concern with isonomy is evident in the work of republican theorists who defend the primacy of democratically elected representative law-making assemblies. These parliamentary republicans' objection to Pettit centres upon the claim that elitist judges and expert commissions will engage in partisan and potentially arbitrary oversight over majority decision-making in legislatures concerning contested matters such as rights and freedoms. The content of rights is best determined by procedures that accord equal weight to each elector's views via mediated structures of representation thereby respecting individual autonomy. Representative assemblies bring a wide range of knowledge and expertise into governing structures. They can check wealthy and powerful minorities. They can provide ongoing revision of rights from a position of democratic authorisation.

Unfortunately, leading defences of parliamentary political processes manage in the main to ignore the distorting grip of wealthy and politically powerful groups over parliamentary processes. To be fair, Urbinati in *Democracy Disfigured* does mention campaign finance reform as an issue requiring attention on account of current unequal opportunities for political advocacy.[104] Outside the issue of political party campaign finance reform, however, she does not identify the several other means by which representative democracies are subject to capture/undue influence by powerful interests.[105] Nor does she consider how reforms to legislative procedure intended to secure greater responsiveness to citizens' interests might

[103] R Hirschl, *Towards Juristocracy – The Origins and Consequences of the New Constitutionalism* (Massachusetts, Harvard University Press, 2004) at 213–14.

[104] N Urbinati, *Democracy Disfigured: Opinion, Truth and the People* at 53–58.

[105] A criticism also made by J McCormick, 'The New Ochlophobia? Populism, Majority Rule and Prospects for Democratic-Republicanism' in (ed) Y Elazar and G Rousseliere, *Republicanism and the Future of Democracy* (New York, CUP, 2019).

be implemented in the face of existing office holders' self-interested defence of the status quo.

Bellamy, in *Political Constitutionalism – A Republican Defence of the Constitutionality of Democracy*, stresses the role played by free elections and political parties in securing decision-making by majority rule.[106] Provided parliamentary scrutiny mechanisms over executive power are appropriately robust, mediated majoritarian rule is said to offer a sufficient means of protecting rights and the rule of law. Parliamentary determinations of rights questions will bring a wide range of knowledge to bear on difficult questions and produce settlements that can be revisited more easily than their judicially determined equivalents. Rights-based judicial review on the other hand is more likely to promote the interests of privileged groups who enjoy relatively easy access to courts at the expense of their disadvantaged counterparts.[107]

Bellamy's defence of representative party politics overlooks 'less visible and more insidious' inequalities between elites and non-elites.[108] He fails to acknowledge, let alone interrogate, how parliamentary rule-making occurs within inegalitarian social structures that undermine any formal equality among citizens. We may each have one vote in the choice of legislative representatives but it is surely a mis-step from here to claim that, in the reality of practical politics, this is mirrored in terms of equal access to ministers and MPs in the formation/application of policy or subsequently in holding the executive to account.[109] Bellamy's account of parliamentary politics assumes at times a genteel and patient form of polite disputation in which sensible and enlightened representatives argue about the common good and reach a compromise after 'hearing the other side'. Like the accounts of deliberative democracy examined in the preceding pages, the successful operation of a political system is thereby defined by its ability to yield a consensus outcome among (a narrow set of privileged) participants.[110]

Aitchison makes the telling point that the defences of the primacy of parliamentary models of law and policy such as outlined by Urbinati and Bellamy offer at best a partial account of citizen engagement with politics. They do not consider or evaluate what he labels the 'more antagonistic modes of claim-making' by ordinary people who confront entrenched power inequalities.[111] Aitchison considers that

[106] R Bellamy *Political Constitutionalism – A Republican Defence of the Constitutionality of Democracy* (Cambridge, CUP, 2007).

[107] Judicial resolutions of rights questions can accordingly constitute a form of domination.

[108] G Aitchison, 'Three Models of Republican Rights: Juridical, Parliamentary and Populist' (2017) 65 *Pol. Sts.* 339, 347.

[109] For a very clear example of privileged access enjoyed by recently departed Ministers see former Prime Minister David Cameron's lobbying of the Chancellor of the Exchequer in April 2020 in order to win contracts for Greensill Capital under the Government's COVID-19 support scheme. Repeated contact was made via informal text messages and personal phone calls to ministers. Mr Cameron held a 'very significant economic interest in the firm' according to a critical House of Commons Treasury Select Committee Report *Lessons from Greensill Capital* at https://publications.parliament.uk/pa/cm5802/cmselect/cmtreasy/151/15102.htm (published 20 July 2021).

[110] R Bellamy, 'Rights as Democracy' (2012) 15 *Crit. Rev. of Int. Soc. & Pol. Phil.* 449.

[111] ibid.

there is scant space in either juridical/parliamentary models for 'non-institutional forms of popular struggles as a creative source of norms and as a countervailing force to corrupt and dysfunctional institutions'.[112] The practices and procedures found in assemblies and legislatures cannot ground a renewal in political claim-making. Groups who lack access to the formal rights of full democratic citizenship (eg irregular migrants, prisoners), or who lack the means or standing to exercise rights of citizenship effectively (the homeless) are thus shut out of parliamentary processes. This is a vitally important perspective to retain when contemplating the regulation of political expression by ordinary people. At their optimal design, the extra-parliamentary fora offered by online speech platforms could facilitate a renewal in claim-making by non-elite speakers and groups.

Conclusion – Ongoing Ineliminable Conflict: Truly Plural, Participatory Politics

Whilst more aligned to a republican vision of politics and popular sovereignty than its Schumpeterian minimalist democracy alternative, I have argued in this chapter that deliberative democracy accounts of participatory politics are defective for a number of reasons that may be tied to the narrowing of political discourse. I am saying here that the various versions of deliberative, reasoning republics are mistakenly aimed at the overcoming of political difference and conflict. Such strategies are suspect on account of their effect of dampening the responsiveness and accountability of elites to citizens. The taming of discord and disagreement that occurs via the contestatory institutions (Pettit) or via parliamentary politics (Urbinati/Bellamy) has lost sight of the vital importance of ferocious and uncivil disharmony to republican politics.[113] McCormick observes in this regard that:

> the constructively participatory and tranquillity-inclined disposition of civic-culture approaches may not generate the required animosity to encourage better responsiveness and greater accountability among elites. Contentiousness over different conceptions of the common good, over more or less just forms of domination, provides this in Machiavelli's Rome.[114]

In this concluding section, I want to set out a brief understanding of the radically pluralist account of participatory politics that is contained in agonist accounts of democracy. This is intended to provide a theoretically informed background to arguments for an inclusive account of expressive freedom that is sketched out later in the book. For Machiavelli, the passions and antagonisms of the popular

[112] G Aitchison, 'Three Models of Republican Rights: Juridical, Parliamentary and Populist' (2017) 65 *Pol. Sts.* 339, 340.

[113] J McCormick, 'Machiavellian Democracy: Controlling Elites with Ferocious Populism' (2001) 95 *Am. Pol. Sci. Rev.* 297.

[114] ibid at 310.

classes are a vital means to protect freedom from a wealthy elite. I examine the highly original Machiavellian approach to political discord towards the end of chapter three. There we will draw further on McCormick's helpful insights about the centrality of class conflicts and discord in the Roman republic. For the present however the centrality of conflict in political life in agonist accounts of democracy can be set out.

Agonist democrat scholarship may be traced via Nietzsche and Arendt back to the tragedies of Ancient Greece. The idea of the flawed central protagonist features in the dramas of Sophocles (*Antigone*, *Oedipus Rex*), Aeschylus (*Agamemnon*, *Libation Bearers*, *The Eumenides*) and Euripedes (*Hipploylte*, *Bacchae*). The character is someone who, on account of his/her disposition, is inevitably bound to endure struggles and conflicts in their relations with others and is ultimately at the mercy of the gods (some of whom are in conflict with each other and use humans to advance their own struggles). The tragic hero/heroine is all of us in our social and political relations with others. This state of personal suffering is not, however, some temporary or intermediate stage through which we pass before enjoying true concord with our fellow human beings. There is no final moment of personal awakening or reconciliation between the conflicting parties. There is no unfolding of a progressive journey towards personal/societal perfection. Neither should it be assumed that the main character is the possessor-in-chief of the virtues. Greek tragedy shows instead the incommensurability of the different sets of values and virtues personified by the various players. By the end of the play, the audience is left with competing and plausible accounts of the good. Deeply irreconcilable accounts would have provoked an open-ended debate among theatre goers.[115] Nietzsche's reading of the message in Greek tragedy was that, amidst the anguish and suffering of the main characters, it taught us about the importance of personal courage in the face of adversity and disaster. In *The Birth of Tragedy* he counsels that we need to be able to look at the 'horror of individual existence without being turned to stone by the vision'.[116] Nietzsche believed nonetheless that art could provide the necessary means of comfort for the vicissitudes of human life.[117]

For all that complex forces act both on and within humans, agonist accounts resist the suggestion that we should be passively resigned to hardships and suffering in the face of overwhelming forces. In other words, the idea that our lives are wholly determined from the outset is rejected.[118] There is an ontological claim here

[115] E Barker, *Entering the Agon: Dissent and Authority in Homer, Historiography and Tragedy* (New York, OUP, 2009) esp. chs 5 and 6.

[116] F Nietzsche *The Birth of Tragedy and The Genealogy of Morals* (New York, Anchor Books, 1956) at 102, and see for a helpful overview M Wenman, *Agonistic Democracy: Constituent Power in the Era of Globalisation* at 33–58.

[117] Kaufmann argues that Nietzsche 'discovers in Greek art a bulwark against Schopenhauer's pessimism' in W Kaufmann, *Nietzsche: Philosopher, Psychologist and Antichrist* (New Jersey, Princeton Classics, 2013) at 131.

[118] M Wenman, *Agonistic Democracy: Constituent Power in the Era of Globalisation* at 37–39.

that humans are thrown into the world in an incomplete state. There are (albeit limited) choices open to us to shape our existences during the struggle against life's privations. These choices extend to the capacity for action in the field of politics. The human capacity for political action is a key idea in the work of Hannah Arendt. The limited contestation of fate brings into the world plural responses. Political action is thus an essential part of the human condition.[119]

[119] H Arendt, *The Human Condition* (Chicago, University of Chicago, 1958).

3

Enlightenment Rationality vs Machiavellian Pluralism

Introduction

Chapter two traced the connections in European free speech regulation between democratic self-government and responsible expression. I argued that the deliberative democratic rationales for speech regulation explain official policy preferences for responsible contributions to public discourse among political equals, contributions that help reach consensual outcomes on the basis of disinterested arguments grounded in public reason. This is not to say that liberal elitist accounts of expressive freedom have been entirely discarded. The residual attachment to elite-guided political discourse is evidenced by those elements of legislative policy and jurisprudence that conceive of ordinary citizens in the main as consumers of professionally produced news and opinion content. Whilst deliberative accounts of political expression creditably seek to overcome the very limited conception of citizen participation in politics that is found in liberal elitist thinking, my claim in chapter two was that the version of political pluralism endorsed by deliberative democrats narrows the range of permitted political expression with the result that meaningful participation by non-elites in public discourse is a chimera. This loss of speech occurs because deliberative democratic accounts at their core share an overriding concern to secure the progressive unfolding of an 'ideal' and cosmopolitan liberal democracy. In this chapter I seek to make more explicit the Enlightenment underpinnings of the turn to deliberative democracy that informs official attempts to regulate political expression. The analysis offered below explores ideas of rationality and public reason in liberal thought from the Enlightenment onwards and its telos of progress towards universal goals that transcend the particularistic/local. Notwithstanding the fact that its ideals have come under intense pressure in the late twentieth century as ethnic, nationalist and fundamentalist religious forces have asserted themselves, Enlightenment thinking remains at the heart of much liberal democratic thinking, especially in the academy, as evidenced by the deliberative turn in political theory. The restoration of a more rational public sphere figures prominently in the work of today's defenders of Enlightenment who argue that it offers an important means of combating the modern phenomenon of 'fake news' and other threats to civilised, happy human lives. Robertson in *The Enlightenment: The Pursuit of Happiness* for example states:

> The Enlightenment, though distant in time, remains vitally important. In an age that seems dominated by 'fake news', widespread credulity, xenophobia and unscrupulous demagogues, it matters more intensely that ever to hold onto reliable knowledge, to be aware of our common humanity, and to pursue the possibility of human happiness.[1]

Opposing arguments premised upon the essential incommensurability of values and the limits of rationality stand in the shadows. Counter-Enlightenment thought emphasises the fact of value pluralism. It disputes the idea that rationality might be able to supply a 'correct' answer when we are asked to choose between conflicting values or goods. In this chapter I show that the arguments of the counter-Enlightenment offer a serious though largely neglected challenge to the strait-jacketed discourse of ever more progress towards perfected liberal constitutionalism on offer from the Enlightenment-inspired deliberative democrats.

My aims in doing so are as follows; first to challenge aspects of the Enlightenment thinking of the sort indicated in the quote from Robertson. From here I proceed to analyse the closing down of substantive political contestation that is present in the work of Rawls on justice and Habermas on communicative rationality that prefigure much deliberative democracy scholarship. A final section on Machiavellian pluralism then sketches out a radical pluralist conception of political participation that can also accommodate an Arendtian notion of the political essence of individual citizens. Informed by the Florentine's *Discourses on the First Ten Books of Titus Livy*, this radical understanding of political pluralism stresses the inevitable and ineliminable nature of conflict and disharmony between classes of person and ideologies. It chimes with the positive valuation of participatory democracy found in Arendt, valuing discordant expression between elites and non-elites that can only ever establish highly contingent, temporary resolutions of political disputes that are bound to recur without any necessary progression towards the universal goals cherished in liberal theory. The agonist component of my argument takes issue therefore with Robertson's fundamental claim about the pursuit of human happiness. I emphatically reject that idea. The authentically republican life – the *vivere politico* defended in Machiavelli's *Discourses* – is bound up with discord and disharmony, with conflict, compromises and transient accommodations with our political opponents. The central contrast in short that is offered in this chapter is that between Enlightenment rationality (and its deliberative democracy progeny) and authentically republican projects of self government that draw upon more radical understandings of political pluralism.

[1] Preface (London, Allen Lane, 2020).

Enlightenment Roots of Deliberative Democracy and Some Counter-Enlightenment Objections

Kant's 1784 essay 'An Answer to the Question: What is Enlightenment?'[2] is usually considered to offer a definitive statement of what lies at the core of the Enlightenment.[3] It is a call to individuals to become courageous and use their own understandings of the world around them to reason for themselves, instead of being guided by others. The activity of thinking in Kant is not confined to the intellectual class only. Each person could and should move beyond the state of immaturity entailed in being guided by others and acquire the resolve to apply reason to the information they already possess by virtue of their senses. Reasoned thinking about societal affairs will enable the thinker to enter conversations with others in the community. Kant's essay famously extolled each of us 'Have the courage to use your *own* understanding!' Kant did not believe late-eighteenth century Europe to be an enlightened epoch, but considered that the freedom of thought which each individual undoubtedly possessed made it an age in which humankind could make progress towards its betterment over the generations. Kant's *Critique of Pure Reason* is a defence of reasoning in institutional settings where free citizens could publicly express their opinions and respond to the ideas of others up to and including their objection and veto. The improving qualities of public deliberation and judgment allow the individual to move past the unthinking prejudices handed down by others that marks out immature thinking. O'Neill notes that this escape from prejudice in Kant's thinking is equated with an

> escape from passive reason, the failure to think for oneself, and hence is a condition of enlightenment. Thus, since the comparison with the judgements of others is required to avoid prejudice, the maxim 'think for oneself' and the maxim 'think from the standpoint of everyone else' are related.[4]

The length of a human life is too short Kant argues for any one individual to develop completely into a perfectly reasoning being. Reason requires trial, error and reflection for progress from 'one stage of insight to the next'.[5] The Kantian project is an evolutionary one to be elaborated incrementally over generations as they progress towards an end point of a consensual and just society. Human freedom of thought is to be pressed into service on behalf of this unfolding rational quest for justice.[6]

[2] In (ed H Reiss) *Political Writings* (Cambridge, CUP, 1991), 54–55.

[3] See thus R Robertson, *The Enlightenment: The Pursuit of Happiness* (London, Allen Lane/Penguin, 2020) 29–31.

[4] J O'Neill, 'The Rhetoric of Deliberation: Some Problems in Kantian Theories of Deliberative Democracy' (2002) 8 *Res Publica* 249, 252.

[5] 'Second Proposition' in 'Idea for a Universal History with a Cosmopolitan Purpose' in (eds G Brown and D Held) *The Cosmopolitan Reader* (Cambridge, Polity Press, 2010) at 18.

[6] M Wenman, *Agonistic Democracy – Constituent Power in the Era of Globalisation* (Cambridge, CUP, 2013) at 43–44.

The varieties of traditional liberal thought developed since Kant's time share a universalist core that prescribes the most appropriate kind of societal institutions and political regime that humans might consciously choose as rational beings to create and function within. Gray comments that the Enlightenment project rests upon a 'philosophy of history which has universal convergence on a rationalist civilization as its *telos*'.[7] Berlin reminds us of the natural law roots of Enlightenment thinking which emphasised the essential sameness of persons through history and across the globe.[8] Current variations in human nature across regions and countries, as well as those revealed by historical research were considered

> unimportant compared to the constant central core in terms of which human beings could be defined as a species … that there were universal human goals; that a logically connected structure of laws and generalisations susceptible of demonstration and verification could be constructed.[9]

Just as the methods of Newtonian physics in the natural sciences were uncovering new truths about the inanimate world, so might the same methodologies be applied in the science of society. Unthinking prejudice and unjustified reliance upon custom and tradition could thus be swept aside. In their place, scientific inquiry would yield up rational and just systems of government. The new systems would usher in a new era of knowledge and virtue, enabling humankind over generations to realise a state of enlightened rule. Robertson's sympathetic account of the Enlightenment stresses the commitment to an ever improving understanding of the world based upon reasoned inquiry and observation.[10] 'Enlighteners', he informs us, 'urge people to be rational, but still more, to be reasonable … in dialogue with others'[11] in social settings. Logical, abstracted thinking (rationality) allied to common sense and reason-giving in debate-style exchanges would thus uncover valuable societal truths and impel human society towards the ideal polity. Enlightenment thought with its reworking of earlier natural law theory is inextricably linked to constitutional liberalism's two most enduring societal designs, namely the French *Declaration de Droits d'Hommes* and the US Constitution and Bill of Rights.[12] The principles of the French and US Revolutions

[7] J Gray, *Enlightenment's Wake* (Abingdon, Routledge Classics, 2007) at 97. He continues 'This is the modern conception of human social development as occurring in successive discrete stages, not everywhere the same, but having in common the property of converging on a single form of life, a universal civilization, rational and cosmopolitan', ibid.

[8] I Berlin, 'The Counter-Enlightenment' in *Against the Current – Essays in the History of Ideas* (London, Hogarth Press, 1979).

[9] ibid at 1.

[10] He argues that the 'best starting-point' is the idea of a 'coherent intellectual movement united by a "commitment to understanding, and hence to advancing, the causes and conditions of human betterment in the world"'. Robertson, *The Enlightenment: The Pursuit of Happiness* at 37 citing his own earlier definition in *The Case for the Enlightenment – Scotland and Naples 1680–1760* (Cambridge, CUP, 2005).

[11] *The Enlightenment: The Pursuit of Happiness*, ibid at 28.

[12] I McGilchrist, *The Master and His Emissary – The Divided Brain and the Making of the Western World* (2018, Yale Uni Press, New Haven) describes the French and American revolutions as 'the two most important and enduring legacies' of the Enlightenment' at 344.

(universal reason, rights, justice) were however as Berlin observes entirely at odds with the later Romantic or counter-Enlightenment themes of individual uniqueness, emotional introspection and the essential difference and dissimilarity between things.[13] One of the aims of this chapter is to address the relative neglect of the counter-Enlightenment challenge to mainstream liberal thinking. I intend to show that the Romantics have given us credible grounds to treat modern enlighteners' claims with more circumspection than they usually receive.

Running to just short of 1,000 pages, Robertson's detailed defence of the Enlightenment's pursuit of human happiness might have been expected to address counter-Enlightenment objections to the idea of ever greater progress towards truth and the ideal society. Although the title appears to confine the subject matter to a relatively brief 110-year period (1680–1790), it is clear from the preface that Robertson's broader aim is to have written something relevant for present times, the era as he defines it of '"fake news", xenophobia and demagoguery'.

It follows that his defence might have been expected to respond to criticisms of Enlightenment thinking in succeeding eras, at least in more detail than the perfunctory references that appear in the book's 11-page concluding chapter. In what follows below, I identify two overlooked strands of counter-Enlightenment objection that are worthy of closer attention. The first strand focuses upon human psychological traits that Enlightenment thinking overlooked and have been raised by existentialist writers including, most remarkably, the Russian novelist Fyodor Dostoevsky. The second strand considers a more philosophically anchored set of arguments from Berlin and Gray in which serious doubt is cast upon the universal, abstracted, rational and ever-unfolding dimensions of the Enlightenment project.

Curiously, Robertson manages to overlook completely Dostoevsky's existential objections to the 'Age of Reason's' carefully calibrated vision of human progress. Dostoevsky's metaphor for the Enlightenment's end point – the 'Palace of Crystal' appears in *Notes from the Underground*.[14] The Palace instantiates the idea of human progress in accordance with universal laws of nature. The magnificent glass structure is confronted head on by its embittered narrator who resists on free will grounds the application of scientific laws to humankind.

> All human actions will then of course be tabulated according to those laws, mathematically, like tables of logarithms. New economic relations will be established, all ready made and worked out with mathematical exactitude so that every possible question will vanish in the twinkling of an eye, simply because every possible answer to it will be provided.[15]

[13] I Berlin, *The Roots of Romanticism* (1999, Princeton Uni Press, New Jersey) 7.

[14] Dostoevsky was writing 13 years after the Great Exhibition (May to October 1851) held in the newly constructed Crystal Palace, a building of glass and iron then set up in Hyde Park to showcase British engineering and manufacturing. Once the exposition was over, the structure was relocated to Sydenham Hill, South London. It was completely destroyed by fire in 1936.

[15] F Dostoevsky, *Notes from the Underground* (1864) VII.

Human beings will thus be reduced to cogs in a machine or piano keys acting in wholly pre-determined ways. The Underground Man's/Dostoevsky's fundamental objection to 'Palace of Crystal' is one based in human psychology, namely that Enlightenment reason overlooks human freedom to act independently, to act in ways at times unfettered by calculations of rational self advantage.

> (Y)ou are fully convinced that … (man) will be sure to learn when he gets rid of certain old bad habits, and when common sense and science have completely re-educated human nature and turned it in a normal direction … Science itself will teach man … that he never has really had any caprice or will of his own, that he himself is something of the nature of organ stop … And how do these wiseacres know that man wants a normal, virtuous choice? What has made them conceive that man must want a rationally advantageous choice?[16]

Such freedom fits within no system of classification devised by Enlightenment thinkers. 'What man wants' he states, 'is simply an independent choice, whatever that independence may cost and wherever it may lead.'[17] Barrett expresses it thus:

> What the reformers of the Enlightenment, dreaming of a perfect organization of society, had overlooked, Dostoevsky saw all too plainly with the novelist's eye: Namely, that as modern society becomes more organized and bureaucratic, it piles up at its joints figures like the Underground Man, who beneath their nondescript surface are monsters of frustration and resentment.[18]

Barrett concludes that existentialism in its various forms forces us to take seriously the whole person, a bundle of emotions that include anxiety, trembling, despair, guilt and consciousness of his/her finitude. Enlightenment thinking by contrast seeks to drag us away from these troubling aspects of the human condition and lift us on towards our more perfect future. Enlighteners who look forward to our happy arrival at the Palace of Crystal will find existentialism's account of the individual depressing but it is the Enlightenment's thin, abstracted version of humankind that is profoundly misleading. Discarding Enlightenment thinking's incomplete account of the person on the other hand is liberating. Those who seek a meaningful life in the present find themselves liberated from having to worship the 'idol of progress' and thus more likely to fashion something out of their actual existences in an imperfect and conflictual world.[19]

The idea of achievable societal betterment that lies at the core of Enlightenment thinking is premised on the claim that human nature 'is the same in all times and places: that universal human goals, true ends and effective means, are at least in principle discoverable …'[20] The hold of local beliefs rooted in mysticism, custom

[16] ibid.

[17] ibid.

[18] W Barrett, *Irrational Man – A Study in Existential Philosophy* (New York, Anchor Books, 1990) at 139.

[19] ibid, at 274–75.

[20] R Hausheer, 'Introduction' in I Berlin, 'The Counter-Enlightenment' in *Against the Current – Essays in the History of Ideas* at xxvi.

and religious authority would be loosened and wither away as Newtonian methods of rational enquiry were brought to bear on matters of morals, politics and societal institutions. As Hausheer observes, Enlighteners sought to devise 'universal unifying frameworks … where everything that occurs should be … wholly explainable in terms of immutable general laws'.[21]

Aside from the forces of custom and religious authority, Enlightenment thinking was also ranged against what Isaiah Berlin labelled a 'relativist and sceptical tradition that went back to the ancient world'.[22] The sophists of Ancient Greece had previously doubted the rational universalism that later came to occupy the centre of Enlightenment thinking. Protagoras, Antiphon and Critias had all doubted the universality of moral and political values across time and place. The variability of the value judgements made by humans and the institutions they give rise to could best be explained by reference to fluctuating human conventions. Fires may well have burned in the same manner throughout history wherever on the surface of the Earth they were set alight. Humans on the other hand had changed their institutions and differed in their opinions over time and across different locations on account of changing conventions.[23]

Sophocles' tragedy of Antigone and Creon, for example, points up the irreconcilable value pluralism that can exist within a society simultaneously. The brothers Eteocles and Polynices had slain each other in a conflict over the Theban throne. The deadly quarrel had arisen after Eteocles, the elder brother and incumbent ruler, had refused to honour his power-sharing agreement with Polynices whereby each was to hold the throne in alternate years.[24] Creon, the new Theban King, decided that Eteocles as the defender of Thebes would be buried with full state honours whilst his brother Polynices as a traitor would be denied the traditional burial rites. Instead, his decomposing body would be left outside the city walls. Creon's denial of a traditional burial in accordance with the laws of the gods condemned Polynices' soul to wander forever in the underworld without rest. Anyone who disputed Creon's decision would be sentenced to death. Antigone, the sister of Eteocles and Polynices, disputed Creon's right to decide how to treat the dead. For Antigone, a higher law, that of the Greek gods, demanded that Polynices be given the sacred family burial rites. Antigone performed the burial rites, was arrested by Creon's men and sentenced to death by being sealed alive inside the family tomb.

To counter-Enlightenment minds, Antigone's predicament lays bare the stark irreconcilability of competing value choices on matters of the most profound significance. Antigone's choice to disobey Creon's law and honour instead of the

[21] ibid.

[22] I Berlin, 'The Counter-Enlightenment' in *Against the Current – Essays in the History of Ideas* at 1.

[23] Berlin cites in this regard the work of Giambattista Vico, the Neapolitan philosopher who defended the idea of cultural uniqueness, and sought to refute the Aristotelian notion of timeless natural law whose truths were in principle knowable to anyone at any time in history and at any place on the Earth's surface, at 4–6.

[24] This agreement was intended to avoid the bloodshed predicted by Oedipus, their father.

gods' sacred burial rites represents a value preference for the ties of family and obligations to the soul of her deceased brother. Others would see in Creon the just demands of a stable legal order. Etxabe's insightful reading of Antigone treats the play as depicting the clash between incommensurable values of 'equal validity at the same time and place, each of which provides in its own right an authoritative answer to a legal issue of substantive complexity'.[25] In the tragic circumstances that Antigone and Creon found themselves, a creative, a form of ad hoc compromise was needed to displace temporarily (that is in this instance) the conflict between the divine law of burial rites and family bonds on the one hand, and the positive law of the state on the other. Such a compromise would tap into the human (Arendtian) capacity for political creativity and action. That future conflicts would require further acts of creativity and compromise highlights the reality of an open agon where no one idea or norm seals off future contestation. By contrast, contemporary Enlightenment thinking would see Antigone's conflict as one in which there was a failure first to identify and then to apply the relevant transcendent determining principle(s) of justice or rationality. In this way the 'just' or 'right' answer to Antigone's position could be articulated and serve as an authoritative precedent for future cases.

The experiences of post-Renaissance Europeans who travelled across oceans and continents appeared to confirm the variability of human societies, their laws, institutions and values. Montesquieu famously commented upon the effect of climate upon the development of society in *The Spirit of the Laws* when he writes:

> If it is true that the character of the mind and the passions of the heart are extremely different in the various climates, *laws* must be relative both to the difference of those passions and the difference of those characters.[26]

McGilchrist fastens on this discovery of difference and incompatibility as the 'weak place' of Enlightenment thinking: 'Since the foundation of all Enlightenment thinking is that all truths cohere, are mutually compatible, non-contradictory, ultimately reconcilable, its weak place is where incompatibilities are found.'[27]

Although the presence of difference points up an unpromising (from an Enlightenment perspective) empirical fact about the world, Isaiah Berlin notes that Enlightenment beliefs about ultimate immutable laws and universal human

[25] J Etxabe, *The Experience of Tragic Judgment* (Abingdon, Routledge, 2014) at 2.

[26] Montesquieu, *The Spirit of the Laws* (Cambridge, Cambridge Texts in the History of Political Thought, 1998) (ed A Cohler) Part III Book XIV 'On the laws in their relation to the nature of climate'.

[27] I McGilchrist, *The Master and His Emissary – The Divided Brain and the Making of the Western World* (New Haven, Yale University Press, 2018) at 353. McGilchrist's pioneering work on the structure and function of the left and right hemispheres of the human brain makes the claim that Enlightenment thinking is heavily left-hemisphere influenced. This is reflected in the rigid pursuit of logical enquiry and truth about discrete phenomena or a particular version of things. For the left hemisphere, the world is 'single, knowable, consistent, certain, fixed therefore finite, generalised across experience, a world that we can master' (ibid). The romantic or counter-Enlightenment tradition is in his view a right hemisphere-led approach to grasping at but never fully comprehending the nature of the changing, multi-faceted world.

purposes nonetheless took hold and gained ground into the eighteenth and nineteenth centuries.[28] Alongside physical needs for security and sustenance, broader claims about convergences upon abstracted notions of peace, happiness, wisdom and justice continued to be articulated by eighteenth-century writers. Although individual thinkers might disagree each other about the precise content of the laws or how they might be arrived at, the fact that such laws *were* discoverable 'remained the central dogma of the Enlightenment'.[29] From our vantage point in the early twenty-first century, the unwarrantedness of the assumption about later convergence seems plain. We can concur with Hampshire that the Enlightenment's promise of a 'step by step' convergence on liberal values, on 'our values'[30] did not occur. Aside from the obvious question about why Enlighteners still hold out the prospect of an eventual coming together on these highly contested political questions, a more immediately useful line of enquiry might be to look in more detail at counter-Enlightenment explanations for value pluralism and non-convergence.

Berlin credits Machiavelli with the initial expression of a fatal objection to the promise of rational resolutions of value conflict.[31] The Florentine sets out two irreconcilable forms of life, two incompatible moral universes that instruct us on how to live well. One can choose to live a life in accordance with Christian values that is inward looking, concerned with the well-being of the soul and rewards in the afterlife.[32] This dictates an attitude of forbearance and meekness in the public sphere. It offers no resistance to tyrannical uses of public power. Alternatively, one can live according to values that are located in our communal existences in the polity and its welfare. A noble society like ancient Rome or Athens is one where glory is sought by strong, proud citizens who through their participation with others in political institutions come to realise their common goals. These two modes of living comprised for Machiavelli two complete ethical codes. They offered mutually exclusive ways of living a moral life. He does not quite say that the personal characteristics he associates with the Christian life are intrinsically bad. It is rather that these virtues are not suited to the survival and flourishing of political communities. It is clear, however, which choice Machiavelli believes to be the better one. According to Villari, Machiavelli was fond of quoting Capponi's maxim

[28] Berlin writes that, despite the pioneering historicist work of Giambattista Vico and renewed interest in the epic poetry of Homer, Norse sagas and Shakespeare and the diverse cultural traditions these writers represented, the various attacks on Enlightenment reasoning were insufficient to dislodge the latter's central claims of universal laws and the abstract individual. See his essay 'Hume and German Anti-Rationalism' in 'The Counter-Enlightenment' in *Against the Current – Essays in the History of Ideas* at 164.

[29] Ibid at 4.

[30] The phrasing is taken from Stuart Hampshire's *Presidential Address to the American Philosophical Association* in 1991 *Proceedings and Addresses of the American Philosophical Association* (1991) Vol 65, 25 and cited by J Gray, *Enlightenment's Wake* at 98.

[31] 'The Originality of Machiavelli' in *Against the Grain – Essays in the History of Ideas*.

[32] Machiavelli was not opposed to religion per se. Where religious beliefs promoted valour and active participation in community affairs as evident pagan era of Ancient Rome, they had a clear role to play in sustaining the polis.

favouring those that 'loved their countries better than the safety of their souls'[33] Berlin summarises Machiavelli's position as requiring a person who chooses the Christian life to 'give up all hope of Athens and Rome, of a noble and glorious society in which human beings can thrive and grow strong, wise and productive'.[34] The major contribution of Machiavelli's work on statecraft and political community is the revelation of this 'insoluble dilemma'.[35] The author of *The Prince* and *Discourses on Livy* had succeeded in

> planting a permanent question mark in the paths of posterity … ends equally ultimate, equally sacred, may contradict each other, that entire systems of value may come into collision without possibility of rational arbitration, and that not merely in exceptional circumstances … but (this was surely new) as part of the normal human situation.[36]

Machiavelli's permanent question renders the Enlightenment search for the one true rational answer to the question of how men and women should live 'conceptually incoherent'.[37] The binary choice he holds out between the Christian life and the politically virtuous life need not be treated as exhausting the plurality of value choices open to citizens. Within liberal forms of political community where ideals of liberty and equality are centre stage, incommensurable accounts of the optimal design of the constitution (and the idea of the role of the citizen within the constitution) abound. Put another way, the fundamental rights and freedoms that characterise the liberal constitution are caught up in conflicts of an irreconcilable and ineliminable quality. There is simply no overreaching common standard or means of discovering whether the gains/losses of the trade-off between rights (and collective interests or other competing rights) in solution A are 'greater' than the gains/losses entailed in the equivalent trade-off proposed by rival solution B. Even assuming there could be a consensus around human well-being and the bundle of rights needed to sustain such a state, the need to make a radical, non-rational choice between incommensurables could not be eliminated.[38] Take the question of how freedom of expression is to be weighed against the right to respect for private life. It seems clear that different persons will rank differently these same interests in ways that reflect their particular conception of the good. The weight attached to each interest across different factual circumstances will reflect a particular conception of human well-being. My commitment to republicanism will steer me towards the widest possible protection for all forms of political expression. My neighbour's primary concerns about the damage done to persons by tabloid intrusions and the greed of corporate media organisations will push her towards a different regulatory stance. Raz argues that these types of dispute ultimately rest

[33] P Villari, *The Life and Times of Niccolò Machiavelli* (London, T Fisher Unwin, 1878) Vol 2, Book 2, ch 2 at 92.

[34] 'The Originality of Machiavelli' in *Against the Grain – Essays in the History of Ideas* at 58.

[35] Ibid at 74.

[36] Ibid at 74–75.

[37] Ibid at 76 and with it any attempt to compel others by force to live accordingly.

[38] See thus J Gray, *Enlightenment's Wake* at 107–10.

upon different conceptions of human interest and well-being. The rights in question do not ground the political morality. They rely at a more foundational level upon rival understandings of human and societal well-being.[39] They do not, it should be noted, collapse into relativism. It remains possible nonetheless, whilst being committed to the idea of incommensurable conceptions of the good life, to maintain as Gray does, that the life of a crack addict is a poor one.[40]

Public Reason and the Reasonable Citizen in Deliberative Democracy Scholarship

Kantian public reason employed in the service of societal progress has been hugely influential in deliberative democracy scholarship.[41] The contributions of John Rawls on justice and Habermas on communicative rationality, for example, share 'Kantian roots' in their respective defences of public reason.

For Rawls the central task of political liberalism is to secure the stable existence over time of a just society comprised of free and equal citizens who disagree on the most fundamental questions of morality and religion.[42] The solution rests upon the idea of political justice in which fair terms of cooperation between these diverging (though rational) citizens are established. The terms include the abandonment of comprehensive world views on the good life upon entering the public sphere. 'Fair cooperation' requires the use of public reason among reasonable persons who argue as rational self-interested citizens from behind the veil of ignorance. Rawls excludes from this cooperative search for just laws those who hold 'unreasonable' views, confining dialogue to those who are fully committed to honoring 'fair terms' of cooperation. As Mouffe remarks, this amounts to nothing other than saying only those reasonable persons who accept the fundamentals of liberalism are to be permitted to participate in the making of just laws and policies.[43] The overlapping consensus on justice as fairness (including the consensus reached on matters of political liberties and socio-economic rights) that emerges among the 'fair-minded' 'rational' and 'reasonable' citizens may not subsequently be called into question. To do so is to question the principles of justice that have been 'authoritatively' settled. Such dissent is obviously irrational/unreasonable.

Rawls' model of justice is blatantly anti-political. It closes off from future contestation in the political realm ongoing and vibrant questions concerning the

[39] J Raz, *The Morality of Freedom* (Oxford, OUP, 1986) ch 8.
[40] *Enlightenment's Wake* at 43.
[41] J O'Neill, 'The Rhetoric of Deliberation: Some Problems in Kantian Theories of Deliberative Democracy' (2002) 8 *Res Publica* 249 at 252–53.
[42] J Rawls, *Political Liberalism* (New York, Columbia University Press, 1993) xviii.
[43] Mouffe herself asks, 'What is this if not an indirect form of asserting that reasonable persons are those who accept the fundamentals of liberalism?' in C Mouffe, 'Democracy and Pluralism: A Critique of the Rationalist Approach' (1995) 16 *Cardozo Law Rev* 1358.

optimal trade-off between the values of equality and liberty and the respective roles accorded to the institutions of liberal democracy in securing this optimised state. In other words, there is no scope for ongoing political agency and the recurring re-authoring of the laws on these fundamental matters since the bedrock principles of justice are accepted by every reasonable citizen.[44] This 'emasculation' or 'hollowing' out of the political sphere in Rawls' account, Gray argues, proves 'fatal to its self description as a form of political liberalism and discloses its true character as a species of legal liberalism'.[45] To seal off the consensus on rights and liberties from future contestation, constitutionally entrenched bills of rights and supreme courts police the democratic agency of the people so that the latter remains subordinated to the constituted authorities and norms.

In ontological terms, the idea that there might be no more political conflict over the nature of protected rights (such as the right to private property or the right to healthcare) or the distribution of wealth appears somewhat utopian. More fundamentally still, it denies the Arendtian notion of the political dimension of humankind.[46] That is that we are uniquely among living creatures given to make (plural) starts and create new forms of living with and conflicting with each other in society in perpetuity. Where, as in a number of liberal democracies, these questions are turned over to and authoritatively settled by constitutional courts, there is on both Arendt's and Gray's views an inevitable diminishment of political life. Gray's primary concern however appears to be a loss of civility in public life and the missed opportunities for compromise among the political actors on contested questions. Arendt's emphasis upon the political citizen on the other hand pinpoints the central objection to Rawls' depoliticised public sphere, namely the diminished scope for political agency.

If Rawls's position ends up prioritising legally defined rights over politically arrived at compromises on rights/interests questions, an explicit attempt to establish the equal ranking of laws (and rights) and democratic agency is to be found in Habermas's dialectical work on private/public autonomy and communicative rationality.[47] Habermas' concern is to provide legitimation for liberal democracy. His account of co-originality has the people as both the authors of law and the users or subjects of law. There must be both democratic self-rule and individual rights. A self-learning process is at play in Habermas' work wherein

[44] As Mouffe puts it in *The Democratic Paradox* 'Rawls' view of the well-ordered society eliminates the democratic struggle among 'adversaries', that is, those who share the allegiance to the liberal-democratic principles, while defending different interpretations of what liberty and equality should mean and to which kinds of social relations and institutions they should apply' (London, Verso, 2005) at 30.

[45] *Enlightenment's Wake* at 114.

[46] H Arendt, *The Human Condition* (London, University of Chicago Press, 1998) see esp ch 2 for her discussion of action in the social realm. Danielle Allen's Foreword to the second edition notes that Arendt's 'revival of politics demands a renewal of the capacities of each and every democratic citizen or civic agent to diagnose the circumstances of human experience – what is possible for them with regard to opportunity for labor and work – and to pursue the political work of responding to those circumstances' at xvi.

[47] *Between Facts and Norms* (MIT Press, Cambridge Mass. 1996).

citizens' competences to arrive at 'better' understandings of how to live together are progressively improved.[48] Over time and generations, people become more accomplished at the ongoing process of making a constitution.[49] The constitution may have been authored by previous generations but each generation has the responsibility to engage in their lifetimes in the task of further elaboration.[50] This means an entitlement/duty to participate politically but, as Habemas makes clear, democratic agency in his dialectical account is constrained by an expectation that there will be 'a public use of reason; as democratic co-legislators, citizens may not ignore the informal demand to orient themselves towards the common good'.[51]

As they author new laws, the people are to acknowledge their indebtedness to their constitution-making predecessors and to 'recognise the project as the same throughout history and to judge it from the same perspective' as their forebears.[52] This capacity for retrospectivity will enable them to see how previous orientations towards the common good were at first 'sharply contested' but came later to be appreciated as the progressive elaboration of the shared constitutional project unfolded. The battles in the United States over Roosevelt's New Deal programme is cited by Habermas as offering a good illustration in this regard.

Honig credits Habermas with attempting to grapple with the inevitable tension between (liberal) rights and (republican) popular sovereignty.[53] Ultimately however, she reads Habermas correctly as cabining public autonomy and self-rule within a unilinear teleological development towards an ever more perfected *liberal* constitution. The agency of the people to make and unmake the laws is subordinated to the demands of this Enlightenment project. A self-correcting process occurs in which citizens acquire a better understanding constitutional norms and are able to instantiate this by authoring new laws that align more closely to the perfected constitution. However, such a progression *cannot* be said to be rooted in the *co-originality* of fundamental individual rights and democratic agency. Honig rightly asks 'in what sense can the people be said to have free authorship … if they understand themselves to be bound to a progressive temporality in and out of which constitutional democracy is required to unfold?'[54]

[48] J Habermas, 'Constitutional Democracy: A Paradoxical Union of Contradictory Principles?' (2001) 29 *Pol. Theory* 766, at 771, 771–74.

[49] ibid, at 768.

[50] ibid.

[51] ibid at 779.

[52] ibid at 775.

[53] B Honig, 'Dead Rights, Live Futures: A Reply to Habermas' "Constitutional Democracy"' (2001) 29 *Pol. Theory* 792. She finds in Habermas 'an admirable attempt to stem the translation tide of liberal constitutionalism and give participation its due' at 801.

[54] ibid at 795. As Larmore puts it, '… democracy is made subordinate to liberal principles precisely because the value of democratic institutions is held to lie chiefly, if not exclusively, in their being the best *means for guaranteeing* liberal freedoms', *Morals of Modernity* (Cambridge, CUP, 1996) at 182. Loughlin summarises liberalism's commitment to rights beyond the reach of democratic agency as reflecting a perceived need 'to be protected against our own base instincts', in 'Rights, Democracy and Law' in (eds T Campbell, K Ewing and A Tomkins) *Sceptical Essays on Human Rights* (Oxford, OUP, 2001) at 46.

In truth, the autonomous agency of the people is hedged by the overriding, rational imperative of moving ever closer to a perfected version of the liberal democratic constitution. Habermas himself at other times explicitly acknowledges this ordering in favour of fundamental rights (and the correlative subordination of the constituent power):[55]

> Because the practice of civic self-determination is conceived as a long run process of realising and progressively elaborating the system of fundamental rights, the principle of popular sovereignty comes into its own as part and parcel of the idea of government by law.[56]

On Habermas' view, 'history' (perhaps in the guise of juristocratic intervention) will judge whether we made advances by enacting the 'good' laws or impeded the perfecting of the constitution by enacting 'bad' ones.

Honig draws our attention to the lop-sidedness at the core of Habermas' progressive dialectic which emphasises 'the importance of constitutionalism to democracy while neglecting to stress *equally* the importance of democracy – of *a*constitutionalism and democratic agency … to constitutionalism'.[57]

By subordinating democratic will formation to previously formulated constitutional norms, Habermas avoids the 'risky tumult of *a*constitutionalism'[58] but at a heavy cost. There is a deadening effect of 'rights-centred' discourse upon spontaneous political action as the documents in which constitutional norms are articulated attain a 'narcissistic, necrophilic' status.[59] Constitutional liberals want us to lose sight of the fact that their cherished settlements are, in fact, the products of specific political conflicts at a particular moment in history and authored by then powerful societal groupings. They would rather have us subscribe like Mr Podsnap[60] to a creation myth in which a divinely ordained set of basic rules was handed to God's favoured people than understand how the complex interaction of political forces combined to produce what is counted today as comprising 'the Constitution'.

[55] This point is entirely missed by some legal commentators, see for example A Young, 'Populism and the UK Constitution' [2018] 71 *Current Legal Problems* 17, 33 where she uncritically takes Habermas 'co-orginality' claim at face value.

[56] J Habermas, 'Constitutional Democracy: A Paradoxical Union of Contradictory Principles?' (2001) 29 *Pol. Theory* 766, at 778.

[57] B Honig, 'Dead Rights, Live Futures: A Reply to Habermas' "Constitutional Democracy"' (2001) 29 *Pol. Theory* 792, 800.

[58] ibid.

[59] ibid. See in this regard Mark Tushnet's work on policy distortion and democratic debilitation in 'Policy Distortion and Democratic Debilitation: Comparative Illumination of the Countermajoritarian Difficulty' (1995) 94 *Mich. L. Rev.* 245. Tushnet discusses the problem where the legislators and electors do not take their own understandings of constitutional norms sufficiently seriously (democratic debilitation) and instead allow judicial readings to shape excessively the formulation of public policy (policy distortion).

[60] A character in Dickens' *Our Mutual Friend*, Mr Podsnap asks a 'foreign gentleman' what he thinks of London before telling him with what is called a sense of 'meritorious proprietorship', 'We Englishmen are Very Proud of our Constitution, Sir. It Was Bestowed Upon Us By Providence. No Other Country is so Favoured as This Country', ch 11.

Wenman's observant summary of the endeavours of liberal constitutionalists notes that much effort has been devoted to 'elaborating rational conditions of validity for the rightful expression of the constituent power and to subsume the creative power of the demos under one set of determinant principles'.[61]

To secure the 'narcissistic, necrophilic' status of the terms of settlement, liberal constitutionalists cast constitutional courts in the role of affirming the transcendent principles (fundamental human rights and cherished liberal doctrines such as the rule of law[62] and the separation of powers) and re-interpreting them in the light of modern conditions. Thus for Habermas, like Rawls before him, the content and meaning of rights are to be taken out of the political realm altogether. Law and courts function to keep democratic politics in check.[63] They capture essentially political disputes and refashion them as adversarial, zero sum legal contests. On Gray's view, this juridification of politics is aimed at the abolition of politics, an objective which he asserts can never be realised on account of the uncertainties and indeterminacies that lie at the heart of political thinking.[64] Instead, he argues that the political struggles inherent in determining rights questions are simply transferred into the legal sphere with the debilitating consequence that the political sphere is itself corroded. Disputes which within the political arena would

[61] M Wenman, *Agonistic Democracy – Constituent Power in the Era of Globalisation* at 76–77. For an example of a UK constitutional law academic who subordinates the creative powers of the demos to the overarching precepts and institutions of liberal constitutionalism, see A Young, 'Populism and the UK Constitution' (2018) 71 *Current Legal Problems* 17, 51–52. Young refers to the importance of constitutional re-imagining by non-elites before, in the same paragraph, privileging a Habermassian need for greater understanding of existing UK constitutional values. The citizens are required to value the importance (or rather Professor Young's preferred account) of pluralism, multiculturalism and the 'delicate balance of power on which the UK constitution is based' as the precondition for becoming eligible participants in the re-imagining exercise. Seen in these terms, Young can be seen to reject the idea of genuinely democratic innovation which is implicit in republican ideas of the constituent power of the citizens (and not just those persons that share precommitments to the liberal democratic constitution) that was discussed in the opening chapter of this book.

[62] Of course in standard liberal constitutionalist writings the 'rule of law' is inextricably linked to the protection of fundamental human rights thus permitting the courts to intervene where they adjudge the political part of the constitution to have failed to show 'adequate respect', see further T Bingham, 'The Rule of Law' (2007) 66 *C.L.J.* 67, 79–80. As Bingham concedes, however, the courts have not always been up to the task liberal constitutionalism sets for them. Judicial failures in this regard cited by Bingham include in this jurisdiction *R v Halliday* [1916] 1 KB 738; *Liversidge v Anderson* [1942] AC 206. It is not in my view difficult to find significant others which then prompt the question whether liberal constitutionalism's defence of judicially articulated rights bears close examination.

[63] Ackerman allows by contrast fleeting moments for the constituent power to assert itself in determining the meaning of the Constitution, but one suspects that his admittedly rare 'constitutional moments' are contingently linked to those occasions where among popular opinion a preponderance of progressive views on constitutional questions is considered to exist; see B Ackerman, *We The People, Vol 1: Foundations* (Massachusetts, Harvard University Press, 1991). Indeed, he views the constituent power in general in a strongly negative light. See his *We The People, Vol II Transformations* (Massachusetts, Harvard University Press, 1998) at 11, where he describes acts of the constituent power as 'arbitrary' noting that 'where law ends … pure politics (or war begins)'. Ackerman's distinction between 'constitutional moments' and ordinary, elite-run politics is rightly seen in the US context of the 1820s and 1830s as belonging to those anti-republican, aristocratic ploys associated with John Quincy Adams and Henry Clay to keep Jacksonian democrats at bay, see L Kramer, *The People Themselves – Popular Constitutionalism and Judicial Review* (New York, OUP, 2004) at 197.

[64] J Gray, *Enlightenment's Wake* at 115.

have been resolved in an ad hoc and compromised manner, only to be revisited subsequently when the balance of political forces had altered are now settled in the lofty environs of constitutional courts in adversarial, zero sum proceedings between legal combatants. One side wins and is granted a favourable reading of their constitutional position. The losing litigant must now regulate his/her affairs in accordance with the victory handed down to his/her opponent. In common law systems, the ratio of the ruling creates a binding precedent until subsequently modified/overruled by another constitutional court. Of course, in Arendtian terms, even such definitive legal resolutions do not extinguish the creative capacity of differently situated humans for political action and bringing new forms of living into existence. Courtroom decisions, even from lauded Supreme Court judges, do not blot out the desire in some political agents 'to start the world again'.

Outside the courtroom, dissenters and losers in this judicially articulated progression have nowhere to go. After the final dispositive pronouncement, they must concede defeat. Where they choose to continue their future expressive and associative activities, this may open them to state sanctions on account of the putative 'harms' that the perpetuation of their errors and falsehoods may pose. They risk additionally being de-platformed or 'cancelled' by private actors (for-profit multinational corporations) who take it upon themselves (often very publicly for strategic commercial reasons) to do their bit to overcome what Habermas labels 'contingent interruptions and historical regressions'.[65] At the same time, it must be doubted as a matter of fact whether it is ever sensible to refer to a *final* conclusion as regards battles over the meaning of the constitution. Does any observer seriously maintain that the triumph of New Deal politics in 1930s United States closed off for all time thereafter disputes about the role of the state in providing welfare and regulating private capital? It may be easy for the victors to assume a uni-directional unfolding of political and economic ideas, but it is by no means clear that older, discarded approaches are incapable of future resurrection. What may be more certain is that the victors at times may resent having to remake their case and would prefer (insist?) that the losers not resume their place on the field of political combat.[66]

Contra Habermas (and with a view to avoiding narcissistic or necrophilic reverence), it may be responded that the very meaning of rights depends upon them to be kept animate, that is subject to ongoing contestation in an unpredictable future. Honig speaks of the need for even entrenched rights to retain a quality of vulnerability so that they achieve temporarily settled, highly contingent meanings only. In her agonistic polity, the scope and content of rights are to be re-fought over and re-envisioned continuously.[67] She defends the opening of constitutions

[65] J Habermas, 'Constitutional Democracy: A Paradoxical Union of Contradictory Principles?' (2001) 29 *Pol. Theory* 766.

[66] B Honig, 'Dead Rights, Live Futures: A Reply to Habermas' "Constitutional Democracy"' (2001) 29 *Pol. Theory* 792, 798.

[67] ibid, at 800.

to more democratic agency. Accordingly, Honig looks favourably on the Canadian Constitution's 'notwithstanding clause' that allows democratic majorities in the provinces to refuse to implement Canadian Supreme Court interpretations for a five-year period. The risks that attach to 'bad majoritarianism'(by which she presumably means democratic reversals of Supreme Court decisions she views as defensible) are more than likely to be offset by reducing the countervailing risks of a juridified constitution in which the courts are able to impose precedent-setting rulings that display 'no ear for context or its own injustices'.[68]

Machiavellian Pluralism – Risky Tumults and Political Liberty in Non-deliberative Settings

> I shall not pass over in silence the disturbances that occurred in Rome from the time of the death of the Tarquins to that of the creation of the Tribunes … I maintain that those who blame the quarrels of the Senate and the people condemn that which was the very origin of liberty … And if it be said that these are strange means to hear constantly the cries of the people furious against the Senate, and of a Senate declaiming against the people, to see the populace rush tumultuous through the streets, close their homes, and even leave the city of Rome, I reply … that every free state ought to afford the people the opportunity of giving vent, so to say, to their ambition.[69]

Machiavelli's *Discourses on First Ten Books of Titus Livy* broke dramatic new ground in analysis of the political institutions and norms of Ancient Rome. As some of its central themes resonate through this book, the short concluding section of this chapter devotes attention to outlining the significance of Machiavelli's defence of popular participation in governing structures and the value of discord and political pluralism. I suggest here that Machiavelli is best read as the prototype non-deliberative, participatory democrat. His defence of discordant, conflictual politics that secures, at best, temporary and contingent moments of consensus only between elites and non-elites has been largely neglected in western political thinking. Such has been the dominance of Enlightenment influence on political thought.

Composed at much the same time as the author's more (in)famous work *The Prince*, *Discourses* sets out to address what Machiavelli in turn saw as the neglect of the ancient republics and the examples of wisdom and virtue these exhibit. Even those who professedly admire them and pay great sums of money to have statues of orators and patricians erected in their locales, fail on Machiavelli's view to ask how we might imitate the glories of the ancients in our present age.[70] His output, *The Prince* notwithstanding,[71] reveals a clear preference for

[68] ibid at 801.

[69] *Discourses on Livy* ch IV The Disunion of the Senate and the People Renders the Republic of Rome Powerful and Free.

[70] ibid First Book Introduction.

[71] *The Prince* should be read as a highly pragmatic response by the author to the ascendency of the Medicis in Florence, not as a principled defence of princely rule.

republican or commonwealth forms of government. In the lesser known *Letter to Zenobius* Machiavelli defiantly accepts the charge of preferring commonwealths to monarchies. It was only his desire to avoid the dogmatism found in others' work, Machiavelli reveals, that prevented from concluding as he wished that 'a Democracy founded upon good orders is the best and most excellent Government, and this without the least fear of confutation'.[72]

Machiavelli's commitment to a vibrant, non-deliberative form of political pluralism is best understood within a set of political structures at a certain point in the history of Rome that facilitated inclusive and robust contestations of policy. The finer details of Roman constitutional design lie beyond the parameters of the present discussion.[73] The structured plurality of ordinary Roman voices in policy formation and law can be clarified, however. Lawmaking in the ancient assemblies such as the *comitia* and the *concilium plebis* allowed every citizen to have a direct say in the passing of laws. Machiavelli notes that 'A tribune or any other citizen could propose a law to the people, and every citizen could speak either in favour or against it before the law was enacted'.[74] When the citizens were mindful of the vital role in defending liberty, this democratic practice worked well since the people could be trusted to propose and endorse good laws whilst rejecting bad ones. As McCormick comments, this extent of popular participation produced 'a more diverse array of views than could be generated by the mind of a single prince or even by the deliberation of a prudent but almost invariably homogeneous small group of elites'.[75]

Viewed from the Roman perspective of a class-based institutional design that safeguards ordinary citizens' contributions to political discourse and law-making, McCormick argues that the representative institutions of modern liberal democracy seem 'insufficiently antagonistic'.[76] Occasional trips to the ballot box and the opportunity to stand for elected office fall far short on this account of controlling socio-economic elites and – to the extent that they are distinct – their political office-holding allies.

In addition to popular participation in law-making, ordinary citizen involvement in Roman public affairs was institutionalised in the system of public accusations that could be levelled against political elites. For Machiavelli this is an important means of checking oligarchic abuses and reveals the people to be capable of sound judgement.[77] He cites the example of the Capuan Republic at the

[72] *Letter to Zenobius* cited in J Burnham, *The Machiavellians – Defenders of Freedom* (London, Lume Books, 2020) at 61–62.

[73] See for the leading exposition J McCormick, *Machiavellian Democracy* (New York, CUP, 2011).

[74] *Discourses* Book 1, ch 18, 'How a Free Government can be Maintained in Corrupt Cities if One Already Exists, or if One Does Not Already Exist, How to Establish It'.

[75] J McCormick, *Machiavellian Democracy* at 77.

[76] J McCormick, 'Machiavellian Democracy: Controlling Elites with Ferocious Populism' (2001) *Am. Pol. Sci. Rev.* 297 at 303.

[77] These are to be distinguished from calumnies against public officials which Machiavelli defines as uncorroborated and anonymously levelled charges.

time the Roman armies had been massacred by Hannibal at Cannae in 216 BC.[78] The crushing defeat brought to a head tensions between the senators and ordinary people across Italy including in Capua. To stave off a plebeian uprising against the nobles that would likely have led to the nobles' slaughter and the city's capture by Hannibal's forces, Pacuvius Calanus, the supreme magistrate in Capua, persuaded the nobles to submit themselves to the judgment of the plebs in a series of public trials. If the people were to vote to execute a senator, they would first have to select and agree upon a replacement. Once the first senator was put on trial, Machiavelli writes that a 'great clamour arose' as members of the assembly accused the senator of being 'proud, cruel and arrogant'.[79] However, when the assembly was then invited to nominate a successor from among the plebeians, the first nomination that was proposed drew only jeers and derision. Similarly negative reactions to each and every subsequent nomination followed: '(S)ome people began to whistle, others to laugh, and still others to speak badly of him in one way or another, and continuing in this fashion, one by one, they judged all those nominated unworthy of the senatorial rank.'[80]

At which point, Pacuvius Calanus, noting the lack of consensus on replacements, invited the assembly to enter into some form of reconciliation with the suitably chastened senators. Public order was restored. The assembly had been able to come to a fuller understanding about the respective qualities of existing and proposed office holders. That this was achieved by popular judgment and in a style of character examination falling considerably short of the ideal of civilised empathetic exchanges much vaunted by deliberative democrats (and others who seek to curate the mode of public discourse) are points that should not be overlooked. A popular desire to limit elite abuses of power is also manifested in the plebeian demand for the creation of tribunes after the collapse of the early Roman monarchs. Plebeian determination subsequently forced the senate to restore the office of the tribunes in 450 BC after the tribunate had fallen away.[81] Elected by ordinary citizens, the tribunes presided over plebeian assemblies. They could indict and prosecute powerful Roman citizens and enjoyed the power of veto over most of the Senate's proposed laws. In this way, noble domination of ordinary citizens could be resisted.

Conclusion

The focus in this chapter has been the influence of Enlightenment thinking upon political discourse and the boundaries of acceptable political expression.

[78] It is estimated that some 50,000–70,000 Roman legionnaires lost their lives at Cannae, see R O'Connell, *The Ghosts of Cannae: Hannibal and the Darkest Hour of the Roman Republic* (New York, Random House, 2011).

[79] *Discourses* Book 1 ch 47. Although Men May Deceive Themselves in General Questions, They Do Not Do So in the Particulars.

[80] ibid.

[81] See generally A Lintott, *The Constitution of the Roman Republic* (Oxford, OUP, 1999).

The normative preferences it holds for public reason, deliberation and rationality link to universal narratives of human rights and progress towards shared goals. The long shadow cast by Enlightenment thought in western political and constitutional discourse has consequently meant that Enlightenment-critical perspectives struggle to command the serious attention that they ought to receive. Aside from important objections from existentialist accounts of human psychology, a more sceptical set of traditions located in Counter-Enlightenment thinking has been neglected. The latter's chief legacy has been the identification of incompatible and incommensurable values that have challenged transcendental principles of rational thought and justice. Machiavelli deserves much credit in Berlin's eyes for placing this particularly jarring spoke in the wheel of Enlightenment thought. Within liberal political communities, the force of this objection means that the optimal configuration of the values of equality and liberty in the constitution can never be settled according to claims of logic and rational inquiry. Instead, rival propositions are bound up in an ongoing and inconclusive clash which no overarching standard may be called upon to determine. Nonetheless, the fidelity of deliberative accounts of democratic decision-making to Enlightenment thought means that much effort has gone into the design of fora and processes in which the 'better' arguments are supposed to win out over time. Whether by effectively taking vital questions concerning the 'just society' out of the political realm altogether and thereby hollowing out the political sphere (Rawls), or by subjecting democratic will formation to rights-centred (juridified and teleological) constitutionalism, respectful dialogic exchange and 'government by law' (Habemas), the loss to citizens' political agency is abundantly clear. In Ancient Rome by contrast, Machiavelli shows us how the institutionalisation of ordinary citizen participation in political life produced tumult and discord that ensured the maintenance of political liberty.

4

Populism and Ochlophobia: The Denouncements of Popular Participation in Liberal Democracy

Introduction

Some of the masses have been revolting. For a while now liberal democratic politics have been witnessing a challenge from marginalised groups and individuals who have been increasingly disinclined to believe that representative politics work for them. Online communications offer disaffected people a vital means of articulating grievances and finding/organising with like-minded others. For some time now, surveys of political preferences in European countries, the US and beyond have suggested a growing disconnect between ruling elites and the citizens they serve.[1] Eatwell and Goodwin note the increasing dominance of a 'highly educated and liberal elite whose backgrounds and outlook differ fundamentally from those of the average citizen'.[2] Ordinary voters for their part are much less likely to show the sort of constancy of political affiliation to mainstream political parties that their parents and grandparents once displayed.[3] The growing divergence in political outlook between large numbers of citizens and the centrist political parties that alternate in office has, in turn, created rising levels of disillusionment among voters with their elected representatives. In the UK recent sets of electoral promises made by the mainstream parties on key issues (student tuition fees Labour 1997, Liberal Democrats (Clegg) 2010; immigration Labour 2001; implementing the result of the EU Referendum Conservative and Labour 2017) were not kept. Widening economic inequalities and less secure employment in an extended period of austerity (itself the product of the elite-curated global financial crash of 2008) fuel the sense of a decoupling between office holders and a significant

[1] In the case of the United States, Frank dates recent popular discontent with governing elites back to the 1970s, see T Frank, *People without Power – The War on Populism and the Fight for Democracy* (London, Scribe, 2020) at ch 7.

[2] R Eatwell and M Goodwin, *National Populism: The Revolt Against Liberal Democracy* (UK, Pelican Books, 2018) at 85.

[3] H Clarke and M Stewart, 'The Decline of Parties in the Minds of Citizens' (1998) 1 *Am. Pol. Sci. Rev.* 357; P Mair, W Muller and F Plasser (eds), *Political Parties and Electoral Change: Party Responses to Electoral Markets* (2004, Sage, London).

section of the electorate. Eatwell and Goodwin contend that this development has been compounded by the emergence of a new 'governance elite', one that is linked through 'informal and formal networks that cut across elected national governments'.[4] They dispute the account of populist political forces as *the cause* of the threat to liberal values such as tolerance and diversity. This is to confuse cause and effect. On their view, large numbers of citizens were previously disillusioned with their political systems and the leaders these produced well before today's populists arrived on the scene.[5] Promised economic benefits to ordinary citizens from globalised trade or membership of a supranational trading bloc have proved chimerical. In this sense populism is more correctly seen as the latest *symptom* of remote, elite rule and a *yearning* for more responsive forms of majoritarian rule-making.

As the rejection of elite and expert/technocrat-led policymaking at the ballot box has become more common across a number of western democracies, a commensurate level of elite unease about 'populism' and the competence and wisdom of the electorate has been expressed across a range of legislative, business, media and academic/think tank platforms. Non-mainstream parties from the Right and the Left have secured power or advanced their legislative representation in Greece, Poland, Hungary, Austria, the Czech Republic, Spain, Italy, the Netherlands and Germany to name but a few polities. The resurgence of popular political expression would seem to pose a particular challenge to liberals. Historically sceptical about majoritarian democracy, liberals have long conceived the 'will of the people' to pose in certain situations a significant challenge not just to centrist political parties but more fundamentally to core liberal precepts such as the rule of law, judicial independence, constitutional courts and minority rights.[6]

One of the aims of the early part of this chapter is to describe some strains of the anti-populist rhetoric that has become a staple of mainstream media explanations of recent electoral contests. The contributory role played here in the UK by prominent figures in the Labour Party in fuelling anti-populism must also be acknowledged. Traditionally the party of working men and women, senior Labour politicians are on record as describing sections of their traditional supporters as ignorant or racist. These developments are significant. They provide a cultural context to official and corporate efforts to tamp down forms of popular political expression at odds with elite preferences and values.[7]

Theorised assaults on popular participation in the academic literature occupy a succeeding section of discussion. Aside from their respective defences of

[4] Eatwell and M Goodwin, *National Populism* at 85.

[5] A fact evidenced in part by declines in voter turnout across Western democracies.

[6] See for a classic statement of liberalism's purely instrumental connection to democracy F Hayek, *The Constitution of Liberty* (Abingdon, Routledge Classics, 2006) at 92–93, 'However strong the general case for democracy, it is not an absolute or ultimate value and must be judged by what it will achieve … the liberal believes that there are definite limits to the range of questions that should be thus decided.'

[7] Examined in more detail in ch 6.

representative party politics, other common features of these accounts are highlighted. Typically, these expositions conflate several distinct forms of anti-elite politics, preferring to see only anti-immigrant and right-wing forms of challenge to the status quo. Anti-populist theorists, share a common set of normative commitments to centrist political programmes and market-friendly economics. They manifest an *anti-pluralist* and *undemocratic* determination to shield existing power holders from their more radical sets of challengers. Although the structures of representative party politics (and a wholly unelected Upper House in the UK) already do much to mediate and modify the political expression of ordinary citizens, liberal democracy shores up its defences against popular majoritarian rule by entrusting selected experts, academics and think tanks to advocate an apparently value-free set of technocratic policy solutions. I argue in this section of the chapter that such counter-majoritarianism lies in fundamental opposition to the principle of isonomia – the idea that each citizen has an equal political weight in influencing the outcomes of law and policymaking in their communities. Of course, the structural and constitutional reforms needed to restore meaningful popular participation in policymaking lie outside the scope of the present work. As a commentary on free speech disputes in the online era however, this contribution critiques restraints faced by citizens in public discourse offering diverse perspectives on policy matters.

To ensure that the processes of policymaking in representative liberal democracy in the UK sustains elite forms of governance, opportunities for unmediated, non-elite political expression must be controlled and limited. Occasional resort to citizens via elections can be helpful from time to time in bestowing the necessary political legitimacy on elite-framed choices. However, popular inputs to political decision-making can be tolerated only so far. When 'irrational' majority sentiment threatens to derail liberal preoccupations with the global market and the accumulation of private property, or, dares to reject membership of supranational free market/neo-liberal organisations then liberals turn to counter-majoritarian institutions such as the courts in the hope that hitherto unelaborated 'constitutional' norms can be discovered that will impede the emotionally unhinged, self-destructive tendencies of the *populi*. The apprehension with which liberals view instances of popular political expression can accurately be gauged by the regularity with which they denounce referenda and issue calls for 'depoliticised' decision-making by expert agencies and committees appointed by the executive. For some liberals, governance problems stem from an 'excess of democracy'.[8] Cass Sunstein, an academic and a key Obama Administration figure, has argued for less partisan politics in US governmental structures and in favour of enhancing the grip of technocrats on policymaking. His civic republicanism has of late taken a technocratic turn in which the role of unelected experts within the executive is emphasised.

[8] M Crozier, S Huntington and J Watanuki *The Crisis of Democracy: Report on the Governability of Democracies to the Trilateral Commission* (New York, NYU Press, 1975).

He has talked for example of 'empowering' Department of Transport staff to help reduce road traffic fatalities.[9] What residual role is left for the citizen voters (a class that includes drivers, other road/pavement users and community groups) prior to/once the expert recommendation is made is unclear. For reasons of democratic legitimacy however, some form of popular endorsement will be needed at some point.

The power and influence of this type of liberal technocratic thinking should not be underestimated, nor should the threat it poses to authentic political pluralism. Michael Lind's *The New Class War* argues that, in the twenty-first century, technocratic neoliberal thinking has replaced democratic pluralism and is overseen by a 'credentialed, managerial overclass whose members simultaneously dominate the governments, corporate suites, universities, foundations, and media of the Western world'.[10] Recall too in the context of regulation of digital expression, the 'revolving door' of bright people who move between the world of government and Silicon Valley-based corporate media platforms. Bartlett charts how numerous policy advisers moved freely between Google and the Obama administration in the US and between Google and the Blair and Cameron/Clegg governments in the UK.[11] In the UK specifically, Burnham notes how the Blair Government's economic policy reflected a shift away from ideological debates between Keynesianism and monetarism to a type of 'technocratic managerialism' in which the need to secure global capital set the perimeters of what policies the government might pursue. Ironically, this depoliticisation was deceptively couched in the language of 'inclusiveness, democratisation and empowerment'.[12] Seen thus, the liberal constitutionalism of dominant US and UK political thinking should remind us that an emphasis upon the settled constitution is a conscious anti-democratic move to preserve acquisitive capitalism against its enemies.

Anti-populist Themes in Mainstream Culture and Politics

> The people are too ignorant to discuss important matters freely and ably in assembly.
>
> Guicciardini Considerations of the Discourses of Niccolò Machiavelli I.2 (1530)

For some time now, concerns about 'populist' (majoritarian) rule-making have been to the fore in mainstream political and academic discourse. In the UK, the

[9] C Sunstein *#Republic* (New Jersey, Princeton University Press, 2017) at 266. And see for commentary M Lind *The New Class War – Saving Democracy from the Metropolitan Elite* (London, Atlantic Books, 2020) at 50.

[10] ibid at 47–48.

[11] J Bartlett, *The People vs Tech* (London, Random House, 2018) at 138–39.

[12] P Burnham, 'New Labour and the Politics of Depoliticisation' (2001) 3 *Brit. Jo. of Politics and Int. Rels.* 127, 129.

victory of the Leave campaign in the June 2016 referendum on continued EU membership took most by surprise.[13] The election of Donald Trump to the US Presidency in November 2016 appeared to confirm the view of the respective demoi in the UK and the US as utterly unhinged. In higher education circles, for example, an easy call-out of expressions of popular opinion as 'racist', 'irrational' or 'ignorant' followed in academic books, articles, blogs and tweets.[14] Thomas Frank has characterised the anti-populist perspective thus:

> When someone moans about populism, we know instantly that they are summoning up a vision of society directed by responsible professionals, always including themselves, always concurring prudently with one another, always doing their best to steer the world through complex problems. These professionals are all highly educated; in fact they probably went to a tiny handful of schools. If it's pundits we're talking about, they work for one of a tiny handful of media outlets, if it's policy advisers, they work for one of a tiny handful of think tanks. They might not all agree with one another down to the letter, but agreement itself –consensus – remains for them the noblest of goals.[15]

Take for example among recent anti-populist tracts Anthony Grayling's *Democracy and its Crisis* (2017),[16] which enjoyed lavish cover endorsements from Nick Clegg (former leader of the Liberal Democrats and later Vice President for Global Affairs and Communications at Facebook), members of the London media commentariat such as Jon Snow (Channel 4 News anchor), and Baroness Helena Kennedy (a peer in the unelected House of Lords), as well as the *Wall Street Journal*. The crisis, Professor Grayling contends, has arisen because the electorate of late has not shown the degree of sophisticated understanding of politics that was required of it. In truth however, Grayling's ochlophobic work goes over some fairly well-trodden and highly selective ground before concluding in underwhelming style by advocating votes for 16-year olds and greater transparency in matters such as political party funding. In common with other defences of centrist, technocratic rule by elites, *Democracy and its Crisis* condemns the masses for failing to take their lead from the guidance offered by Professor Grayling and other like-minded people.[17] When the people show their unsuitedness to take constitutional decisions, Grayling

[13] Galston himself wrote 'I will never forget June 23, 2016 the date of the Brexit vote. I stayed up most of the night watching the BBC, absorbing the mounting shock of political commentators and elected officials as the returns trickled in'. W Galston, *Anti-Pluralism: The Populist Threat to Liberal Democracy* (New Haven, Yale University Press, 2020) at 64.

[14] Out of many possible examples in academic publishing see the facile equation of Leave supporters with fascists in R Bradford, *Orwell – A Man of Our Time* (London, Bloomsbury, 2020).

[15] T Frank, *People without Power – The War on Populism and the Fight for Democracy* (London, Scribe, 2020) at 168.

[16] London, Oneworld Publications, 2017.

[17] As a serious commentator, Professor Grayling might have been expected to take on board counter arguments from academics who defend the wisdom of democratic crowds on epistemic criteria. See, for example, Landemore's account of the superior cognitive diversity of larger groups of citizens over smaller groups of experts. For Landemore, this enhanced cognitive diversity allows democracies to produce smarter outcomes than their oligarchic counterparts. See H Landemore, *Democratic Reason: Politics, Collective Intelligence and the Rule of Many* (New Jersey, Princeton University Press, 2011).

supports entrusting experts and courts with final judgements regarding 'constitutionality morality'. His contempt for popular opinion is a leitmotif through the text.[18] When he laments the absence of judicial review of primary legislation to enforce his version of 'constitutional morality',[19] he objects that it is 'too much of a convenience (for the Executive) … to have the flexibility to make things up constitutionally'.[20] This neglects, of course, the fact that the UK executive enjoys a current political legitimacy since it is headed and directed by the winning party in the most recent General Election. Grayling's thin analysis further omits any reference to the existing set of political checks and balances that constrain the elected government in the House of Commons, including (though not limited to) the need to maintain the 'confidence' of a majority of elected MPs and the existence of Baroness Kennedy and her fellow peers in the mainly appointed though still partially hereditary House of Lords where a clear anti-Government majority exists at the time of writing. The author's barely concealed disregard for rule-making by ordinary citizens is perhaps most forcefully confirmed by something he does not say. From the 1970s onwards, the executive used its treaty-making powers to confer *additional* law-making competencies on EU bodies. As for the necessary translation into domestic law, this was achieved on occasion merely by the device of laying a packaged motion before the Commons and Lords, thereby avoiding the heightened legislative scrutiny attendant on the passage of primary legislation through Parliament.[21] In Grayling's terms however this convenient flexibility enjoyed under the Crown prerogative did not amount to an abuse of the executive's powers or point up a lack of legislative scrutiny. It facilitated further European integration without burdensome resort to popular endorsement. 'Constitutional morality', thus revealed, is whatever Professor Grayling wishes it to be. Presumably the electorate was at fault again (and deserved a renewed bout of scolding) when in the December 2019 UK General Election it failed to support those parties calling for a rerun of the 2016 referendum (eg Labour) or, more directly, a straight reversal of the result without any further plebiscite (eg the Liberal Democrats).[22]

Self-interested pieces on the deference that should be accorded to 'expert' voices drawn from the pro-EU consensus across academics and think tanks could also be seen flowing onto the pages of *The Guardian, The Observer* and *The Financial Times* in the aftermath of the 2016 referendum result. Outraged broadcast journalists on

[18] It is not difficult to imagine Orwell rebuking Grayling in similar terms to those in which he admonished George Bernard Shaw in *The Road to Wigan Pier* 'how much understanding of working class life … (does he) display? … At best his attitude to the working class is the sniggering *Punch* attitude, in more serious moments … he merely finds them contemptible and disgusting' (London, Penguin Modern Classics, 2001) at 166.

[19] A phrase incidentally left undefined by the author.

[20] ibid at 106.

[21] See thus HM Government (2013). 'Decision pursuant to Article 10 of Protocol 36 to the Treaty of the Functioning of the European Union', on bringing EU criminal justice measures into domestic law.

[22] There is an obvious irony here in the Liberal *Democrats* advocating the overthrow of the result of the 2016 EU Referendum without a further referendum.

the BBC's flagship *Newsnight*[23] programme and *Sky News*[24] did little to hide their contempt for the majority verdict. Public intellectuals on mainstream broadcasters denounced the 17.4 million who voted to leave. London-based novelist Will Self encapsulated this level of disdain. 'You don't have to be a racist or anti-Semite to vote for Brexit', he argued, 'it is just that every racist and anti-Semite in the country did'.[25] Self was looking at (but crucially failing to understand) economically powerless groups and communities who had concluded that the economic benefits of 'ever closer union' with other European economies had passed them by. Instead these marginalised communities perceived, quite accurately as it turned out, that they lived out their lives at the sharp end of austerity programmes (taking the form of diminished public services and zero hours employment contracts) that followed swiftly on from the elite-managed financial crash. On trying to understand why these groups had voted as they had however, Self could only see racism and anti-semitism. He was joined by another public intellectual Professor Richard Dawkins in the chorus of critics of the referendum outcome. Professor Dawkins tweeted: 'Yes OF COURSE there are people who voted Leave for reasons other than xenophobic bigotry or fading imperial jingoism. I've met at least four.'[26]

Awkwardly for Dawkins and Self, the survey by Clarke, Goodwin and Wheatley of Leave voter demographics reveals that this group was more ethnically and educationally diverse than is commonly believed. One quarter of graduates voted to leave as did one third of black and ethnic minority citizens.[27] Among Sikh and Jewish voters, Leave enjoyed majority support.[28]

When analysing the causes of anti-populist sentiment in mainstream political discourse (and the willingness to close down non-centrist opinion), the change in the demographic make-up of the parliamentary Labour Party in the UK is especially rewarding of close attention. This change helps explain the party's current estrangement from its traditional core support among the less affluent classes in British society.[29] Paul Embery's *Despised – Why the Modern Left Loathes the Working*

[23] See www.pressgazette.co.uk/bbc-europe-editor-breached-impartiality-guidelines-with-tweet-calling-michael-gove-delusional/.

[24] See www.standard.co.uk/news/politics/sky-s-adam-boulton-caught-saying-b-ks-to-brexit-when-he-thought-cameras-had-stopped-rolling-a4104341.html.

[25] Seehttps://inews.co.uk/news/uk/will-self-mark-francois-brexit-row-bbc-video-racist-anti-semite-267337.

[26] See http://twitter.com/RichardDawkins/status/1010775795646779392?s=20. Among Black and Asian voters around one-third voted Leave. See www.statista.com/statistics/519308/eu-referendum-voting-intention-in-uk-by-age/.

[27] H Clarke, M Goodwin and P Whiteley *Brexit: Why Britain Voted To Leave the European Union* (2017, CUP Cambridge) ch 7.

[28] See www.spiked-online.com/2019/03/26/many-ethnic-minority-voters-backed-brexit-too/.

[29] In the December 2019 General Election, Labour lost traditional seats in the Midlands and the North of England to Boris Johnson's Conservatives. Astonishingly, former pit villages such as Bolsover, Blyth Valley and Workington returned a Conservative MP to the House of Commons as Labour's 'Red Wall' collapsed. See www.bbc.co.uk/news/election-2019-50771014. The number of Labour MPs in the Commons tumbled from 262 in 2017 to 203 in 2019. For analysis see D Cutts, M Goodwin, O Heath and P Surridge, 'Brexit, the 2019 General Election and the Realignment of British Politics' (2020) 91 *Pol. Quarterly* 7.

Class usefully describes elitist strains in the modern party once considered to be *of* and *for* the working man and woman.[30] Born out of the trades union movement in Victorian/Edwardian Britain, today's Labour MP is however a very different person to the 26 MPs who won their seats in the 1906 General Election. Likely to be university educated and a committed Europhile who, in the aftermath of the 2016 EU Referendum, believes that Leave supporters had voted without understanding the issues properly.[31] Some of the current crop of senior Labour MPs have expressed themselves quite robustly on the matter. David Lammy MP infamously referred to the 'will of the people bollocks'[32] and said that pro-Brexit Conservative MPs were 'modern day Nazis'.[33] Lammy then doubled down and said his comments about the Conservative MPs had not been 'strong enough' – meaning perhaps that the MPs were in fact more evil than the genocidal National Socialists.[34] Huddersfield MP Barry Sherman said that the Remain cause had been vindicated because the more intelligent section of the population had voted Remain.[35] Denigration of ordinary working-class voters by senior Labour Party figures predates, however, the 2016 vote.[36] In 2014, Emily Thornberry MP (Islington South) was obliged to resign her Shadow Cabinet Attorney-General post on tweeting a picture of a house and van in Rochester where she was campaigning for Labour at a by-election. The house and van were festooned with St George flags. Thornberry tweeted the photo with the caption 'Image from Rochester'.[37] The sneer at working-class voters was both intended and understood. The house owner himself called Thornberry 'a snob' and explained the flags were there to show support for the England football team. Labour came a distant third in Rochester, suffering a 11.7 per cent drop in its share of the vote. The defeated Labour candidate said that Thornton's tweeted image had shown just how much Labour was becoming detached from its roots.'[38] A few

[30] Cambridge, Polity, 2021.

[31] Embery argues cogently that Labour's conversion to a pro-EU stance was borne out of a defeatist air after four successive election defeats in 1979–97 when they came to believe in the idea of a 'workers' Europe', at 43.

[32] See https://twitter.com/DavidLammy/status/1022243897253289986.

[33] See www.theguardian.com/politics/2019/apr/14/comparing-erg-to-nazis-not-strong-enough-says-david-lammy.

[34] ibid.

[35] See www.youtube.com/watch?v=JiRbRWgPKjs&ab_channel=OldQueenTV. It is curious in this regard to recall as David Goodhart does in *The Road to Somewhere* (2017, Penguin, London) how, when less affluent voters in Sunderland backed Leave in the 2016 Referendum they were deemed to be self-harming whilst, when rich people back increased taxation on the wealthier sections of society, they were typically considered noble and deserving of praise, at 52.

[36] In *The Road to Wigan Pier* (1937) George Orwell provides an acerbic account of a branch meeting of the Independent Labour Party in London well before Emily Thornberry's time: 'I remember my sensations of horror on first attending an ILP branch meeting … every person there, male and female, bore the worst stigmata of sniffish middle-class superiority. If a real working man, a miner dirty from the pit, for instance, had suddenly walked into their midst, they would have been embarrassed, angry and disgusted; some I should think would have fled holding their noses' (London, Penguin Classics, 2001) at 162–63.

[37] See www.bbc.co.uk/news/uk-politics-30139832.

[38] Cited in P Embery, *Despised – Why the Modern Left Loathes the Working Class* (Cambridge, Polity, 2021) at 33.

years previously at the 2010 General Election, then Labour leader Gordon Brown was caught on a microphone in Rochdale complaining that a lifelong voter he had just spoken to was a 'bigoted woman'.[39] Brown later apologised. Labour's patrician disdain for its support base was by then a well-established feature of centre-Left politics. Upon learning of the outcome of the June 1975 EEC Referendum, Roy Jenkins (then Home Secretary in the Wilson Government) reacted approvingly by saying on camera that the electorate had taken 'the advice of the people they were used to following'.[40] More recently in 2021, a new nadir was reached. Chris Emmas-Williams the Labour leader of Amber Valley Council who had just lost his seat in council elections (and his party overall control of the council) wrote without any hint of irony 'The people have let us down. I hope they don't live to regret it.'[41] The Left's failure in the UK and elsewhere to defend minorities who have suffered from the discriminatory impacts (economically and socially) of COVID policy on lockdowns and vaccine passports on the poorer and elderly sections of the community may offer a further instance of the growing disconnect between progressive politicians and their electorates. A sustained analysis of the UK Left's accompanying silence on enhanced digital surveillance and crackdowns on public protest and their complicity in rushing through Parliament emergency limitations on personal freedom in the name of public health is now needed.[42]

In the US, elite progressives' disdain for ordinary voters was exemplified by Presidential candidate Hillary Clinton's 'basket of deplorables' remark. This assessment doubtless played some part in the movement of votes from the Democrat column into the Republican one in 2016.[43] In the Clinton worldview these voters were 'to be scolded, not championed'.[44] Clinton supporters among the literati and intelligentsia could be found asserting that Trump supporters should be ashamed of their ignorance, stupidity and moral grotesqueness.[45] The contrary suggestion

[39] See www.theguardian.com/politics/2010/apr/28/gordon-brown-bigoted-woman.

[40] Cited in P Mair, *Ruling the Void: The Hollowing of Western Democracy* (Cambridge, Polity Press, 2011) at 114.

[41] Cited by Mick Hume in 'Labour: The voters let us down', see www.spiked-online.com/2021/05/10/labour-the-voters-let-us-down/. Hume neatly draws the parallel with Bertolcht Brecht's 1953 poem *Die Lösung* in which a Communist Party official in East Germany responds to workers' revolt by declaiming that the people of East Berlin 'had forfeited the confidence of the Government'. The poem concludes by asking:

> Would it not in that case be simpler
> for the government
> To dissolve the people
> And elect another?

[42] For an early and highly insightful piece from a left-of-centre perspective, see T Green and T Fazi, 'The Left's Covid Failure' at https://unherd.com/2021/11/the-lefts-covid-failure/.

[43] The remark was reported on CBS News on 10 September 2016 and is available on youtube. See www.youtube.com/watch?v=PCHJVE9trSM&ab_channel=CBSNews. This part of the speech was greeted by uproarious laughter by members of the audience.

[44] T Frank, *People without Power – The War on Populism and the Fight for Democracy* (London, Scribe, 2020) at 233.

[45] There are many sources to quote from here, but those cited by Frank at 236–37 include the novelist Garrison Keillor, Charles Taylor an academic at NYU and Jamelle Bouie a columnist for *Slate*.

that the electoral choice made in 2016 by US voters might require a more careful analysis was conspicuous by its absence. That the life circumstances and anxieties of some of the have-nots were deserving of some closer inspection and understanding was somehow beyond these reasoning, tolerant and decent liberals.[46] The lack of enthusiasm for Clinton among more radical sections of Democratic party supporters was also overlooked in the rush to explain the result. The Clinton camp's strong support among superdelegates at the Democratic National Convention (Democratic Party establishment figures drawn from governors, senators, congressmen/women and members of the Democratic at the Democratic National Committee) meant that primary victories for the Sanders camp among grassroots Democratic Party supporters were easily nullified at the final count of delegates.[47] Sanders' supporters were quoted as saying that the system was 'rigged' in favour of Clinton.[48]

In the aftermath of the Biden victory in 2020, the levels of contempt and condescension for popular decision-making abated as the voters were considered to have come (temporarily in the US at least) to their senses in sufficient numbers when the centrist Democrat defeated Trump. In truth however, as Furedi observes, the dominant representation of democracy in much of our political culture in the UK and elsewhere as 'populist' is 'entirely associated with negative characteristics …'[49] It is a representation that is required to be reproduced on an ongoing basis to justify holding popular expressions of political opinion in check.

Not all academic opinion denounced the outcome of the 2016 EU Referendum in the UK or joined in the denunciation of working and lower middle classes in the US after the election of Trump. Writing in the immediate aftermath of the UK's EU Referendum result, Gray accurately observed that 'populism' had become a 'term of abuse used by establishment thinkers to people whose lives they have not troubled to understand (and) … at whom they like to sneer'.[50] The referendum result followed in Gray's view from an accurate diagnosis by ordinary men and women that the purportedly 'safe option' of the EU had proved anything but. From the dysfunctional Eurozone currency, to its destructive austerity policies and the sheer incompetence of EU institutions to deal with the migrant crisis, the EU had 'demonstrated beyond reasonable doubt that it lacks the capacity for effective action and is incapable of reform'.[51] At an even more fundamental level, however, it

[46] Lest it be misunderstood, I am not for a moment arguing that Trump's victory was beneficial to ordinary US citizens. I am critical of liberal responses to his success. The overwhelming tone of condemnation is misplaced. A more productive use of time might have been to try to understand voters' various sources of disillusionment with the Democratic candidate, Hillary Clinton, and the policies she represented.

[47] See theguardian.com/us-news/2016/apr/19/democratic-party-superdelegates-history-rules-changes.

[48] See www.nytimes.com/2018/05/17/us/politics/democratic-party-superdelegates.html.

[49] F Furedi, *Democracy under Siege* (Winchester, Zero Books, 2021) at 11.

[50] J Gray, 'The Strange Death of Liberal Politics' *New Statesman* (2016) 5 July at www.newstatesman.com/politics/uk/2016/07/strange-death-liberal-politics.

[51] ibid.

was the popular and accurate perception that rule-making in the European Union was profoundly lacking in democratic accountability that foreshadowed the Leave verdict. Political scientist Peter Mair's description of EU policymaking as lying with a political system constructed by national leaders to 'evade the constraints imposed by representative democracy' carries resonance here.[52] The structures of EU power, Mair notes, allow the decisions of transnational political elites to be taken 'with more or less a free hand'.[53] The capacity of national legislatures to enact policies in areas of EU competency are severely limited. At the same time, the preferences of citizens neither mandate nor constrain EU policymakers. 'It is in this sense', Mair concludes, 'Europe appears to have been constructed as a protected sphere, safe from the demands of voters and their representatives'.[54] From the user perspective of citizens, this protected sphere equates to ruler remoteness and unresponsiveness.

Social historian Christopher Lasch's earlier critique of elites, *The Revolt of the Elites and the Betrayal of Democracy*, presciently identified in the US in the 1990s something that he termed the 'growing insularity of elites', a consequence of which was that 'political ideologies lose touch with the concerns of ordinary citizens'.[55] He described the emergence of a new upper middle class, privately (and expensively) educated at the best schools and universities whose subsequent professional careers were centred on the manipulation of information. They were to be found across a broad range of occupations – bankers, brokers, real estate agents, consultants of all sorts, systems analysts, scientists, doctors, artists, writers, university professors, writers, television producers and entertainers.[56] What unified this otherwise disparate grouping according to Lasch was their reliance upon global markets. Their fortunes were inextricably linked to the success or otherwise of transnational companies or structures. Their loyalties were international, not local or even regional.

Chiming with Lasch's account of US social attitudes is David Goodhart's binary division between the 'somewheres' and 'anywheres' in the UK. In *The Road to Somewhere* Goodhart offers an explanation of the contrasting outlooks between those who identify themselves as rooted in particular communities and/or extended families ('somewheres') on the one hand and the individualist outlook of the more highly educated ('anywheres') who conceive of themselves as 'citizens of the world' enjoy managerial careers and are prepared to travel and work well away from the places they were born into.[57]

[52] P Mair, *Ruling the Void – the Hollowing of Western Democracy* (London, Verso, 2013) at 99.

[53] ibid. at 109.

[54] ibid.

[55] C Lasch, *The Revolt of the Elites and the Betrayal of Democracy* (New York, WW Norton, 1995) at 80.

[56] ibid at 34.

[57] D Goodhart, *The Road to Somewhere – The New Tribes Shaping British Politics* (London, Penguin, 2017), especially ch 2.

In both Lasch's and Goodhart's theses, members of the professional classes see themselves as having more in common with their peers in Brussels or Hong Kong than with ordinary citizens in their own countries.[58] Lasch notes how this new governing class were lauded by admiring onlookers as the 'brightest and the best'.[59] They had reached their current high status in a meritocratic fashion. Through dint of their own intelligence and hard efforts, they had escaped the drudgery of the lot of the common people left behind and joined a higher class. Meritocracy, as Lasch remarks, has an important effect on the self perceptions of those who advance upwards through society. Having escaped from a manual/repetitive labour fate through hard work and study, these success stories view their elite status securely. The left-behinds had also had their chances for self-advancement. The difference being that the left-behinds failed to take those chances.[60]

The cosmopolitanism of the 'anywheres' draws at a theoretical level upon an abstracted sense of the individual in which people are global citizens and equally entitled to the same moral respect and concern (and legal privileges) regardless of their family history and ties to a particular polity through work and residence. Cosmopolitans wish to weaken ideas of belonging to a particular country or territory. They are suspicious of local cultures that are transmitted through immersion in a particular community and that confer on many a sense of who they are. Appeals to universal norms go hand in hand with criticisms of popular sovereignty and the nation state. A cosmopolitan legal order, Ober observes, 'regards state-based restrictions on immigration and rights of citizenship as inherently illegitimate'.[61] Universal norms, counter majoritarian institutions (some of which will be supra-national like the EU) and a culturally abstracted notion of the citizen can help weaken national majorities and their inclination to oppress and discriminate against others. Cosmopolitans struggle however to articulate how, in a world shorn of national governing institutions and sovereign state legislatures, there might be any vestige of a democratic form of life through which power holders are made politically and electorally accountable to those they make rules for.[62] As debates about the EU continue to show, cosmopolitans look to constrain national, democratically elected authorities and will happily disregard or play down the lack of democratic legitimacy of the supranational power structures in their commitment to free markets and cross-border flows of capital and people.

[58] *The Revolt of the Elites and the Betrayal of Democracy* at 35.

[59] See, thus, the remarks attributed to Robert Reich, Secretary of State for Labour in the Clinton Administration 1992–96 at 39.

[60] ibid at 43.

[61] J Ober, *Demopolis: Democracy before Liberalism in Theory and Practice* (Cambridge, CUP, 2017) at 168.

[62] F Furedi, 'Why the People Must Be Sovereign'. See www.spiked-online.com/2018/03/02/why-the-people-must-be-sovereign/ and by the same author *Populism and the European Culture Wars* (2018, Routledge, Abingdon).

Populism in Political Theory – A Response to Modern Representative Democracy and Redemptive Possibilities

It is possible to seek alternative accounts of the rise of non-mainstream, anti-elite political expression, ones that place it normatively in a healthier, dynamic relationship with the pragmatism of mainstream representative and establishment politics. Margaret Canovan's notion of the pragmatic and redemptive sides of politics in liberal democracy offers an example. On Canovan's view, mediated politics conducted through mainstream parties, pressure groups and lobbying firms can point to the non-trivial accomplishments of the orderly and peaceful resolution of political conflict. This stability is especially important after an election when the non-violent handover of power to the victors occurs. Canovan suggests however that, over time, such stability can lose its value in stable democracies. This occurs where stability and order are seen increasingly to favour existing power holders who act largely out of self-interest and, in some cases, become prone to corrupt conduct. Mainstream news organisations on this view can be complicit in buttressing established political opinion and ignoring/marginalising non-elite viewpoints.

Repeated failures to keep election promises fuel a sense of the unaccountable nature of representative politics on the part of ordinary citizens. Unable to finance their own campaigns for public office, citizens are compelled to become the clients of parties and pressure groups and business organisations who alone have the financial muscle to shape political agendas.[63] Votes are thus traded for the promise of benefits from the party once in power. Clientelism subverts the orthodox idea that in democracy citizens hold the governing authority and opposition parties to account. Instead the more powerful party machine exercises considerable influence over voters by threatening that a promised benefit will not materialise (ie the voters will be punished) if a rival party wins the contest.[64] Populism is, in McCormick's apt phrase, 'modern representative democracy's "cry of pain"'.[65] A system of representative democracy is supposed to permit the majority to rule but fails in any substantive sense to ensure popular direction of the organs of state. When the recent performance of elites in office is examined, the emotional 'cry of pain' could hardly be described as unwarranted. Whether one takes in the parliamentary expenses scandal of 2009, foreign policy catastrophes in the Middle East, or the conscious choice to under-regulate the financial sector and responses to the ensuing global economic collapse from 2008 onwards (including the decade-long

[63] J McCormick, 'The New Ochlophobia? Populism, Majority Rule and Prospects for Democratic-Republicanism' in (ed) Y Elazar and G Rousseliere, *Republicanism and the Future of Democracy* (Cambridge, CUP, 2019).

[64] For evidence about widespread nature of clientelism in democratic practice beyond Latin America, see S Stokes, 'Perverse Accountability: A Formal Model of Machine Politics with Evidence from Argentina' (2005) 99 *Am. Pol. Sci. Rev* 315.

[65] J McCormick, 'Democracy, Plutocracy and the Populist Cry of Pain' at www.academia.edu/22225287/Democracy_Plutocracy_and_the_Populist_Cry_of_Pain.

set of austerity programmes), or the tranche of allegations of dishonesty that go to the very heart of the Johnson Government in the UK,[66] the critics of elite custodianship would seem to be spoilt for choice. And that is merely the UK domestic scene.

Populist programmes promise a reconnection between the demos and the exercise of political power. Canovan notes how this redemptive view of politics taps into the idea of the sovereign people – the constituent power – creating a better world. An earlier encapsulation of this optimistic sentiment is to be found in Thomas Paine's averment in the appendix to *Common Sense* 'We have it in our power to begin the world over again'.[67] It is there too in the US Declaration of Independence's confident proclamation of the constituent power of the people 'to alter or abolish' oppressive constituted authorities and 'to institute new Government …'[68]

Of course, where populist parties themselves acquire political office and direct government departments a similar popular disillusionment with institutional representative forms of power is likely to recur. Leaders of populist parties may/may not actually improve the economic well-being of ordinary voters. Some might fail to eliminate corrupt practices and become less responsive to the demands of voters over time. They might even close down the political freedoms of their opponents. For Canovan, modern representative liberal democratic society cannot in any case function without institutions that are captured by political elites and technocratic experts. It follows for her that citizen alienation from the daily practice of politics is a fact of political life. Nonetheless, Canovan advances a relatively positive valuation of redemptive politics as a self-correcting component in liberal democracies.[69] Expressive outlets for anti-establishment opinion are vital mechanisms through which liberal democracies are replenished and maintained. Populist discourses tend, as others have observed, to be 'relentlessly optimistic about people, about political possibilities, about life …'[70] It follows on this view that any attempt to remove/stifle forms of populist, anti-establishment expression is likely to trigger a more fundamental crisis for such states.

Although she thus recognises the unfortunate tendency of constitutional liberals to 'curb popular access to politics' in ways that frustrate the replenishment

[66] J Pickard, S Payne and J Cameron-Chileshe et al 'Probe into Flat Deepens PM's Woes' (2021) *Financial Times* 11 December 2021.

[67] Coming from an advocate of representative, non-direct democracy, Paine's world-anew building project is to be mediated by an elite political class.

[68] See also James Madison's defence of the Philadelphia Convention which gathered without authorisation from the constituted powers in terms of the 'transcendent and precious right of the people to abolish or alter their government …', *The Federalist No 40*.

[69] That said, Canovan accepts that the working out of political tensions between elites and non-elites has to occur within liberalism's Enlightenment frame. Progress towards the better society must always happen within the horizons of the liberal constitution led by those with a clearer vision of its end goals and steadfast in their commitment to acquisitive capitalism, private property and individual rights. See *The People* (Cambridge, Polity Press, 2005) ch 4.

[70] T Frank, *People without Power – The War on Populism and the Fight for Democracy* at 242.

of liberal democracy,[71] Canovan remains however anchored to a 'complex set of political practices and discourses, institutions and ideas' in which rights-based constitutional limitations on the exercise of the power of numerical majorities is in order. There is, as with Habermas, a lexical ordering of private autonomy over and above public autonomy – the people not primarily as constituting authors of the law but as the constituted subjects of law whose only legitimate moves consist in the making of enlightened liberal laws that respect universal rights, the rule of law, private property and acquisitive capitalism.[72] This is made evident in the sections of her writings that query any shift towards majoritarian politics that removes or lessens the enlightened grip of progressive political elites, constitutional courts and technocrats. It is not merely that she considers that appeals to 'the people' lack conceptual clarity and are not easily rendered into institutional forms.[73] Canovan worries separately that the liberal political project of an ever more progressive society led by the enlightened and liberated can be derailed by those laggardly groups and individuals whose lives and cultures are not valued by progressives.[74] She is concerned that, in a less deferential society, acceptance by ordinary citizens of the 'tutelage' of their more educated betters can no longer be taken for granted.

A concluding section of this chapter goes on to offer a different and, I maintain, considerably stronger endorsement of popular participation in republican political theory than that outlined in Canovan. It is derived from Machiavelli's groundbreaking *Discourses on Livy* that challenges much in the thinking of aristocratic/patrician republican thought, and places ordinary citizens centre stage in isonomic rule-making and in checking the self-aggrandising tendencies of socio-economic elites. The *Discourses* can be deployed to ground a more robust agonistic defence of ongoing, popular contestation of political decision-making. In the absence of institutional reforms to liberal democratic constitutions that could secure greater popular participation (fixed-term public office holding by lottery, plebeian-only assemblies, vetoes on legislation held by modern day tribunes) that are in any case beyond the scope of the present study,[75] the discussion presented in this conclusion defends a non-derogatory and extra-institutional meaning of populism that challenges elite restrictions on popular expression designed to

[71] *The People* at 85.

[72] See further M Canovan, 'Taking Politics to the People: Populism as the Ideology of Democracy' in Y Meny et al (eds) *Democracies and the Populist Challenge* (London, Palgrave MacMillan, 2002) where she argues that they are also redemptive energies in the 'rich' liberal doctrines of universal rights and the rule of law and that these energies should be released to modify the concepts of sovereignty, people and majority rule, at 38.

[73] Noting that populist assumptions about contemporary politics include the ideas that 'the ultimate source of political authority is the 'sovereign people', and that all legitimate political power is based on the consent of the people', she comments that 'these truisms of modern political culture inadvertently show up their embarrassing obscurity', *The People* at 84.

[74] ibid at 87.

[75] See for a full and engaging treatment of the issue J McCormick, *Machiavellian Democracy* (Cambridge, CUP, 2012).

maintain the status quo. It looks to the participative possibilities of challenging and disturbing the dominant neo-liberal market, *post*-politics worldview of society where the diktats of financial capitalism endorse 'responsible' austerity packages. It calls for a rebalancing of the inherent tensions in liberal democracy away from liberalism and its exclusionary practices. The latter have largely hollowed out the democracy (popular sovereignty) component to episodic manifestations of free elections in which the distorting influences of corporate expenditure and mainstream media organisations (and increasingly for-profit social media platforms) drown out minority and dissenting opinions. Agonistic republicanism of the form defended here disputes at its core a Hegelian analysis in which late advanced capitalism, free markets and possessive individualism represent the culmination of human progress.[76] It concurs with Arendt's conclusion that dialectical/teleological accounts of humankind downplay particular events in recorded history as 'functions in an over-all process'.[77] Such accounts are reductive of the particular significance of the free acts of humans. As Arendt puts it, 'single events and deeds and sufferings have no more meaning here than hammer and nails have with respect to the finished table'.[78] Viewed thus, dialectical and deliberative notions of progress sit in opposition to ideas of human agency. Arendt's rejection of the teleological accounts represent a liberation that 'goes hand in hand with the agonistic stress on freedom and with restoration of the idea of the priority of politics and of the constituent power.'[79] My overall aim in this later section of writing is to defend a more disrupting, conflictual set of political exchanges between differently situated groups and their irreconcilably distinct projects. As elsewhere in the analysis, this chapter develops the claim that a vibrant, meaningful political pluralism is under constant threat from dominant elites that try to close down political disagreement. The constituent power of the people to freely remake their society may augment an existing set of constitutional understandings by emphasising the thread of continuity that links the new settlement to themes and values in earlier versions of the settlement. Alternatively, the constituent power may bring about the 'absolute beginning' in which 'time' begins anew from the moment of the revolutionary event. A commitment to radical, agonistic pluralism entails that both modes of the constituent power be considered legitimate.

Before embarking upon that defence, two sections on anti-populist ideology are presented. The first sets out the venerable tradition of anti-populism and traces overarching themes that link the hostility of Plato and Thucydides to critics of mass culture in the twentieth century. A second section then examines current anti-populist strains in republican theory. In this section, whether it be through

[76] See, for example, F Fukuyama, *The End of History and the Last Man* (London, Penguin, 1992).

[77] H Arendt, 'The Concept of History: Ancient and Modern' in *Between Past and Future* (New York, Penguin, 1977) at 63.

[78] ibid at 80.

[79] M Wenman *Agonistic Democracy: Constituent Power in the Era of Globalisation* (Cambridge, CUP, 2013) 299.

a reliance upon counter-majoritarian institutions such as courts or representative institutions such as legislatures, distrust of unmediated popular participation in political decision-making is writ large. What this amounts to can be stated in the starkest of terms. Constituted forms of authority are beyond the reach of the constituent power. Liberalism will continue to demand that individual political agency be subordinated in pursuit of the progressive realisation of the liberal ideal.

Defending Oligarchical Rule Down the Ages – From Thucydides and Plato via Madison and Tocqueville to the Twentieth-century Critics of Mass Culture[80]

> When Adam delved and Eve span, who then was the gentleman?
>
> John Ball (1381) itinerant preacher and leader of the Peasants' Revolt

Current denunciations of popular participation outlined in an earlier part of this chapter tap into a venerable tradition of defending elite rule and doubting the capacity of ordinary citizens for sound judgement. The one-sided accounts of participatory decision-making in Greek city states by Thucydides and Aristophanes have been handed down and received uncritically. Plato's ship of fools in Book IV of *The Republic* treats the practice of ruling as beyond the capacity of non-experts. Statecraft is a skill that has to be learnt and cultivated in those few competent individuals capable of being instructed and cultivated. In *Gorgias*, Plato has Socrates criticise public speech as practised by persuasive orators (rather than the men of 'real information' such as physicians in matters of bodily health) and as being able to appeal to the desires of the ignorant crowd, thereby in the process enslaving the now corrupted speaker to the mistaken viewpoint of the people.[81] In Plato's thought, the intellectual and other character deficiencies of the 'mob' inevitably precipitate a descent into tyranny out of which demagogic rule emerges.

As Melissa Lane comments, these received narratives point up the supposed failings of the Athenian demos as comprising arbitrariness and stupidity. These deficiencies were evident in the events at Arginusae, Sicily and the treatment of captured Mytelline men.[82] If only the ignorant and insufficiently deferential

[80] For an accessible and helpful overview, see F Furedi, *Democracy under Siege* (Winchester, Zero Books, 2021). Furedi highlights the negative psychological assessments of ordinary citizens that pervade much of anti-popular discourse over time.

[81] 'And so likewise in respect of all the rest of arts the case is the same with the orator and with rhetoric; there is no occasion, that is to say, for them to be acquainted with the things themselves, but it is enough for them to have discovered some instrument of persuasion which may enable them to present the appearance to the ignorant of knowing better than the well informed', *Gorgias* 21.

[82] M Lane, *Greek and Roman Political Ideas* (London, Pelican, 2014) at 116.

Athenians had been replaced by men of wisdom and superior understanding, these disasters might have been avoided. Lane's more nuanced account by contrast shows that, at times, the Athenian assembly *was* capable of recognising and acting upon good advice.[83] She argues that the near-exclusive focus of critics on law-making leads them to overlook other aspects of policymaking in this popular body. Herodotus for example in *The Histories* is read as offering a defence of Athenian democratic practice by associating popular rule with strong societies in contrast to weak societies led by tyrants:[84]

> [78] So Athens flourished. Now, the advantages of everyone having a voice in the political procedure are not restricted just to single instances, but are plain to see wherever one looks. For instance when the Athenians were ruled by tyrants, they were no better at warfare than any of their neighbours, but once they had got rid of the tyrants they became vastly superior. This goes to show that while they were under an oppressive regime they fought below their best because they were working for a master, whereas as free men each individual wanted to achieve something for himself.[85]

Where the beneficial effects of popular and inclusive forms of rule/policymaking in the later Roman period are acknowledged, these are expressly attributed to the well-designed 'republic' and its virtuous, enlightened leadership rather than any system of popular checks on oligarchical power and the input of the demos. By the eighteenth century when the claims of representative republics were being championed,[86] Athens was regularly served up as an exemplar to be avoided. US Founding Father James Madison's dismissal of direct unmediated rule in *Federalist Paper* 55 could not have been clearer: 'In all very numerous assemblies, of whatever character composed, passion never fails to wrest the sceptre from reason. Had every Athenian citizen been a Socrates, every Athenian assembly would still have been a mob.'[87]

Federalist Paper 55 picks up Madison's earlier denunciation of 'pure democracies' in *Federalist Paper* 10. These, he stated, were 'ever spectacles of turbulence and contention; … incompatible with personal security, or the right of property …'[88] His defence of representative forms of democracy rests upon the capacity of

[83] See the examples provided by Lane at 110–15 of following Themistocles' advice to build up the Athenian navy and strategic decisions to (i) commute the death sentences upon the captured Mytelline men and (ii) confer a generous amnesty on those soldiers who had participated in an oligarchic uprising.

[84] *The Histories* Book Five and see for commentary S Forsdyke, 'Athenian Democratic Ideology and Herodotus' "Histories"' (2001) 122 *Am Jo Philology* 329.

[85] *The Histories* Book Five (Oxford, OUP, 1998) (translation R Waterfield) at 82.

[86] Lane cites Thomas Paine as a leading and influential proponent of representative democracy who wrote in *The Rights of Man* that Athens would have 'surpassed' itself had it adopted a representative form of democracy. Lane argues that Paine's position rests upon a mistaken assumption that the Athenian assembly's main activity was the enactment of laws, when in fact more important functions included settling questions of public policy such as war and peace, agriculture and food and national security, at 117–18.

[87] J Madison, A Hamilton and J Jay *The Federalist Papers* (London, Penguin, 1987).

[88] ibid.

elective institutions to mediate and overcome the short-sightedness of popular opinion. The true public good could best be identified by the election of educated and disinterested people capable of reflective and civilised debate in a representative assembly. Madison is also on record as having resisted the extension of the franchise to all adults without regard to property. Even those who owned small parcels of land should not be included on the register of voters, since this would give too much power to those who would not know how to use it or else would sell their votes to the rich.[89]

This account of Madison's aristocratic republicanism has been challenged in recent times by scholars who have argued that other parts of Madison's published works indicate that his position was less straightforward than a simple endorsement of enlightened elite rule.[90] It is argued that Madison placed far greater emphasis upon popular opinion as the basis of (and setting the limits of) republican government. These revisionist versions of Madison's thought are considered more fully in chapter five in order to ascertain how far, if at all, they absolve him from the charge of aristocratic republicanism.

Madison's concern to protect the minority from the tyranny of the majority found an interested reader in Alexis de Tocqueville whose *Democracy in America* also devoted considerable thought to the problem. However, instead of seeing like Madison a majority who might at any point trample over the minority, if left constitutionally free to do so, de Tocqueville articulated a different anxiety about the demos. He saw in America a stable society where social equality prevailed and thus no scope for permanent political disagreement between its different citizens. What disturbed de Tocqueville was the cultural uniformity that social equality had produced. 'The man you left in New York you find again in almost impenetrable solitudes: same clothes, same attitude, same language, same habits, same pleasures.'[91] The tyranny of the majority for de Tocqueville was expressed in how public opinion exercised control over the individual mind.[92] The formal laws might permit a range of opinion and thought, but the censoring effect of societal mores produced a degree of conformity and unanimity. The majority's cultural norms were unthinkingly adopted by the rest, thus stultifying any progress and pursuit of excellence that might result from the clash of values and ideas in more diverse, pluralist societies. 'Despotism … had arrived at a new stage of perfection since those who were oppressed glorified their oppression and honored their oppressor.'[93]

[89] R Matthews, 'James Madison's Political Theory: Hostage to Democratic Fortune' (2005) 67 *The Review of Politics* 49, 53. Matthews' article makes clear just how worried Madison was by the prospect of the day when the propertyless become the majority in society, see especially the discussion at 55.

[90] Instructive explorations of this side of Madison are to be found in R Martin, *Government by Dissent* (New York, NYU Press, 2014) at ch 5 and C Sheehan *James Madison and the Spirit of Republicanism* (New York, CUP, 2009).

[91] A De Tocqueville, *Democracy on America* (ed I Kramnick) (London, Penguin New Classics, 2003) at 880.

[92] M Horwith, 'Tocqueville and the Tyranny of the Majority' (1966) 28 *The Review of Politics* 293.

[93] ibid at 303. Arendt develops this point in *On Revolution* noting how public unanimity removes the possibility of freedom of opinion since the individual is prevented from forming his/her own views without being able to access the varied opinions of others (London, Penguin, 2006) at 217.

De Tocqueville's negative assessment of mass culture and individual psychology in nineteenth-century America and how the demos was fundamentally unsuited to the task of exercising political power set a powerful theme that was to carry over into the twentieth century. The grudging extensions of the franchise that occurred in the nineteenth and early twentieth century were accompanied by warnings about how mass opinion needed to be led by more enlightened minds. Elements among elite opinion became anxious, fearing that the ability of superior intellects to influence the mindsets of the expanded electorate would be diminished. Politicians would then become corrupted if, instead of shaping public discourse, they became enslaved to popular opinion and, opportunistically, gave the masses what they foolishly wanted as opposed to what they actually needed.[94]

Approaching Ortega y Gasset's denunciation of mass culture in *The Revolt of the Masses*, it is difficult now to comprehend that this work was written by a member of the Spanish Republican government in 1930 who, at some fundamental level, must have been committed to the idea of democratic self-government.[95] Like the aristocratic de Tocqueville before him, Ortega y Gasset speaks of the homogenising masses as a force which 'crushes beneath it everything that is different, everything that is excellent, individual, qualified and select'.[96] He adopts a rigid binary distinction between the minority – people of intellect who enjoy the faculty of wonder – and the majority, that is the others in whom this faculty is absent.[97] 'The ordinary man, hitherto guided by others, has resolved to govern the world himself.'[98] *The Revolt of the Masses* looks back nostalgically to an earlier epoch when 'democracy was tempered by a generous dose of liberalism and of enthusiasm for the law'.[99] The masses understood their limitations and were happy to defer to the elite minority in whom actual political power was vested.[100] By the 1930s, however, the mass had come to believe that it had 'the right to impose and to give force of law to notions born in the cafe'.[101] The ensuing displacement of cultural elites meant that the one section of society capable of living up to the demanding ideals of twentieth-century civilisation was no longer at the helm.[102]

[94] F Furedi *Democracy under Siege* (Winchester, Zero Books, 2021) at 62–66.

[95] Ryan writes that Ortega y Gasset provides us with a 'despairing account' of the rise of the masses and 'ascribes to it most of what he disliked about the first three decades of the twentieth century', *On Politics* (London, Penguin, 2012) at 833.

[96] J Ortega y Gasset, *The Revolt of the Masses* (New York, WW Norton, 1993) at 18. See further J Carey, *The Intellectual and the Masses – Pride and Prejudice among the Literary Intelligentsia 1880–1939* (London, Faber & Faber, 1992) for an excellent critical analysis of Ortega y Gasset and other academic and artistic denouncements of mass culture emanating from British authors such as DH Lawrence, George Bernard Shaw, HG Wells and Virginia Woolf.

[97] 'The faculty of wonder is the delight refused to your football "fan"' Ortega y Gasset asserts on 12.

[98] ibid at 97.

[99] ibid at 17.

[100] Ortega y Gasset was influenced by the French sociologist Gustave Le Bon who in 1895 had ascribed irrationality, savageness and impulsiveness to crowds. When exposed to education, matters merely became worse on Le Bon's account. The masses merely developed grievances about their lot in life and were inclined to support socialist ideas. *La psychologie des foules* (1895) (trans. *The Crowd – A Study of the Popular Mind* now available in English (New York, Dover Publications, 2002).

[101] *The Revolt of the Masses* at 17–18.

[102] ibid at 26.

An era of barbarism had begun in which good manners, courtesy, restrictions on sexual relations – all things that made living in common possible – were falling away. Without a sense of the fragility of civilisation, without a sense of wonder, the ordinary man in Ortega y Gasset's scheme of thinking was destined to act selfishly like 'the spoiled child of history'.[103] Much that had been gained would now be lost.

Arguably however the most damaging attribution made about popular democratic rule and the psychological and intellectual failings of ordinary individuals was made in the years immediately before and after World War II by the Hungarian-born, German sociologist Karl Mannheim. The significance of Mannheim's work lies in the link he claimed existed between the move to universal suffrage and the rise of totalitarian political movements in Germany, Italy and elsewhere.[104] Mannheim argued that democracies by definition create opportunities for more 'impetuous' contributions to political debate that can easily provoke crises and stalemates. Previously in the early stages of democratisation but prior to full universal suffrage, political decision-making was still in the hands of 'more or less homogeneous economic and intellectual elites'.[105] This pragmatic cadre of leaders understood what was politically achievable, as opposed to the various utopian and delusional schemes of the massed ranks of newly enfranchised voters. As the influence of the latter increased and clashes between the two outlooks occurred, 'disturbances' were inevitable. Inevitably, Mannheim argued, the 'irrational' dreams of the masses would not be capable of realisation. In the accompanying personal insecurity and psychological crisis this fact induced, ordinary citizens would turn increasingly to messianic leaders and authoritarian regimes to replace democratic governments. Thus, as societies became more democratic and economic inequality grew, the stand-off between the masses and the elites would only be resolved in one way. Subsequently, working at universities in both the UK and the US, Mannheim turned his attention to how democracies might avoid the slide into illiberal authoritarianism. Having identified how widening economic inequalities led to class antagonisms, Mannheim argued for state planning to ensure that technological innovation might be made to work for the good of all.[106] The pressing objective in the UK and the US in the post-war years was thus to ensure an effective planned economy that ensured all shared in the benefits of technological progress. His generalised ascription of irrationality and utopianism to ordinary citizens and their tendency to embrace totalitarian regimes sent out a chilling warning. After all, Mannheim had seen at close quarters the rise to

[103] ibid at 98.

[104] K Mannheim, 'Present Trends in the Building of Society' in (eds. R Cattrell, J Cohen, R Travers) *Human Affairs* (London, Macmillan, 1938); K Mannheim *Diagnosis of Our Time* (New York. OUP, 1944) and see overview by J Albini, 'Crisis or Reconstruction: Mannheim's Alternatives for Western Democracies' (1970) 3 *Sociological Focus* 63.

[105] K Mannheim, 'The Democratization of Culture' in (ed K Wolff) *From Karl Mannheim* (2nd edn) (London, Transaction Publishing, 1993) at 448.

[106] K Mannheim, 'Democratic Planning and New Science of Society' in (ed J Brumwell) *This Changing World* (London, Routledge, 1944).

power of the Nazis via democratic elections. Though accepting the inevitability of mass universal suffrage, it spoke to the need for liberal elites to closely manage and supervise economic development. Mannheim referred to the attitude that was required from the managing class. It was to act as democracy's sober stock-taker, demonstrating an 'awareness of the possible defects of democracy as a prerequisite for correcting them'.[107]

Mannheim's account does, however, raise certain difficulties of its own. A principal difficulty centres upon the masses' unfulfilled political/economic expectations. If the masses in democratic states do hold 'irrational' and thus unrealisable expectations about how the economy can be run to benefit them, it does not, as a matter of empirical truth, seem to be the case that these unfulfilled expectations ineluctably drove the masses everywhere to embrace totalitarian parties and their anti-democratic ideologies. Take, for example, the Great Depression in the 1930s following the Wall Street Crash of 1929 when in the UK and US and elsewhere millions of workers and their families experienced crushing levels of poverty. Did the 'irrational and unrealistic' masses switch their political allegiances away from mainstream liberal democratic parties in order to back authoritarian parties led by messianic leaders? Obviously not. In US elections, the 1930s saw the New Deal Democrats led by Roosevelt win election after election, by crushing margins both in the popular vote and Electoral College over their Republican opponents.[108] In the UK, the 1931 General Election saw the voters decisively reject Labour's manifesto that had declared 'capitalism has broken down' voting in large numbers to support a National Government composed of Conservative and former Labour politicians including the first Labour Prime Minister Ramsay MacDonald. The Communist Party fielded 26 candidates, none were elected and only two received more than 10,000 votes. In the 1935 national elections the National Government under the Conservative leader Baldwin was returned to power with a comfortable if reduced majority.

It seems clear therefore that Mannheim's thesis about a generalised, inherent instability of systems of universal suffrage is simply not supported by the evidence of election outcomes at times of great economic suffering. It also flies in the face of George Orwell's anecdotal account of working-class attitudes in *The Road to Wigan Pier*. Among the miners and factory workers that Orwell encountered in his journey around the depressed towns and cities of Northern England in the 1930s, the author found no interest in the theoretical and revolutionary Marxism of the intellectuals. Instead their 'socialism' centred upon eliminating the worst abuses in their daily lives and keeping at the centre of things family life, the pub, football and local affairs. Put thus, Orwell's observations could hardly be considered

[107] K Mannheim, 'The Democratization of Culture' in (ed K Wolff) *From Karl Mannheim* (2nd edn) at 449.

[108] In the 1936 General Election, Roosevelt was returned, winning 523 electoral college votes as against just 8 votes (Maine and Vermont) for his Republican challenger Alf Landon.

a confirmation of Mannheim's unstable, delusional proletariat given to endorsing fantasist politicians and messianic leaders.

Even in the most egregious examples of the slide from democracy into authoritarianism on the European continent, evidence about the majority appeal of messianic leaders is lacking. It needs restating that in the final days of the Weimar Republic, Hitler's National Socialists actually failed to secure an overall majority of seats or votes in the two national parliamentary elections in 1932. Indeed they fell back from winning 230 seats (out of 600) in the June 1932 election to 196 five months later in the November election. It is simply mistaken to assert that the majority of the German people either voted for or gave an overall majority in seats in the Reichstag to Hitler's party, although they were the largest single party. Moreover, the German working class was less inclined to support the Nazis than the middle classes comprising university graduates, civil servants and shop owners. Ullrich notes that, despite aiming much of their propaganda at blue-collar workers, the NSDAP 'did not do well with that demographic group'.[109] The elevation of Hitler to the Chancellorship in January 1933 represents a catastrophic failure of the very containment strategy devised by the knowledgeable and pragmatic elites entrusted by Mannheim to avoid the descent into totalitarianism.

Denying Isonomia Today – Ochlophobia in Liberal and Republican Political Theory

> Democrats should worry when philosophers employ the language of 'republicanism'. When philosophers espouse purportedly objective principles, such as the common good, the rule of law, depoliticization – that is normative standards that they claim will make democracy operate more justly – democrats should be very worried indeed.
>
> J McCormick *Machiavellian Democracy* (New York, CUP, 201) at 141

The discussion that follows explores some leading arguments in political theory today for limiting or endorsing popular participation in liberal democracy. Initially, the focus falls upon leading liberal and republican defences of mediated political expression. Concerned by the anti-pluralist strands of some populist groups and the threat these pose to ideas of political equality, liberals and aristocratic/patrician republicans make the case for institutional intermediaries and devices that interpolate between the people and the levers of government. A key argument made in this chapter is that, far from preserving the goal of political equality among citizens and hence political pluralism, these defences manage paradoxically in various ways to tamp down popular and politically diverse forms of engagement in the making of the laws. Moreover, the mediation and minimising of popular

[109] V Ullrich *Hitler: Ascent 1889–1939* (New York, Vintage, 2017) at 117.

participation cannot on any measure be said to have conduced to outcomes that have 'tracked the common good', serving instead to bolster the interests of existing power holders. This is hardly surprising. The logical consequence of minimising popular participation is to buttress existing structures of elite influence and control. These are particular problems for modern scholars in the republican tradition (such as Phillip Pettit) who fall back on a Madison-/Guicciardini-style defence of aristocratic/expert rule that is inherently doubtful of citizens' capacity for sound judgement.

Popular Political Activity as the Deformer/Disfigurer of Liberal Democracy

The nuanced redemptive account of anti-elite, populist contributions to politics offered by Canovan stands in sharp contrast to more recent and hostile analyses of Galston and Urbinati.[110] For these scholars, populism 'deforms' (Galston) or 'disfigures' (Urbinati) liberal democracy and threatens a reversion to forms of authoritarian rule in which the rule of law, political pluralism and minority rights are variously jeopardised.[111] I make the argument in this section that the respective defences of representative forms of politics by Urbinati and Galston each carry substantial adverse implications for non-elites' political participation in governance structures. These reasoned exclusions from political power share with more ostensibly 'republican' accounts such as those of Pettit a distrust of unmediated popular expression that is examined shortly. Pettit has even gone so far as to call for a 'depoliticised democracy', whereby the popular passions and sectional interests of majoritarian politics can be quietened by a combination of tribunals, monitoring bodies staffed with appointed experts and a Bill of Rights.

[110] W Galston, *Anti-Pluralism: The Populist Threat to Liberal Democracy* (New Haven, Yale University Press, 2020).

[111] Another prominent liberal political thinker, Jan Werner Müller *What is Populism?* (London, Penguin, 2017), likewise stresses the anti-pluralist nature of 'populism'. Müller explicitly warns his readers against conflating 'populism' with 'irresponsible or fearful' citizens since this plays into the image of elites as 'condescending'. On Müller's view, advancing (as for example Machiavelli did) the interests of ordinary citizens against societal elites does 'not automatically' make one a populist (at 20). It seems clear enough, however, that Müller dismisses class-based politics that seek radically redistributive economic programmes. He is accordingly unwilling to countenance either institutional or more spontaneous forms of checks upon elite dominance, preferring to hope instead that inclusive policymaking structures will build consensus across political divides. In republican terms, his parting claim that 'Populism … should force defenders of liberal democracy to think harder about what the current failures of representation might be' (at 103) is short on detail regarding how greater confidence on the part of non-elites in elite representative rule is to be attained. Of course, it does not show why we should strive for consensus (or at least a consensus that is acceptable to Müller) in the first place. Like Galston, however, Müller defends a constrained form of political pluralism in which some (not all) of those currently excluded can be brought into the fold and made to see the benefits on balance of free markets and globalised movements of capital and labour.

Galston, a former adviser to Bill Clinton, has revised his earlier account of the causes of populism in which he emphasised *post* the financial crash of 2008–09 the role of economics and growing income inequality. He now argues that this account ignored (i) the waves of immigration experienced in the US, EU and UK that were never satisfactorily submitted to citizens for approval[112] and (ii) the increased numbers of university graduates that created new cultural divides, with non-graduates feeling that they had less control over the direction of their lives and had now become more alienated from mainstream politics. In the final analysis, Galston's policy solutions to alienation and the absence of express democratic consent for changes in immigration policies adopt a familiar liberal patrician tone. No attempt is made to involve citizens more fully in the decision-making structures that purportedly execute policies in their name. Instead, what is offered is more efficient markets and better government regulation (to reduce economic inequality) allied to a renewed liberal spirit of compromise, self-restraint and toleration of others (although how this new spirit is to be ushered in is not clear). The admiration for elite centrist politics is underscored by Galston's praise for the French President Emmanuel Macron[113] and the accompanying plea for leaders who can help the people 'better understand their long term interests'.[114] Galston's focus on ethno-nationalist forms of populism leads him to under-analyse popular support for leftist, anti-austerity movements and parties in Europe such as Syriza and Podemos that do not threaten minority rights or political pluralism. The latter are given a single and inaccurate mention as 'self-proclaimed Marxists' in one paragraph out of 150 pages.[115] Thus, for Galston these electorally successful challengers to supra-national, financial market-imposed cuts to welfare and social assistance programmes are just another (though evidently minor) dimension of the problem of populism.[116] His commitment to political pluralism does not, it seems, extend beyond the range of political parties and movements that endorse technocratic mainstream liberal economics and acquisitive capitalism of the sort promulgated by Blair, Clinton and Obama.[117] This might be termed the

[112] In his preface, Galston writes that 'Denouncing citizens concerned about immigration as ignorant and bigoted does nothing to ameliorate either the substance of the problem or its politics', at xviii.

[113] Described as a 'determined leader with clear ideas', ibid at 1.

[114] ibid at 6. The implication that voters do not always know where their true interests lie or are easily misled by charismatic politicians of the 'wrong sort' is borne out at various places in *Anti-Pluralism* including a section of analysis on the Brexit vote where the author states at 17, 'Many British citizens said they voted to leave the European Union in order to regain democratic self-government, which *they thought had been surrendered to un-elected bureaucrats in Brussels*' (emphasis added). One wonders just how cognisant Galston is of the provisions of s 2 of the European Communities Act 1972 or the House of Lords ruling in *Factortame No 2* [1991] 1 AC 603.

[115] ibid at 42.

[116] For a more rounded analysis of leftist popular movements see J Sola and C Rendueles, 'Podemos, the Upheaval of Spanish Politics and the Challenge of Populism' (2018) 26 *Jo. of Contemporary European Studies* 99.

[117] Galston's influence on the political programme of the US Democrats in recent decades is well known. In 1998 he co-wrote a manifesto for the party in which he urged them to seek the votes of university educated, upper-middle class and increasingly wealthy Americans. These would be the type of voters who would have moved out of city centres to the suburbs and sent their children to private

'Henry Ford' approach to political pluralism. You can advocate for any kind of social/economic policies you like, provided it is centred on free markets, propped up by counter-majoritarian institutions and directed by an elite class of representatives who hold citizens at arm's length away from the locus of decision-making. In truth, this is an ersatz account of political pluralism shorn of meaningful conflict between competing societal visions. It comprises a radically truncated version of what authentically contested pluralistic democracies might look like.[118]

A normative commitment to mainstream liberal economics is also to be found in Mudde and Kaltwasser's *Populism: A Very Short Introduction*.[119] Initially, Mudde and Kaltwasser strike a sympathetic note in recognising the difficulty faced by a number of national governments in the European Union elected on the basis of anti-austerity, inequality-reduction programmes. For these administrations, the room to carry out election promises has been heavily curtailed through Eurozone 'deficit to GDP' ratio rules. Although offering a more nuanced account of populism than Galston,[120] the authors' account goes beyond a purely descriptive account of the pro-market design of the laws and institutions of the EU however.[121] On their view there is a disconnect between the actions that the voters want (and authorise) their political leaders to take and what the 'responsibility' of leadership demands. Citizens may well have desired that their political leaders tackle growing levels of inequality and reverse austerity programmes but for Mudde and Kaltwasser these are not demands that a 'responsible' government could or should have implemented.[122] The notionally socialist administrations of

schools. He and co-author Elaine Kamarck urged Democrat leaders to go after the support of the '(m)illions of Americans (who) are surging into the ranks of the upper middle class and wealthy', in (ed A Giddens) *The Global Third Way Debate* (Cambridge, Polity Press, 2001) at 102.

[118] The claim by Kratsev and Holmes that the origins of populist uprisings in Central and Eastern Europe have to be seen against the background of EU-choreographed efforts to impose an anti-pluralist liberal order on post-Communist societies is interesting in this regard. The 'very conceit' that there is no way other than the EU's way of moving away from the Communist pasts of these countries towards liberal democracy has played in their view a significant part in the rise of anti-liberal forces, I Kratsev and S Holmes, *The Light that Failed – A Reckoning* (London, Penguin, 2020) see especially 4–6. That this insight has not gained traction among federalist defenders of the EU is hardly surprising.

[119] Oxford, OUP, 2017 at 101–02.

[120] This is evidenced throughout the short book, but see inter alia at 13 concerning (i) Hugo Chavez's contention that economic elites were obstructing his economic programme in Venezuela and (ii) Syriza's claim that oligarchic forces in Greece were undermining the Tsipras Administration. Neither allegation, the authors concede, 'was unfounded' and subsequently at 79 in the statement that 'populism per se is neither good nor bad for the democratic system'. In this latter section the greater involvement of citizens in political fora is highlighted as a positive feature of populism.

[121] See for a much more critical account D Nicol, *The Constitutional Protection of Capitalism* (Oxford, Hart Publishing, 2010).

[122] Mudde and Kaltwasser at 102. The theme of 'irrational' demands by populists is also replicated in legal academics' work. See for a recent example A Young, 'Populism and the UK Constitution' [2018] 71 *Current Legal Problems* 17, who is troubled by what she sees as emotion-based populist challenges to experts and expert-led deliberation. Unfortunately Professor Young fails to acknowledge both (i) her own self-interest in defending expert-led public discourse and (ii) the policy failures of elite-rule in the UK and beyond. Young shows no consciousness of how elites have dominated and manipulated political discourse in favour of the status quo. The resultant *narrowed* range of political choices on offer to electorates paradoxically mirrors the very anti-pluralist criticism she makes of populist

Zapatero (Spain 2004–11) and Papandreou (Greece 2009–11) are therefore lauded for acting as 'responsible' agents in overseeing what transpired to be increasing economic inequality across the classes. Mudde and Kaltwasser have nothing to say about the institutional and structural reforms that might facilitate greater participation by ordinary citizens in policymaking thereby rendering political elites more responsive to electors' concerns. The elite-driven focus of their account of democratic politics is confirmed in a concluding section. Here Mudde and Kaltwasser encourage 'practitioners' (presumably those politicians who hold power) to engage in an open dialogue with populist actors and supporters to discover which of the populists' proposed policies 'have merit within a liberal democratic regime'.[123]

The contribution by Mudde and Kaltwasser embraces an underlying set of political values that treats critics of late advanced capitalism, globalised free markets and austerity programmes as irrational and economically illiterate.[124] It is for existing political elites and power holders to decide which claims from the non-mainstream parties and organisations have 'merit' for the purposes of open dialogue. Stressing in the classic liberal manner the threat posed by political majorities to minority rights (rather than critically exploring the failure of minority elites to safeguard majoritarian interests), they predictably end up recommending that judicial determinations on rights questions be entrenched, forever to lie beyond the amendatory reach of democratic political processes.[125] Just how far the 'unmeritorious' claims of populists should be given a platform or left unregulated in the online world is not clear. This is a political realm in which permissible pluralism and disagreement is reduced to what power holders consider acceptable (and unthreatening to existing dominant economic structures and ideologies).[126] Moreover, there is no recognition that the very centrist, technocratic policies that follow the logic and constraints of finance capitalism and dominate the *post-politics* world of liberal democracy (the only 'rational' option on the political/economic menu) might be causal factors behind the non-mainstream movements and the political polarisation which has then followed.

Thomas Frank has acutely observed that anti-populist defences of elite representative rule such as those proffered by Galston, Mudde and Kaltwasser all share a curious blindspot. They find it very difficult to identify and own up to catastrophic

political programmes, see especially at 34–36. For Young, borrowing from Canovan's earlier plea for a re-energised commitment to a liberal rule of law/universal rights programme, it is clear that all forms of democratic innovation *must* occur and unfold within the horizon of liberal constitutionalism with its overriding juridified commitments to the rule of law, individual rights and possessive individualism. The apparatus of the liberal capitalist regime is thus forever placed beyond the amendatory reach of the citizens.

[123] *Populism: A Very Short Introduction* (Oxford, OUP, 2017) at 118.

[124] See ibid in this regard from the same concluding section of *Populism* which states 'populism often asks the right questions but provides the wrong answers . . .'

[125] ibid at 90. The authors label the process of placing of rights in counter-majoritarian institutions as a form of 'democratic deepening'.

[126] It is thus at odds with the Arendtian notion of pluralism and human political freedom that was touched upon in the previous chapter.

failures in elite policymaking. Take for example de-industrialisation in the 1980s or the global financial meltdown in 2008 (and the under-regulated financial services sector which give rise to the meltdown). It is as if these events happened when the economic advisers, technocratic policy wonks and centrist party leaders were away on annual leave. What of the disastrous military interventions in Middle East politics in Iraq, Afghanistan and elsewhere? What of the migrant crisis that overwhelmed southern European states after the collapse of the Libyan regime of Ghadaffi and the Syrian conflict began? In these epic policy failures, the usual political elites in Europe and the US were in charge, formulating and implementing disastrous foreign policies. As Frank perceptively notes, 'anti-populists find it harder to criticize their colleagues for fouling things up than they do to deride the voting public … for being angry over these foul ups'.[127]

Urbinati in *Democracy Disfigured* shares with Galston both (i) a limited and largely episodic conception of citizen participation in politics, and (ii) an account of populism that emphasises its most regressive and reactionary emanations rather than recognising its positive energising and participation-enhancing qualities. In *Democracy Disfigured* she contends that representative democracies are far better at upholding the isonomia (equal rights) of all citizens to political liberty including freedom of expression and association than more participative and activist accounts of democracy.[128] Populism, it is claimed, is 'an assault'[129] on representative and parliamentary party politics which mobilises collective forms of expression as the will of the 'people'. Its charismatic leaders employ craft and rhetoric to achieve convergence on issues which are at odds with the true interests of citizens. Individuals are blurred into the anonymous totality of the mass from where public reason is absent.[130] Democracy under populism is 'stripped of its isonomic character.'[131] Politics is polarised as the people are asked to take sides against the corrupt elites. On achieving power populists aim to strengthen executive power via the weakening of checks and balances that ordinarily constrain governments.

At the outset, Urbinati appears to be unsure about precisely who or what constitutes the threat to representative democracy. Popular social movements with radical programmes such Occupy Wall Street and more recently Black Lives Matter are not populists according to Urbinati since they do not *seek state power* to implement programmes that are hostile to liberalism and constitutional democracy. Instead, these groups merely espouse 'populist rhetoric'. The Tea Party on the other hand became a fully formed version of populism when it mutated from a mere social movement into an organisation that put up candidates for election to

[127] T Frank, *People without Power – The War on Populism and the Fight for Democracy* at 17.

[128] Of course, Urbinati's defence of representative structures of government necessarily commit her to discarding the value of isegoria or equal right of all citizens to participate in the business of the assembly.

[129] *Democracy Disfigured* (Massachusetts, Harvard University Press, 2014) at 149.

[130] ibid at 164.

[131] ibid, at 165.

US state and federal legislatures. It is thus only when a mass movement stands for elected office that it acquires the potential to disfigure liberal democracy.[132] The fact, for example, that a movement which opts out of electoral contests declares an area 'police-free' and seeks to prevent ordinary criminal law enforcement does not in Urbinati's view amount to a populist disfiguring of democracy even though it may strike at core ideals in liberal democracy such as the right to hold private property and the rule of law. Conversely, the moment a grassroots group such as Podemos in Spain that is critical of elite mismanagement of the economy and puts its members forward at the ballot box to seek change via new laws, this signals per Urbinati a populist defacement of democracy.[133]

Most problematically for Urbinati, however, is the fact that many of the criticisms she levels at populist parties concerning moves to concentrate executive authority and diminish the range and effectiveness of balancing mechanisms within the constitution might *equally* be laid at the door of mainstream political parties in representative liberal democracies.[134] Examples in recent times abound. Take the UK, for instance, where executive domination of the legislature (and, consequently, the timetabling of parliamentary business) effectively allows the government of the day to decide how much scrutiny from opposition parties it is prepared to tolerate. Conservative and Labour administrations have both controlled the business schedule of the House of Commons to limit opportunities for parliamentary scrutiny of executive action. In August 2019, for example, the minority Conservative Government of Boris Johnson announced an extended prorogation of Parliament that effectively reduced the number of occasions when Opposition MPs and Conservative rebels were able to scrutinise the Government's Brexit proposals.[135] This recent example fits a broader pattern of political gaming by the incumbent party. Previously, the Blair Government was criticised by the Power Commission in 2006 for making the executive more powerful at the expense of elected representatives. Almost a decade into the Blair Premiership, the Commission considered that political decision-making in Whitehall had become 'more opaque, hidden and complex'. This was said to be a primary factor behind the alienation of citizens from democratic processes.[136] It is difficult either to

[132] This is somewhat ironic given that the Tea Party's programme consists in the main of supporting lower taxation, smaller government and greater immigration controls, none of which are necessarily inconsistent with the tenets of liberal democracy.

[133] I am assuming that Urbinati would label Podemos as populist, since it wants to gain political power in representative institutions to reform Spanish society in favour of non-elites.

[134] See further J McCormick, 'The New Ochlophobia? Populism, Majority Rule and Prospects for Democratic-Republicanism' in (eds) Y Elazar and G Rousseliere, *Republicanism and the Future of Democracy* (New York, CUP, 2019). McCormick cogently exposes Urbinati's endorsement of representative democracy's skewing of electoral politics in favour of powerful elites.

[135] See, however, *R (on the application of Miller) v Prime Minister* [2019] UKSC 41 for a successful (if hugely controversial) legal challenge to the prorogation at www.supremecourt.uk/cases/docs/uksc-2019-0192-judgment.pdf.

[136] *Power to the People: An Independent Inquiry into Britain's Democracy* (2006) www.jrrt.org.uk/wp-content/uploads/2019/06/PowertothePeople_001-2006.pdf at ch 5 'ReBalancing Power'.

disagree with that assessment, or to argue that things have altered in the direction of greater transparency in the intervening years.

Urbinati's invariable focus on ethno-nationalist populist groups whose charismatic leaders are able to 'dupe' voters to act in ways that are contrary to their own interests connotes a degree of naivety and credulousness on the part of the demoi that is curiously absent in her account when, in different times, these voters have sensibly preferred mainstream parties. Urbinati discounts the possibility that the rejection of mainstream parties could, at times, be a defensible choice on the part of disillusioned voters. *Pace* Urbinati, one is tempted to offer a counter explanation. After decades of economic mismanagement by the established parties, proven instances of corrupt conduct by office holders (such as the MPs and peers expenses scandals in 2009 and 2021 and the revolving-door between ministerial office and related private sector directorships/consultancy),[137] growing inequality in societal income levels and a heightened alienation from governing structures, the appeal of non-mainstream political groupings might be fairly easy to diagnose.

Undergirding Urbinati's account of the disfigurement of democracy is her claim that populism repudiates the principle of isonomia, that is the equal worth and political liberty of each citizen in a democracy. When, under populist structures of government, individuals become merely part of the 'anonymous totality' of the mass and are conceived of as a united whole, then the equal political liberty of each citizen to shape the laws by which all are governed is forfeit. But precisely how convincing is this commonly stated objection to populism? It is by no means clear that all popular, mass movements seek to silence all those who dissent from their preferred reform programmes.[138] Certainly Urbinati would be hard pressed to find evidence that Podemos or Syriza have advocated the use of the state's coercive powers to shut down the political expression of their neo-liberal opponents. More damaging, however, to Urbinati's argument is the fact that representative democracies fail to measure up to her core precept of isonomia. That is to say they demonstrably and repeatedly fail to honour the principle of the equal political liberty of each citizen. Take those constitutional democracies where unelected Supreme Courts have the power to strike down laws made by the elected representatives of the people. This cannot be rendered consistent with the equal political liberty of each citizen. Neither can the design of the US Senate where voters in the state of California (25.3 million eligible voters)[139] share the same number of senators (2) as the neighbouring state of Nevada (1.6 million eligible voters).[140]

[137] See thus R Mason and H Stewart, 'Half of Tory Ex-ministers Take Jobs in Sectors Relevant to Former Department' *The Guardian* (2021) *The Guardian* 15 November, www.theguardian.com/politics/2021/nov/15/half-of-tory-ex-ministers-take-jobs-in-sectors-relevant-to-former-department?utm_term=Autofeed&CMP=twt_gu&utm_medium&utm_source=Twitter#Echobox=1636956094.

[138] The same charge is made by Young, 'Populism and the UK Constitution' [2018] 71 *Current Legal Problems* 17.

[139] See www.ppic.org/publication/californias-likely-voters/.

[140] See https://lasvegassun.com/news/2020/may/01/nevada-gop-registered-more-voters-than-democrats-i/.

Worse still, in the UK, the upper chamber of the legislature is composed of life peers (nominated and appointed by the mainstream political parties), *ex officio* Church of England bishops and a residue of hereditary peers. How faithful then is the 'Mother of Parliaments' to isonomia? A glance at the social backgrounds of elected and elite-nominated/appointed members of the legislature in liberal democracies reveals the fallacy that opportunities to exercise political power are equally spread among the citizenry. These underlying structural inequalities are then compounded by campaign finance rules framed by existing power holders that allow multinational corporations and wealthy individuals to dominate election advertising and drown out minority and unpopular viewpoints.[141] It could be concluded that *it is the absence of isonomia* in many liberal democratic states which engenders the very condition of narrowed political discourse that Urbinati associates exclusively with populism. A theorist who was more fully committed to isonomia would thus condemn not only the anti-pluralism of authoritarian regimes claiming popular support, but also elitist institutions and governance structures found in modern liberal societies which privilege the viewpoints of the wealthy and existing office holders. Loughlin for example observes that 'Representative democracy sanctions a mode of government by elites, subject only to an often inadequate form of retrospective accountability.'[142] That Urbinati is seemingly unable to discern the limited and unequal participation of ordinary citizens in daily political life is perplexing and, as such, leaves unexplored the control exerted and perpetuated by political elites in representative democracies.[143] The failure to envision (after Canovan) a 'redemptive' strand of popular engagement in law-making ultimately marks Urbinati as unconcerned with the widespread levels of scepticism induced by pragmatic politics. It is accordingly quite difficult to see how Urbanati's stance might lead to a renewal of democratic engagement.

From the perspective of more participatory schemes of self-government that are defended in the present monograph, there is nonetheless a partially redeeming

[141] Urbinati notes that the deployment of private economic resources at election time is a vexed question and is aware that such expenditure undermines claims to isonomia. Whilst she is critical of the US Supreme Court decision in *Citizens United v Federal Elections Commission* 558 US 310 (2010), she cannot quite bring herself to endorse a ban on the use of private wealth/income in election campaigning which she describes as a 'sensitive' issue. This ambivalence is best explained by her view that '(s)ince its liberal inception in the seventeenth century, property rights and freedom of expression have been mutually supporting allies of political liberty', at 239. Her concern about the distorting effect of private resources is in any event confined to corporate campaign expenditure. It neglects those disfigurements caused by the personal expenditure of wealthy individuals. No concrete proposal is made to address the isonomia-adverse impact of corporate election expenditure.

[142] M Loughlin, 'Rights, Democracy and Law' in (eds T Campbell, KD Ewing and A Tomkins, *Sceptical Essays on Human Rights* (Oxford, OUP, 2001) at 51. See also B Manin *The Principles of Representative Government* (Cambridge, CUP, 1997) who denies that representative democracy allows for 'the community to govern itself, but a system in which public policies and decisions are made subject to the verdict of the people', at 192 (cited by Loughlin ibid).

[143] As Dunn states, modern representative democracy could be said to have been deliberately created 'for the purpose of denying that any given population, any people, had either the capacity or the right to act for themselves', in J Dunn (ed) *Democracy: The Unfinished Journey 508 BC to AD 1993* (Oxford, OUP, 1992) at 247–48.

feature of *Democracy Disfigured*. This centres on its helpful refutation of the claims made by the epistemic subset of deliberative democrats which were discussed earlier in chapter two.[144] There I argued that Urbinati's criticisms of rational, scientific decision-making in political matters are effective in showing that epistemic deliberativists' instrumental concern is with the design of procedures that deliver up morally correct/true outcomes. The epistemic deliberativist is unwilling to include in political discourse a speaker who is unable to establish the moral truth of his/her contribution. It demands a degree of intellectual rigour that is absent from the Habermassian version of deliberation where what is stressed is the capacity for empathetic reflection and revision of one's initial inputs to public discourse on the basis of having listened carefully to others' contributions. As Urbinati remarks, democracy does not require for legitimacy reasons that a speaker's contribution be shown to be correct or true. A necessary feature of legitimate democratic decision-making is that it entails the freedom of speakers and societies to advocate and endorse policy positions that turn out subsequently to have been mistaken.[145] The epistemic deliberativists by contrast seek a perfectionist version of public discourse and democracy. How many good faith contributions to political debate might be screened out by the criterion of truth? This constitutes a utopian republic of experts and even then a fair number of the aforementioned will find themselves disqualified from making public utterances on account of a rival, irreconcilable expert view being considered to have authoritatively demonstrated the requisite degree of moral truth.

Authors and Editors – Pettit's Non-isonomic Account of Republicanism

A more self-consciously republican set of arguments about citizen participation in politics is to be found in the work of Philip Pettit. Where liberal thinkers are inclined to see rights atomistically as vital mechanisms to protect the set of individual freedoms that existed pre-politically (and attach no special importance to rights required for an active political life), their republican counterparts conceive rights as being historically and contingently derived from a polity's attempt to found and maintain self-government and the public freedoms this entails under the rule of law. This distinction apart, Aitchison rightly observes that liberals and republicans nonetheless both endorse similar political and constitutional constraints in the form of institutions that check and impair more democratic impulses on the settlement of rights questions.[146] Pettit's writings fall into this category and are

[144] The author in this tradition most discussed by Urbinati is David Estlund, see his *Democratic Authority: A Philosophical Framework* (New Jersey, Princeton University Press 2008).

[145] *Democracy Disfigured* at 88.

[146] G Aitchison, 'Three Models of Republican Rights: Juridical, Parliamentary and Populist' (2017) 65 *Pol. Sts.* 339.

grounded in the republican ideal of freedom as meaning (i) non-domination and (ii) the equal legal status of each citizen. He defends a republican account of democratic legitimacy in which the citizens enjoy 'a suitable range, kind and degree of control over government'.[147] At the same time, this is categorically not an account of freedom as active self-government or a defence of ongoing, radically plural forms of political participation. His republican democracy assumes a mediated, representative form, one that is judicially policed and fed with policy inputs from expert commissions appointed from among the same set of technocratic, centrist leaning elites that currently advise governments.[148] Whilst it is true that Pettit is alive to the distortions of democratic practice by wealthy and influential citizens, his primary emphasis rests on the nature and design of institutional mechanisms that can secure non-domination and ward off the dangers of majoritarian tyranny from ordinary citizens that previously troubled Madison and de Tocqueville. In ways that are different to Urbinati, Pettit's prescriptions also fall well short of equalising each citizen's ability to shape the laws. Sometimes, Pettit is saying, the institutions and laws of the republic need protecting from the people. Democratic inputs *may* play a role in preventing governmental domination, however in Pettit's own words they are 'never presented as the center-piece of the republican polity'.[149]

Just as with Urbinati, Pettit's prescriptions scarcely leave a dent on current levels of elite dominance of political discourse. His faith in advisory expert commissions' and the contestatory institutions of courts and senates would entrench and deepen yet further the non-isonomic character of the public sphere.

For Pettit, the two roles of the citizens in a republican democratic state are to act as authors and editors of laws and policies. The authorial role is exercised via voting for parties at election time. In truth, of course, this is an indirect authorial role. Electors vote for representatives who will actually author the law. Ultimate control over the content of the laws rests with legislative members who for the most part can be relied upon to pursue the common good. After all, parties have to remain responsive to (or track in republican terms) the views of the people (and gain newer constituencies of voters) if they wish to stay viable. Nonetheless, there is a danger that elected representatives cease to act in the public good. Political parties may be captured by sectional or majority interests. Pettit's avowed concern is to guard against over-responsiveness on the part of elected representatives to the concerns of popular majorities. He pays virtually no attention to the scenario where elected groups of law-makers in fact depart *as a legislative majority* from the majority will of the electorate and enact laws and policies at odds with non-elite

[147] *On The People's Terms – A Republican Theory and Model of Democracy* (Cambridge, CUP) 179–80.

[148] In this vitally important sense, Pettit's view of democratic legitimacy does not embrace the ongoing, unencumbered authorship claims of the citizens to re-constitute the political authorities from time to time. This distinguishes his work from more radical republican positions, see thus J Colón-Ríos, *Weak Constitutionalism: Democratic Legitimacy and the Question of Constituent Power* (Abingdon, Routledge, 2012), 107 et seq.

[149] 'Republican theory and political trust' in (eds V Braithwaite and M Levi) *Trust and Governance* (New York, Russell Sage Foundation, 1998) at 303.

interests. This blindspot is a major deficiency in Pettit's account and naturally steers his analysis away from the vital discussion around how to secure popular participatory oversight of remote elite rule-making that might fail to track majoritarian interests. Pettit's failure to address the self-serving, anti-majoritarian nature of elite rule stands in contrast to Machiavelli's analysis in his *Discourses on Livy*. The Florentine's arguments on this point are developed below.

To prevent the potential for representatives to pass off a majority interest as in the public good, Pettit makes the case for contestatory institutions and procedures that facilitate an 'editorial' or negative checking role for citizens in challenging the policy outcomes reached in the legislature. Contestatory routes are to be available via judicial review, ombudsmen, senates, tribunals and Bills of Rights. Pettit assumes that these counter-majoritarian institutions are likely to protect the interests of vulnerable minorities rather than the privileged, well-financed elites (including corporate elites) who already enjoy superior access to both legislatures and courts. It is not clear how disadvantaged groups are to rise to the task of mobilising and sustaining a challenge to sectional policymaking in Pettit's scheme of various counter-majoritarian institutional settings. The confidence that Pettit has in these institutions is illuminating. It presumes a degree of knowledge and a litigator's strategic sense of how to operate the various levers of contestation. Pettit does not show us why such a presumption is justified. In short, vulnerable individuals and groups whose interests are not tracked by the policymaking process in the political sphere are likely to be cut adrift in this model. Neither should hopes be raised of a vastly expanded legal aid budget to finance professionally represented judicial review actions on behalf of penurious community groups (or even access to specialist legal advice on a pro-bono basis).[150] Pettit's account also relies on liberal constitutionalists' arguments that defend a central role for courts in the defence of minority rights. In this he endorses substantive accounts of the rule of law that extend to the adequate protection of fundamental human rights. He would endorse Bingham's claim that 'a state which savagely repressed or persecuted sections of its people could not in my view be regarded as observing the rule of law …'[151] Yet Bingham was aware of an 'element of vagueness about the content of this sub-rule, since the outer edges of fundamental human rights are not clear-cut'.[152] Moreover, it is not clear that the judicial branch has always proven itself fit for the counter-majoritarian labours entrusted to it by substantive conceptions of the rule of law when beleaguered minorities finally get to have their day in court. Citing the cases of *R v Halliday*[153] and *Liversidge v Anderson*,[154]

[150] McCormick notes that in these counter-majoritarian fora, however, privileged minorities have typically been more proficient at securing their preferred outcomes than under-resourced and vulnerable groups, J McCormick, 'The New Ochlophobia? Populism, Majority Rule and Prospects for Democratic-Republicanism' at 128.

[151] T Bingham, 'The Rule of Law' (2007) 66 *C.L.J.* 67, 76.

[152] ibid at 76–77.

[153] [1916] 1 KB 738.

[154] [1942] AC 206.

Bingham concedes that the UK courts have not always lived up to the role of effective protectors of minority rights. He notes Justice Brennan's remarks that the US Supreme Court has likewise failed on important occasions to live up to liberal constitutionalists' expectations. In a line of leading cases that include *Dred Scott*,[155] *Whitney v California*,[156] *Korematsu v US*[157] and *Dennis v US*,[158] the US Supreme Court has shown itself unwilling to check major incursions into minority rights at vital moments in US history.

At bottom, Pettit's desire to settle disputes through Bills of Rights and other juristic forms is driven by a desire to remove policy choices out of the political arena. Hirschl's comparative analysis of Bills of Rights'-centred constitutionalism in Canada, South Africa, New Zealand and Israel observes that such a move is

> tacitly supported, if not actively initiated, by political actors representing hegemonic elites and established interests ... (and) driven in many cases to maintain the social and political status quo and to block attempts to seriously challenge it through democratic politics.[159]

Martin Van Buren's criticism of anti-republicans in his posthumously published *Inquiry into the Origin and Course of Political Parties in the United States* (1867) applies to the Pettit position. Van Buren, the founder of the Democratic Party in the US and the nation's eighth President articulated the popular constitutionalist anxiety thus:

> In a large degree wealthy and proud of their social position, their fear of the popular will, and desire to escape from popular control, instead of being lessened, is increased by the advance of the people in education and knowledge. Under no authority do they feel their interests to be safer than under that which is subject to the judicial power, and in no way could their policy be more effectually promoted than by taking power from those departments of the Government over which the people have full control, and accumulating it in that over which they may fairly be said to have none.[160]

Pettit's anxieties about the irrational masses surface in another aspect of his constitutional design. Expert commissions may also be deployed to head off *ex ante* the malign influence of popular passions and something Pettit labels 'moral fastidiousness' on members of the legislature as policy on matters such as criminal sentencing or prostitution is being written into draft legislative form Pettit's trust in the ascertainment of the public good by panels of experts sitting in 'depoliticized' fora stands in contrast to his wariness of majoritarian decision-making.

[155] 60 US (19 How) 393 (1857).
[156] 274 US 357 (1927).
[157] 323 US 214 (1944).
[158] 341 US 494 (1951).
[159] R Hirschl, *Towards Juristocracy – The Origins and Consequences of the New Constitutionalism* (Massachusetts, Harvard University Press, 2004) at 213–14.
[160] New York, Hurd & Houghton, 1867 at 352.

The important role he confers on appointed expertise working in spaces not regularly opened up to the public gaze supplies another reason to place Pettit firmly at the aristocratic end of the spectrum of republican thinkers.[161]

Pettit separately argues that unmediated forms of popular participation in rule-making are to be distrusted for the reason that, over time, plenary assemblies fail over time to produce rationally *consistent* legislation. Doesn't much the same happen in representative democracies when the Blue Party takes office after a period of rule by the Red Party or when 'moderates' at senior levels in the governing party are replaced by less moderate colleagues? Or vice versa? Some would maintain that changes in policy direction are in any case inevitable and desirable where external realities have changed. At a more profound level, Pettit's normative commitment to the unilinear unfolding of the good society via rationally consistent legislative policy harks back to Enlightenment ideas of progression. Once this is acknowledged, it becomes clear why the disruptive jarring caused by the operation of popular passions and diverse opinions must be minimised. In Pettit's scheme of mediated/depoliticised, institutional democracy, rival viewpoints must at the very least be made to conform to the dictates of deliberative politics and associated notions of reasoning in the public sphere in order to progress towards consensus.[162] Pettit belongs thus with other anti-populist theorists of liberal democracy. His concerns about the popular passions unleashed in majoritarian systems of rule-making lead him to assume that (rather than examine whether) the political sphere reflects those majoritarian viewpoints. The same concerns guide him towards a Madisonian faith in representative structures of government where socio-economic elites can channel and mediate popular opinion. His faith in a raft of unimpassioned counter-majoritarian fora including courts and expert commissions speaks to a deeply depoliticised, technocratic and non-isonomic account of republicanism.[163] A rival, isonomic version of political participation is, however, available to those egalitarian republicans drawn to a more actively participatory conception of politics. It draws upon Arendt's idea of citizenship that is sketched immediately below (and is returned to and developed more fully in chapter five on the Democratic Republican societies in the early American Republic and the preservation of the revolutionary spirit). Rights of equal political participation to contest forms of self-interested elite rule are also heavily implicated in Machiavelli's account of liberty in the *Discourses on Livy*. The largely passive, acclamatory role of the people in the works of Pettit, Urbinati and others will be contrasted against more radical accounts of political contestation in the discussion which follows below.

[161] J McCormick, *Machiavellian Democracy* (Cambridge, CUP, 2012) at ch 6.

[162] ibid at 58–59.This last point tends to undercut Pettit's assertion in *On The People's Terms* that he is committed to an active, agonistic political culture, at 280–92.

[163] P Pettit, 'Depoliticizing Democracy' (2004) 17 *Ratio Juris* 52.

Countering Ochlophobia – Popular (Arendtian) Participation and the Value of Roman Discord

> Cherish therefore the spirit of our people, and keep alive their attention .... If once they become inattentive to public affairs, you and I, and Congress and Assemblies, Judges and Governors, shall all become wolves.
>
> Thomas Jefferson (1787 January 16) Letter to Colonel Edward Carrington[164]

The mediated and highly episodic accounts of popular forms of political participation respectively defended by Pettit and Urbinati fall well short of enjoining citizens to be the on-going authors of the laws under which they live. Neither account holds much that would cause socio-economic elites to be unduly concerned about an imminent loss of effective control over political decision-making. Neither account proposes greater democratic control of law and policy. For theoretical envisionings that do offer radical accounts of popular political participation, this concluding section of the chapter turns to the accounts of political agency and popular participation in Hannah Arendt and Niccolò Machiavelli.

For Arendt, political agency – that is action (speech and collective endeavour) in the public sphere – is the thing that confers meaning and significance on the lives of individuals.[165] As citizens come together for the advancement of political goals, they venture with others to create something that is new. The provision of a common public space for the formation and testing of plural political opinion in open argument and debate is central to Arendt's understanding of democratic citizenship. To a pre-digital audience, this spatial dimension of plural public discourse in the Arendtian model of democratic citizenship is Speakers' Corner in Hyde Park replicated across the polity. For today's speakers and audiences, entry to the park is controlled by the shareholders and employees of Facebook, Twitter, Youtube among others on terms that are not open to democratic oversight. The problematic features of privatised platform spaces within which digital communication on public issues is produced and disseminated are the focus of chapter six.

In its fullest and most dramatic form, human action in Arendtian terms means founding a new political beginning. Having come together to create the new political settlement by the exercise of public freedoms of speech and collective action however, Arendt was only too aware that this very revolutionary spirit might also

[164] (1787) 16 January available at https://founders.archives.gov/documents/Jefferson/01-11-02-0047.

[165] Cooper remarks that politics in Arendt's work is 'a vehicle for man's self-expression and collective endeavors within the framework of civic life … The political realm should be one in which each citizen has the opportunity to share in political power, not one which is subordinated to some other goal or overriding transcending vision – platonic or otherwise – of the way in which the community should be organized' (L Cooper, 'Hannah Arendt's Political Philosophy: An Interpretation' (1976) 38 *The Review of Politics* 145 at 148).

sweep away in turn the new foundation and so on *ad infinitum*. This was the paradox of freedom to act. Arendt expresses it thus.

> (N)othing seems to threaten the very achievement of revolution more dangerously and more acutely than the spirit which has brought them about. Should freedom in its most exalted sense as freedom to act be the price to pay for foundation?[166]

The pressing need for stability after the revolutionary upheaval of mass political action preoccupied the authors of *The Federalist Papers* in the early American Republic. For them, stability required entrenched systems of government in a constitutional settlement where the popular will is mediated through representative structures. Jefferson saw, however, that the 'sanctimonious reverence'[167] with which the Constitution was looked at was unjustified.[168] Entrenched constitutions conferred upon an earlier generation an unjustified power to settle foundational questions for later generations. This quest for stability was likely moreover to induce a withdrawal of ordinary citizens from the exercise of public freedoms. Arendt argues that Jefferson's seemingly radical proposition for finite 19-year-long constitutions was borne out of an awareness that the Founders' representative system of government had failed to create a space for the exercise of public freedoms. The Revolution's republican objective of obliterating the ruler/ruled distinction had been displaced by a government of the few, those disinterested, selfless men of public service. The 'wolves' in the federal and state branches of government would happily conduct public affairs among themselves (albeit 'checking' and 'balancing' one another if they functioned as per the Founders' intention). Jefferson, alone among the Founders, is credited by Arendt as having the perspicacity to see the democracy gap in the constitutional design. No provision had been made in the formal structures for the town hall meetings that were the 'original springs' of ordinary citizens' exercise of public freedoms.[169] Ironically, Arendt notes, it was the Constitution – their 'greatest achievement'[170] – that became the instrument by which ordinary citizens were denied an ongoing participatory role in government.

Until comparatively recently, the dominant reading of Niccolò Machiavelli's contribution to republican political theory tended to emphasise his defence of the mixed constitution and the traditional republican preoccupation with non-domination.[171] The newer reading of Machiavelli's analysis of liberty in Ancient Rome stresses in contrast his practical advocacy of (i) mechanisms of popular control over self-interested socio-economic elites and (ii) the role played by plural,

[166] H Arendt, *On Revolution* (London, Penguin, 2006) at 224.

[167] Jefferson used the phrase in a letter to Samuel Kercheval (1816) 12 July.

[168] 'We have not yet so far perfected our constitutions as to venture to make them unchangeable …' *Letter to John Cartwright* (1824) 5 June.

[169] *On Revolution* at 231.

[170] ibid.

[171] eg P Pettit, *Republicanism – A Theory of Freedom and Government* (Oxford, OUP, 1999) at 71; Q Skinner, *Liberty before Liberalism* (Cambridge, CUP, 2010) at 66.

animated and discordant political expression in republican forms of government. The remaining part of this conclusion builds upon chapter three's closing sketch of political pluralism in Machiavelli. This revised treatment owes much to the Machiavelli scholar John McCormick.[172] What follows draws explicitly upon the latter's insights into the democratic strands in *The Discourses on Livy*.

It is important to note at the outset that Machiavelli's defence of popular participation and office-holding does not rely on an account of the psychology of individuals or what Arendt would say gives a profound meaning to human lives. The exercise of public freedoms for Machiavelli serves instead to protect the state of liberty for all citizens, especially in respect of the threat to the public good posed by the economically powerful sections of society.

Machiavelli's starting point is the claim that socio-economic elites on the whole seek political power in order to advance their own private interests. Lower socio-economic classes, by contrast to their dominating social superiors, are better able to discern where the public good lies. 'The desires of free peoples' he observes, 'are rarely harmful to liberty, because they arise either from oppression or from the suspicion that they will be oppressed'.[173] However these ordinary citizens tend to be disengaged from the political life of their communities, wishing on the whole to be left alone. Crucially however, that is not to say that ordinary citizens are incapable of being made more lively defenders of liberty.[174] The lesson of the Roman Republic was that the plebeians and the tribunes could be trusted as active and regular participants and office holders in government. The tribunes, for example, were appointed by and reflective of popular opinion with a power of veto over the self-aggrandising schemes of the grandi put forward in the Senate. Institutional mechanisms were therefore of paramount importance in ensuring the participation of ordinary people in the law-making and administration of the republic. From Machiavelli we understand that the central task facing the designers of the contemporary republican polity is how to inculcate and sustain ideas of the *vivere politico* among those unschooled in the practice of regular participation in politics. At the core of McCormick's revised reading of Machiavelli is the suggestion that elites cannot be made sufficiently attentive to popular opinion and the common good through the disciplining mechanism of regular elections alone.

[172] See inter alia by the author *Machiavellian Democracy* (New York, CUP, 2012); J McCormick, 'The New Ochlophobia? Populism, Majority Rule and Prospects for Democratic-Republicanism' in (ed) Y Elazar and G Rousseliere, *Republicanism and the Future of Democracy* (Cambridge, CUP, 2019); 'Machiavellian Democracy; Controlling Elites with Ferocious Populism' (2001) 95 *Am. Pol. Sci. Rev.* 297.

[173] *Discourses* Book 1 ch 5.

[174] Machiavelli notes that the selfish behaviour of elites may on occasion stir the ordinary citizens out of their passivity. See, for example, the impassioned and aggressive responses of the citizens in the case of the agrarian laws. These were passed to strip nobles of lands they had acquired from recently conquered enemies. *Discourses* Book 1 ch 37.

Machiavelli's originality extended beyond giving ordinary citizens institutional platforms in the republic.[175] He broke new ground in valorising the discord and disharmony given expression in the public sphere by plebeian speakers.[176] The liberty of Rome was attributable in no small part to the tumults that erupted between the different strata of Roman society. The passage *Discourses* where he makes this argument is worth restating:[177]

> And suppose someone were to say: the means were extraordinary and almost barbarous – see how all the people are crying out against the senate, the senate against the people; how they are running wildly through the streets, closing the shops, how all the plebeians of Rome are leaving the city altogether – events which terrify even those who read about them; I will respond that every city must possess its own methods for allowing the people to express their ambitions …

This commitment to vibrant political pluralism is centre stage in *The Discourses*. It is a vital feature of republican government not only that a tribune or any citizen could put forward a proposal for a new law but also that anyone could speak in favour or against the proposal.[178] As Machiavelli himself puts it, this equality in freedom of expression across the social classes is vital to a republic where the powerful threaten to subvert the public good. Through emboldened acts of expression and dissent against powerful, organised interests, ordinary people are capable of disrupting elite efforts to dominate policy outcomes. If, conversely, the citizens become fearful of the powerful or deceived by them, then they will collude in their own destruction either by failing to resist the self-interested proposals of the *grandi* or, when taken in by the scheming of the latter, consent to their own demise.[179] Machiavelli's warning to later polities is clear. The ordinary citizens are more inclined than their socio-economic superiors to take policy stances that favour the common good.[180] An educated, vigorous and energetic citizenry ought therefore be accorded access to political fora in order to be fully watchful over the machinations of the great names and the wealthy that predominate in holding high office. They must be able to dissent from and challenge elite-initiated policies. Whilst his institutional prescriptions for greater contestation are obviously beyond the scope of the present inquiry, it is clear that Machiavelli accords an indispensable role to popular political expression in public fora to flush out

[175] For analysis and translation to modern-day political life, see J McCormick, *Machiavellian Democracy* (New York, CUP, 2013) ch 7.

[176] As has been noted previously, Machiavelli's emphasis on the value of conflict is at odds with much republican writing before and after *The Discourses*.

[177] J Maynor, *Republicanism in the Modern World* (Cambridge, Polity Press, 2003) at ch 5.

[178] M Viroli, *Machiavelli – Founders of Modern Political Thought* (Oxford, OUP, 1998) at 129.

[179] *Discourses* Book 1 ch 18.

[180] That is not to say, however, that Machiavelli believed that commoners' ability to identify the common good was unerring or that the nobles' tendency to deliberately misrepresent the common good was ever present. Machiavelli does, however, point up the quick learning facilities of ordinary citizens.

the self-aggrandising projects of the *grandi*. Plurality of political opinion in the Machiavellian public sphere is its very essence. At no point are the constraints of 'rationality' or 'reasonableness' introduced as pre-conditions for speech in public.

> I must say that it appears to me that those who condemn the disturbances between the nobles and the plebeians condemn those very things that were the primary cause of Roman liberty and that they give more consideration to the noises and cries arising from such disturbances than to the good effects they produced ...[181]

The zone of public participation is thus much more inclusive than the deliberative democrats would approve. Tumult and discord among the masses are appreciated for what they contribute to the control of elites and the preservation of the state of liberty. Ultimately, what is attractive about Machiavelli's way of looking at politics may be summarised in two linked claims. First (contra Pettit, Urbinati, Galston etc), his refusal to accept that laws and policies that are produced in the institutions of representative democracy automatically track the interests of the majority. Put slightly more directly, we could say that Machiavelli usefully recognises that public office holders are prone to act in ways that reflect the interests of more powerful groups. Second, he rejects the claim that public office holders are to be shielded from vigorous and robustly expressed popular criticism. He would be deeply sceptical of attempts by the *grandi* of today to police the content and tone of political debate. He would be forthright in querying the wisdom of having powerful state and corporate elites determine the boundaries of acceptable political expression. Machiavelli sees all too clearly the dangers to non-elites' interests of allowing these *grandi* to define and police terms such as 'fake news' and 'harmful expression'. His prescription for political liberty rests upon a positive valorisation of popular participation and discord in the making of the laws that comes much closer to realising the ideal of isonomy than those ersatz republican models that fall back on elite-dominated forms of counter-majoritarian rule (judicial, expert commission) or wholly representative systems of parliamentary sovereignty.

Conclusion

For those looking to resist current moves to cabin non-mainstream political expression and advance the democratic republican ideal of active participation in law-making among political equals, the respective contributions of Machiavelli, Jefferson and Arendt repay close attention. Much liberal political thinking patronisingly dismisses non-elite speech where it dares to challenge existing free market economic/political orthodoxies. It misappropriates to itself the mantle of defender of political pluralism, whilst also seeking to present the liberal-capitalist state as

[181] *Discourses on Livy*, ch IV The Disunion of the Senate and the People Renders the Republic of Rome Powerful and Free.

'permanent, eternal and necessary'.[182] Aristocratic forms of republican thought for their part share a distrust of unmediated political expression and endorse counter-majoritarian checks and controls on popular opinion that safeguard elite interests in the status quo from democratic review. The next chapter explores further the Arendtian/Jeffersonian commitment to active authorship of the laws by the citizens through an analysis of the Democratic Republican Societies that flourished in post-revolutionary America during the period 1790–1800. Here for a brief moment was witnessed the most active and robust contestation of laws and policies by non-elites.

[182] Hardt and Negri *Empire* (Massachusetts, Howard University Press, 2001) at 11.

5

Popular Participation and Political Dissent in Post-Revolutionary America: A Case Study of the Democratic Republicans

Introduction

The previous chapters explored some critical theoretical differences between liberals and deliberative/patrician republicans on the one hand and their more participatory (Machiavellian/agonist) opponents on the other. In chapter four the ochlophobic nature of current treatments of popular political expression was traced back to a venerable tradition stemming from Plato, Aristophanes and Aeschylus. In the *Oresteia*, for example, democratic bodies in 5 BCE are portrayed as poor decision-makers that operated chaotically. Yet, as Melissa Lane has shown, the Athenian record of popular rule was not always as short-termist and ignorant as the defenders of oligarchic rule would have us believe. The dominant view passed down through the generations, however, condemned democracy and popular participation. As the eighteenth century dawned, Dunn notes that democracy was a word that was still shunned.[1] When more popularly based forms of rule-making emerged at the end of the eighteenth century, these were considered to be 'republican' not democratic.[2] Today, the opponents of democratic rule typically indicate their disapproval of exercise of sovereign decision-making by ordinary citizens by employing dismissive references to 'populism'. Openly disdainful of the 'dance of the dunces',[3] a number of these critics sit in universities and think tanks where they elaborate and defend epistocratic forms of decision-making.[4] It is a curious fact, as Frank notes, that the critics of popular sovereignty often fail to acknowledge their own considerable self-interests in articulating schemes of expert-led/dominated policymaking.

[1] J Dunn, *Setting the People Free – The Story of Democracy* (London, Atlantic Books, 2006) 71.

[2] See thus James Madison in *Federalist Paper* 65 in *The Federalist Papers* (ed I Kramnick) (London, Penguin 1987). Madison's objections to what he called 'pure democracies' are discussed in Dunn, ibid at 77–83.

[3] The phrase is taken from J Brennan's *Against Democracy* (New Jersey, Princeton University Press, 2016) at viii.

[4] T Frank, *People without Power – The War on Populism and the Fight for Democracy* (London, Scribe 2020).

This chapter examines the idea of the political citizen through the lens of three contrasting accounts of popular participation in politics in the early days of the American Republic. These are respectively elaborated in Federalist accounts, rival Republican writings of leading figures such as Jefferson and Madison, and finally (and most radically) in the writings and speeches of local Democratic Republican societies that sprang up in the new republic from around the late 1780s onwards. A central strand of enquiry that is pursued below concerns the differences between the distinct set of arguments for broad political participation offered by national figures in the nascent Republican Party on the one hand, and those developed by artisans and labouring men in their local communities on the other. My reason for devoting a separate chapter to this pre-digital era of political communication in a different continent is to draw out some common themes and anxieties that have arced across the intervening years into the digital era when online political speech from non-elites is regularly treated as ill-informed and unworthy of being taken seriously. The analysis presented here emphasises that the Democratic Republican societies were counter-publics in which those outside the elite governing classes organised themselves politically. Dotts has shown how the members of these societies were possessed of a 'new' sense of self. They rejected the idea that they were defined as 'subjects' of elite rule-making, considering themselves instead to be 'citizens who could alter their government to reflect their understanding of what a republic should be'.[5] The interest that members of the societies were devoting to political matters was not however welcome. Members of the governing elite considered the new civic mindedness to be in breach of established conventions of deference and not respectful of the fixed status and roles allocated to each upon birth.[6] Then, as now, coercive legal means of preventing political speech were deployed against these counter-publics. Then, as now, practical means of suppressing the distribution/dissemination of critical expression were engaged. From the present era's reliance upon West Coast tech giants' blocking and deleting of posts and tweets on social media platforms, we can look back to the Federalists' documented efforts to close down the distribution of 'scurrilous' Republican newspapers and to intercept the mail that passed from Republican to Republican. Back in the early days of the US Republic, the main Federalist response to the attacks in print and speech from the Republican presses and the members of Democratic Republican societies was the enactment of new criminal laws in the Sedition Act 1798. Prosecutions, convictions, fines and imprisonment followed. Later, when the 1798 Act had expired, Republican state prosecutors would, in their turn, use criminal libel laws to silence Federalist opponents in New York and Pennsylvania.

The challenge in political theory terms that the Democratic-Republican societies or 'counter-publics' posed to the more patrician accounts of representative government found in the works of Thomas Jefferson or James Madison occupies

[5] B Dotts, 'The Democratic-Republican Societies: An Educational Dream Deferred' (2010) 88 *Educational Horizons* 179, 183.

[6] Dotts ibid at 185.

a later section of the chapter. To begin with, however, a brief sketch of the respective Federalist and Republican approaches to the relationship between the citizen and the constituted authorities is set down. This is followed by a detailed look at the concern in republican theory to preserve the 'revolutionary spirit' in post-colonial America. Hannah Arendt's notion of 'human action' as the capacity of individuals (in concert with or opposition to others) to act spontaneously and thus contribute in unexpected ways to the political life of their communities is central to this section of analysis.[7] Arendt aligns herself with Jefferson's criticisms of representative government in the new republic and the state of citizen lethargy it induces. Jefferson's 'ward-republic' remedy to preserve the revolutionary spirit is subsequently considered. Though politically associated with the republicanism of Jefferson, the counter-publics of the Democratic Republican Clubs of the 1790s merit separate attention in this chapter, representing as they did a more radically pluralist envisioning of participatory politics. The origins of the Democratic Republican Clubs are recounted as are ensuing Federalist anxieties about popular expression. Attention is also paid to the Federalists' legal/constitutional strategies of containment that included the passing into law of the Sedition Act in 1798 but extended further to the articulation of novel ideas about judicial review. Anticipating a time in the near future when their Republican opponents would hold legislative majorities, Federalist thinking about the place of the judiciary in the new republic evolved to the point where (federalist appointed) judges might be needed to save the people from themselves. The chapter concludes with analysis of the underlying political theory in the published works of leading Democratic-Republican thinkers. We will see that these non-elite speakers consciously strove to preserve freedom to dissent and the collision of opinion in the public domain. Ordinary citizens such as Tunis Wortmann, John Thomson and Thomas Cooper wrote republican tracts that drew directly on ideas of political equality and the citizen as the source of all governmental authority. They disputed the prevailing account of representative politics which relegated the citizenry to the role of passive onlooker only, episodically called upon to renew the mandate of national politicians. It is argued here that they understood much better than Madison and Jefferson the ongoing, tragic, conflictual dimension of politics and were intent on challenging liberalism's subordination of democratic agency. They were, in short, prototype agonist democrats. This is suggested by commonalities around the emphasis upon popular sovereignty, and the commitment to open-ended, non-conclusory political discourse. As Dotts remarks, the members of the societies had a new consciousness that they were 'no longer subjects but citizens who could alter their government to reflect their understanding of what a republic should be'.[8]

[7] *The Human Condition* (Chicago, University of Chicago Press, 2018) 2nd edition.

[8] B Dotts, 'The Democratic-Republican Societies: An Educational Dream Deferred' (2010) 88 *Educational Horizons* 179, at 183.

Federalist and Patrician Republican Accounts of the Political Citizen

Within Federalist accounts an intermittent and extremely limited form of citizen participation in political life is defended. These accounts are premised overtly upon an elitist disdain for the competences and political wisdom of ordinary persons. Having gone through a period of seismic political upheaval, Federalists advocated a period of stability and calm in which the elected authorities (coincidentally in the hands of Federalists at least initially) would be left to get on with the business of governing. They expected that the lower, less educated sections of society would not presume to step beyond the role allotted to them by societal convention. Having cast their ballots once every few years, ordinary voters were expected to remove themselves entirely from the political arena.[9] For Federalists, their Anti-Federalist opponents were beneath contempt. Critics who dared to find fault with the 'great men' of the new Republic such as General Washington, Benjamin Franklin and Alexander Hamilton were mere scribblers who lacked the credentials to be taken seriously. Federalist-owned presses condemned Anti-Federalists as British Tory agents who were undermining the project to create a strong central government and who aimed at the restoration of the Hanoverian dynasty. The Federalists' repeated invocation of the 'heroic' and 'statesmanlike' figures such as General Washington and Benjamin Franklin undoubtedly made it harder for critics to voice doubts about government policy.[10] The reverence that was owed to the wisdom of the Founders ought to have ensured the ready ratification of the Federal Constitution by the states' conventions. The respectful polity the Federalists wished to sustain did not need the contributions of labouring men. Federalists were highly nervous about the activities of the Democratic-Republicans who interposed themselves between the political elite and citizens.[11] That the latter sought to organise and influence public opinion outside of election periods was perceived to threaten the very stability of government. Kramer cites one overwrought federalist Oliver Wolcott who asserted that the gatherings of anti-federalists intended to exert 'general influence and control' over the elected authorities were 'unlawful'.[12] Moreover, the political gains of Jefferson's supporters in the 1790s when state and federal legislatures fell into the hands of anti-Federalists (contrary to the expectation in *Federalist No 10* that local factions would be

[9] After the Revolution, Steinfeld notes that many states enfranchised some men who were leaseholders and wage earners (and thus deemed 'independent') whilst disenfranchising those deemed 'paupers' (and thus 'dependent' on others), R Steinfeld, 'Property and Suffrage in the Early American Republic' 41 *Stan. L. Rev.* 335, 337–38.

[10] R Martin, *Government by Dissent: Protest, Resistance and Radical Democratic Thought in the Early American Republic* (New York, NYU Press 2013) at 64.

[11] L Kramer, *The People Themselves: Popular Constitutionalism and Judicial Review* (New York, OUP, 2004) at 128–30.

[12] ibid at 130.

controlled by the geographical size and plurality of the polity) focused Federalist minds on how best to suppress the popular outpouring of republicanism. A two-pronged assault on the Democratic-Republican societies followed in which the federal legislature and the courts were deployed to quell popular, anti-Federalist feeling. This attack is considered in more detail below.

The anti-Federalist tradition that developed in opposition to Federalist thinking and was represented among the Founders in the writings of Jefferson and Madison was committed to a more activist account of citizen participation in political decision-making. It was, however, steeped in the rationalism of Enlightenment thinking that pre-conditioned entry into the public sphere upon a commitment to respectful public reason in the service of the common good. Popular passions needed to be excluded from these civilised and disinterested exchanges if anything valuable in terms of societal progress was to emerge from them. Dissent was possible, but only within certain constraints. That Jefferson and Madison and their fellow Enlightenment thinkers would champion a form of politics and constitutionalism whose contours were entirely derivable from reason and logical enquiry is thus hardly surprising.[13] As Robertson confirms in *The Enlightenment – The Pursuit of Happiness 1680–1790*, 'the Enlighteners who wanted major social changes expected those changes to be made from above, not below'.[14] Many ordinary persons would lack the discursive skills and background education to be able to satisfy the pre-conditions set for entry into realm of daily politics. They would be considered unable and/or unwilling to abstract themselves from their own parochial sets of interests and concerns to argue for 'national' or 'common' interest solutions. Thus, by their content alone, ordinary persons' contributions to public discourse would be seen as not meriting equal consideration alongside those utterances that revealed the speaker to be capable of more elevated and abstracted forms of rational thinking. The sometimes crude and poorly phrased forms of expression employed by labourers and artisans would be taken as stylistic confirmation of the inherent unsuitedness of ordinary citizens to the demands of the governing public sphere. The patrician strain in Republican thinking in the works of Madison and Jefferson is returned to and developed in a later section of this chapter. In terms of the overall themes of this monograph, the commitments and values of the patrician Republicans can be seen to prefigure norms associated with modern-day deliberative democrats. Through a responsible and enlightened societal dialogue guided by men of wisdom exercising public

[13] Jefferson's broad-ranging interests included astronomy, paleontology, botany, agriculture and chemistry. His biographer Jon Meacham describes quarters occupied by Jefferson during the latter's time as Secretary of State in Washington's administration where on the walls were three portraits of the Enlightenment figures Sir Francis Bacon, John Locke and Sir Isaac Newton. When asked by Hamilton who the men were, Jefferson later recalled that 'I told him they were my trinity of the greatest men the world had ever produced'. Hamilton, by way of response, asserted 'The greatest man that ever lived was Julius Caesar', cited in J Meacham, *Thomas Jefferson – The Art of Power* (New York, Random House, 2013) at 260.

[14] New York, Allen Lane, 2020, Preface xx.

reason, these Republicans hoped that factious dispute would be overcome and common good solutions emerge and be apparent as such to all.

The anti-Federalists struggled to disseminate their criticisms of Federalists' plans. Few papers supported the Anti-Federalist cause. Those that did were subject to boycott actions organised by Federalists reducing the communicative reach of such pieces. Martin notes how from October to December 1787 across the whole of Connecticut just six anti-Federalist opinion pieces were published. Imported pamphlets from New York were seized and burnt.[15] Mail from Anti-Federalists did not always reach its intended recipient. The anti-federalist Samuel Bryan who wrote pseudonymously as Centinel[16] complained that interference by Federalist supporters had effectively muzzled the anti-federalist presses.[17]

Arendt, Human Action and the Mediated (Oligarchic) Political Life – The Failure of the US Founders to Preserve the Revolutionary Spirit

In earlier chapters, I made the argument that political pluralism and individual freedom of the agonistic kind defended in the present account is threatened by liberalism. The dominance of centrist political parties and their technocratic managerial programmes in national and supranational (eg EU) governance structures stifles political participation and thus political choice. Arendt presciently noted in *The Human Condition* (1958) that the liberal technocratic state was increasingly one in which genuine politics was being eradicated.[18] The neo-liberal capitalist state today is presented as 'permanent, eternal and necessary'.[19] Governance and decision-making can be left to a narrow set of centrist political elites and a technocratic class of administrators to manage with just a passing, infrequent nod to the need for renewed support at the ballot box.

To be meaningful in Arendtian terms, citizenship requires individual active participation in the daily political life of one's community. Effective political agency is gained from these exercises of public freedom. In her view representative

[15] R Martin, *Government by Dissent, Protest, Resistance & Radical Democratic Thought in the Early American Republic* at 65.

[16] Anonymity or pseudonymity is a feature of both Federalist and Anti-Federalist contributions at this time, although it is clear that Federalists also tended to write under their real names in an effort to command respect on the basis of *who* they were, irrespective of *what* they had to say. Anti-Federalists wrote under such names as 'A Friend in Harmony', 'Philadelphiensis', and 'A Maryland Farmer'. Among the Anti-Federalists, the practice was seen to encourage robust expression by non-elites about the conduct and proposals of officer holders and those seeking office. See further R Martin, *Government by Dissent, Protest, Resistance & Radical Democratic Thought in the Early American Republic* 70–77.

[17] Centinel XII, *Independent Gazetteer* (1788) 23 January and cited in Martin ibid at 65.

[18] Chicago, University of Chicago Press, 2018, 2nd edition.

[19] The quote is from M Hardt and A Negri, *Empire* (Massachusetts, Harvard University Press, 2000) at 11.

structures are a poor substitute for popular, direct forms of political agency. The political parties that mediate the opinions of the people cannot be regarded as 'popular organs ... on the contrary, they are the very efficient instruments through which the power of the people is curtailed and controlled'.[20] For Arendt, representative government was a form of oligarchy, not in the ancient sense of elites ruling in the interest of elites, but rather in the sense of a few ruling 'at least supposedly, in the interest of the many'.[21] Whilst representative governments sought to advance the public good and private happiness, the effective determination of what these amounted to rested in the hands of a few people.[22]

The foundation of a new constitutional settlement in 1787 (and 1791) established a prototype representative liberal democracy. It also gave rise in the following decade to an extended republican moment as ordinary citizens burst into public spaces to participate in sometimes rambunctious political discourse. The advent of the Democratic Republican societies across the states of the new republic marked a moment when the citizens exercised political agency in non-elite counter publics to become in Jefferson's phrase 'participators in government'. In *On Revolution* Arendt offers a penetrating critique of the US Founders' constitutional design. She remarks upon the almost exclusive focus at Philadelphia on the mechanism of representation in the new Constitution. There was, however, in Arendt's view a failure to envision how the Constitution might be designed to preserve the 'revolutionary spirit'.[23] Instead, a liberal constitutional emphasis upon limited government, the separation of powers and the protection of civil rights came to the fore. Structures to ensure ongoing political participation by the citizens were, by contrast, conspicuous by their absence. It was as if the founders had lost sight of the potentiality of human action and desire for public freedom which had propelled the original break from the mother country. However, as Arendt notes, this was in fact no accidental oversight. Now that the republic had been established, the idea that the people might retain a formally recognised power to use this public freedom threatened 'the very achievement of revolution'[24] and must for the sake of constitutional stability be shelved. '(F)reedom in its most exalted sense as freedom to act ... (became) the price to be paid for foundation ...'[25] The founders knew too well that the revolutionary spirit which was responsible for the successful rupture could also threaten the new constitutional settlement that they were trying to found. At the beginning, it was essential for the success of the revolutionary project of overthrowing British colonial rule that the people act as

[20] H Arendt, *On Revolution* (1977, Penguin, London) 261.

[21] ibid.

[22] Arendt does not at this point elaborate upon who the 'few' are, but she cannot be understood as referring to persons other than socio-economic elite classes which have tended to occupy public office in western liberal democracies.

[23] ibid ch 6.

[24] ibid at 224.

[25] ibid.

free innovators, unconstrained by the traditions of the mother country and able to create a new polity *ex nihilo*. But once both the rupture and act of innovation had occurred, the newly founded polity had no need for ongoing revolutionary acts. Quite the reverse in fact. Popular sovereignty needed to take a back seat whilst the constituted authorities began their work of stabilising the revolutionary state.

Jefferson to his credit saw all too clearly the constitutional lacuna. He, more than anyone else at the time, identified and lamented what he termed the 'vanity and presumption' of the Founding Generation, namely to subject succeeding generations to the former's conceptions of public freedom and public happiness.[26] Jefferson's denouncement captured the subordination of the citizens' democratic agency to the Founders' vision of progressive societal development via entrenched rights and settled institutions and norms. He bemoaned the fact that the founders had failed to carve out a public space where public freedoms to express, debate and discuss might be preserved. The Founders' grand design amounted to an 'abstract political system of democracy (that) lacked concrete organs'.[27] The absence of concrete organs guaranteeing a regular and broad freedom to participate in government complemented the desire for stability. The liberal constitutionalism of the Founders was now, as Wolin memorably puts it, nothing more than 'an ideology seeking repose'.[28] In questioning the Founders' stress upon the importance of constituted forms of authority *to* democracy, Jefferson might be considered to be deprecating the costs to democratic agency entailed *in* constitutionalism.[29] And it is accordingly not too far a stretch to see Jefferson as having endorsed a riskier, less stable form of constituted authority that was prone to *aconstitutional* rupture as and when the constituent power re-emerged.

Some might argue that the positions of Arendt and Jefferson fail to give due credit to the revolutionary potential of the First Amendment of the Bill of Rights (in particular) to facilitate new acts of political innovation and rupture. This is perhaps unfair. A fuller appreciation of the First Amendment's capacity for protecting radical dissenting expression would not have been not possible until some time after the early Holmes and Brandeis dissents in the early twentieth century prosecutions against anti-war, anti-capitalist and syndicalist speakers. Principally, it was the Warren Court, notably in cases such as *New York Times v Sullivan*[30] and

[26] Leading to his oft-quoted remark on hearing of Shay's rebellion in Massachusetts that 'God forbid we should ever be twenty years without such a rebellion … The tree of liberty must be refreshed, from time to time, with the blood of patriots and tyrants.' Letter to William Stephens Smith (1787, Paris) available electronically at www.loc.gov/exhibits/jefferson/105.html.

[27] L Mumford, *The City in History* (Harcourt, Brace & World, 1961) at 332.

[28] S Wolin, 'The Liberal/Democratic Divide: On Rawls' Political Liberalism' (1996) 24 *Pol. Theory* 97, 108.

[29] And see, in like terms, Honig's notion that 'dead rights require live futures – promisingly and dangerously unscripted futures if they are to come back to life', in 'B Honig, 'Dead Rights, Live Futures: A Reply to Habermas's Constitutional Democracy' (2001) 29 *Pol. Theory* 792, 800. For Honig, a constitution that wishes to prevent the risk of aconstitutionalism becomes 'a narcissistic, necrophilic document', ibid.

[30] 376 US 254 (1964).

Brandenburg v Ohio,[31] that opened up the constitutional opportunities for accommodating dissensus. More fundamentally, however, an Arendtian might retort that the First Amendment *itself* constrains how the people are to agitate for change. In opting to bring First Amendment challenges to state/federal laws, the challengers implicitly recognise (rather than subvert) the overall project of constitutionalism as laid down by the Founders and are helping as actors to play their part in the working out of that project. The channelling of the claim for political participation via the juridical route itself ultimately accepts judicial determinations of both the scope and extent of participation interests.

For Arendt, it was the failure to incorporate into the Constitution those public spaces where the revolutionary spirit had first taken root and found expression that would sound its death knell.[32] It was not, however, that representation by political elites per se was un-republican. What was decidedly un-republican was the accompanying failure to provide ongoing opportunities for successive generations among the represented classes to exercise and hone their political capacities.[33] Arendt and Jefferson (more than any other founder although as we shall see Madison endorses a more qualified form of public participation and opinion) articulate a conception of the human need for political activity in community affairs. That is to say, without an outlet for political action, humans are, in some important sense, incompletely realised. Of course, this Aristotelian view of human perfectability stands in contrast to neo-Roman accounts of the value of the demos' participation in the political life of communities where the preservation of a state of liberty is emphasised, or more recent agonist accounts that rest upon a foundational commitment to pluralism. In chapter two, I argued that the perfectibility component of accounts of political participation requires that the content and style of citizens' expression be somehow conducive to their civic improvement. In deliberative accounts of democracy, for example, this requires commitments variously to self-reflection, respectful empathetic exchanges between political equals and reaching consensual, common good outcomes. By these normative standards, the citizen becomes a better interlocutor.[34] It is telling however that deliberative democrats are quite comfortable with the exclusion from public discourse of those who cannot or will not conform to their preferred styles of discourse. Those that do not envisage themselves empathetically engaged in a dialectical process through which universally acceptable outcomes are to be progressively revealed are simply screened out of the conversations that will build the deliberate democrats' better world.

[31] 395 US 444 (1969).

[32] H Arendt, *On Revolution* (London, Penguin, 1977) at 231.

[33] For endorsement in the writings of the Democratic Republican Societies, see further E Link *Democratic-Republican Societies, 1790–1800 – Number 9 of the Columbia Studies in American Culture* (New York, Octagon Books) at 105.

[34] Whilst the liberal critics of 'populism' see all too clearly the 'mote' of narrowed political pluralism under charismatic, populist regimes, deliberative democrats often fail to perceive the highly constrained form of political exchanges that constitute their own 'beam'.

Jefferson's Ward-republic: Preserving the Revolutionary Spirit

> Where every man is a sharer in the direction of his ward-republic or of some of the higher ones, and feels that he is a participator in the government of affairs, not merely an election one day in the year, but every day; when there shall not be a man in the State who will not be a member of one of its councils, great or small, he will let his heart be torn out of his body sooner than his power be wrested from him by a Caesar or Bonaparte.
>
> Thomas Jefferson *Letter to Joseph C Cabell* February 2, 1816[35]

The question for Jefferson then is how might a self-governing society avoid the state of lethargy and inattention to public affairs that systems of representative government tend to induce. The positive experiences of 'freedom' as understood by Arendt require the people as political agents to be involved in the speech acts of expression, discussion and debate in public spaces.[36] Jefferson's search for 'concrete organs' to enable direct citizen participation in governmental affairs led him to endorse the political unit he called the 'ward-republic'. He had in mind a version of the townships found in New England. These were the 'wisest invention ever devised by the wit of man for the perfect exercise of self-government, and for its preservation'.[37] These would be of such a small scale that every citizen could attend and speak in person. Their jurisdiction would extend over local matters such as education, policing and other numerous matters that were among the 'interesting concerns of the neighborhood'. Jefferson's plan was for a four-tiered pyramidal structure.[38] The national government is at the apex setting foreign policy and maintaining the defence of the nation. At the level below, Jefferson somewhat elliptically describes state governments as making and administering law and policy on matters that concern the states, including civil rights.[39] In the same vein, the counties address themselves to 'local concerns' of the counties. Below the counties sit the ward-republics at the local level where every office holder is elected by the citizens. As Matthews observes, each level of the pyramid would be 'dependent on the next subordinate level for its authority and guidance from instructed representatives who reflect the balance of arguments in local communities' as expressed in public meetings.[40] Jefferson understood that unless the state provided some system of schooling for its young, the new Republic would founder. He had long

[35] P Foner (ed), *Thomas Jefferson – Selections from his Writings* (New York, International Publishers Co, 1943) at 58.

[36] H Arendt, *On Revolution* (London, Penguin, 1977) at 231.

[37] *Letter to Samuel Kercheval* (12 July 1816).

[38] ibid.

[39] Although given that Jefferson largely confined the national government to foreign policy and defence, it may be supposed that his state-level governments would focus on internal policies.

[40] R Matthews, 'The Radical Political Philosophy of Thomas Jefferson: An Essay in Retrieval' (2004) *Midwest Studies in Philosophy* XXVIII, at 18.

campaigned for publicly funded schooling in his native state of Virginia but his proposals before the Virginia General assembly in the 1770s were unsuccessful.[41] His attempt to set up publicly funded libraries met a similar fate.[42]

In Arendt's view had Jefferson's local government ward scheme been adopted it would have 'exceeded by far the feeble germs of a new form of government .... (detectable) in sections of Paris Commune and the popular societies during the French Revolution'.[43] It amounted to the 'salvation' of the revolutionary spirit. Through it the citizens would be freed to carry on doing what they had done during the revolutionary war 'namely to act on their own and thus to participate in public business as it was being transacted from day to day'.[44] Jefferson's politically active citizen harks back to the *zoon politikon* in the Greek/Athenian tradition. The public space provided by the ward-republics would not only check abuses/misuses of public power by exposing malpractice and incompetences, it would develop the political craft of the citizenry so that each person might fulfil their republican duty.[45]

The Counter-Publics of Democratic Republican Clubs

> The societies interpreted 'public concerns' broadly and pursued humanitarian as well as political causes. Much of their activity involved creating a new public space for discussion of controversial political issues, and the dissemination of circulars and memorials, as well as remonstrances to the president and Congress ... They aimed to build from the bottom up ... new networks of political intelligence that would challenge the prevailing Federalist point of view. This required full freedom of assembly and the press.
>
> S Wilentz *The Rise of American Democracy* (New York, WW Norton & Co., 2006) 57.

The Origins of the Democratic Republican Clubs

The federal government's tacit support for Great Britain in the latter's war against revolutionary France divided both the Founders and public opinion. On one side President Washington and Treasury Secretary Alexander Hamilton took the cautious (mercantilist) position of avoiding aggravation with the nation's major trading partner. Additionally, the mounting total of executions in the French

[41] J Conant, *Thomas Jefferson and the Development of American Public Education* (California, University of California, Berkeley and Los Angeles, 1962).

[42] D Staloff, *Hamilton, Adams and Jefferson: The Politics of Enlightenment and the American Founding* (New York, Hill and Wang, 2007) at 273.

[43] *On Revolution* at 241.

[44] ibid at 243.

[45] See R Matthews, 'The Radical Political Philosophy of Thomas Jefferson: An Essay in Retrieval' (2004) *Midwest Studies in Philosophy* XXVIII, at 19.

Republic was viewed with increasing alarm. On the other side of the emerging divide among the Founders, Jefferson and Madison wanted official policy to offer support to the French. Jeffersonians viewed the French Republic sympathetically, engaged as it was in a similar republican project to their own and in need of assistance against the same oppressor that the American colonists had overcome.

Encouraged by Jefferson and his supporters, ordinary citizens – joiners, farmers, shoemakers openly challenged the patrician rule of the disinterested gentlemen of landed wealth.[46] Choosing not to defer politely to the 'superior' wisdom of their social betters, elements of the represented class began to contest the policies and rule-making of their representatives. This was a vibrant period in the new republic when men who had daily to sell their labour entered the public sphere as citizens. Eugene Link's account of the emergence of the Democratic-Republican Societies identifies German settlers in Philadelphia as having constituted the first such association.[47] The value attached to constant popular engagement in political debate as a means of maintaining a state of liberty is immediately apparent from the society's first circular.[48] Other societies followed in Norfolk (Virginia), Lexington (Kentucky), Charleston (South Carolina), Ulster County (New York) New Haven (Connecticut) and Boston (Massachusetts).[49]

The new class of political actors went into print to publish their criticisms of their political leaders. They made speeches and organised marches to condemn and even disrupt the actions and decisions of the 'virtuous' and leisured gentlemen holding public office. Debating clubs, newspapers and pamphlets sprung up in which arguments about national taxation and foreign alliances were played out. There emerged an 'unruly, rambunctious democracy-in-the-making … Suddenly everyone apparently felt entitled to express an opinion.'[50]

The noisy clamour of the streets, meeting places and the dissemination of printed criticisms of their political leaders put into sharp relief the fundamental disagreement between liberals and patrician republicans on the one hand, and their participatory republican counterparts on the other. Federalists' expectations of quiescent governance in the post-Revolutionary period had been shattered. Their preference for a limited degree of popular engagement in politics (periodically at election time) were plainly out of kilter with the demands of farmers

[46] Not all members of Congress were plantation/estate owners like Jefferson, Alexander Hamilton and George Mason. Some were lawyers with busy city practices, who soon found the time and financial costs of holding public office to be unviable, prompting a number of them to resign from Congress, see G Wood, *The Radicalism of the American Revolution* (New York, Vintage Books, 1993) at 287–305

[47] E Link, *Democratic-Republican Societies, 1790–1800 – Number 9 of the Columbia Studies in American Culture* (New York, Octagon Books, 1965) ch 1.

[48] Link ibid quotes from this first circular 'In a republican government it is the duty incumbent on every citizen to afford his assistance, either by taking part in its immediate administration, or by his advice and watchfulness, that its principles may remain uncorrupt; for the spirit of liberty, like every virtue of the mind is to be kept alive only by constant action …' at 6.

[49] A fuller list for the years 1793–98 is provided by Link, ibid at 13–15.

[50] Kramer, *The People Themselves: Popular Constitutionalism and Judicial Review* at 133.

and labourers for greater inputs into decision-making at state and federal levels. In Gordon Wood's *The Radicalism of the American Revolution* accounts of the speeches and writings of artisans and labourers are recorded.[51] In 1797, one artisan, George Warner a sailmaker from New York, spoke from the pulpit of the New Dutch Church in New York to encourage the 'industrious classes of society' who had hitherto believed themselves to be of 'TOO LITTLE CONSEQUENCE to the body politic' to become active participants in holding public office holders to account. Warner expected that the ordinary citizen would contribute on the basis of the community's interest not private gain.[52]

Arguments for popular participation in the daily politics of the new republic such as Warner's reside within a broader class of speeches, orations and political activity that sit within the burgeoning Anti-Federalist tradition of the 1790s. Unwilling to trust to the expertise and 'better' judgment of a political elite who had attained elected office, anti-federalists believed that the cause of liberty and the public good was best served by a close and continuing association between rulers and ruled. 'Brutus' in *Essay XV* argued for this position noting that legislators would have to explain their preferred reading of the Constitution 'at their peril' since the people would be able to remove those lawmakers whose reading they disapproved.[53] Ketcham sees anti-federalist arguments here as going beyond a system of close control by citizens over constituted authority and extending into a form of dialogue that blurred the distinction between elected official and constituent.[54] Public liberty for these anti-federalists was synonymous with regular political participation in the life of the community. Democratic republican societies challenged passive notions of the represented citizen.[55] Elected congressmen were expected to take heed of and act upon the instructions of popular meetings when back in the federal legislature. Notions of political accountability of elected representatives developed at this time stressed the ongoing, regular nature of democratic oversight. The Kentucky societies requested that their Congressional representatives appear at local meetings when next back in the state.[56] The demand

[51] G Wood, *The Radicalism of the American Revolution* (New York, Vintage Books, 1993) at 276.

[52] The text of Warner's oration is to be found at *Means for the Preservation of Public Liberty: An Oration Delivered in the New Dutch Church on Fourth of July 1797* (Boston, Gale Sabin Americana, 2012); see also S Wilentz, *Chants Democratic: New York City and the Rise of the American Working Class* (New York, OUP, 2004) at 92.

[53] Brutus XV (March 20, 1788) disputing Publius' argument in *Federalist No 78*, where an argument is made to insulate federal judges from popular influence.

[54] R Ketcham, *The Anti-Federalist Papers and the Constitutional Convention Debates* (New York, Signet, 1986) at xxix.

[55] See thus Centinel *To the People of Pennsylvania* 9 April, 1788 who argued for the widespread dissemination of information and opinion if popular participation in politics was to be meaningful. Centinel believed that the social dimension of popular engagement was vital to the struggle against the great names and other elites. Energised and enlightened political clubs ('democratic societies') were needed to form a bulwark against 'aspiring despots and avaricious office-hunters … (with) their dark intrigues, and deep concerted schemes of power and aggrandisement'. Centinel *To the People of Pennsylvania* 9 April 1788 www.consource.org/document/centinel-xviii-1788-4-9/.

[56] E Link *Democratic-Republican Societies, 1790–1800 – Number 9 of the Columbia Studies in American Culture* at 162–63.

for access to official information was a recurring feature of the societies' campaigns. Federalists in response doubted the intellectual capacity of working men to make sense of the documents and reports that were sought. Contemporaneous local newspaper reports of a Newark, New Jersey club meeting noted that its members had derided the 'slavish doctrine' that the complexity of affairs of state were too complex for the common man to understand.[57] Kramer remarks that the new societies and an increasingly partisan press

> organized and voiced opinions as never before. They mounted petition campaigns and called conventions; they paraded in the streets, planted liberty poles, and burned effigies, they held feasts and delivered public toasts. The popular voice changed and grew more insistent as these new institutions and practices became the means by which that voice was defined and refined.[58]

Their Federalist targets would respond by enacting laws and erecting other barriers to hold forms of popular opinion at bay.

'Jacobins and Terrorists' – Federalist Anxieties about Popular Political Expression

> But in Kentucky you have a Democratic Society – that horrible sink of treason, that hateful synagogue of anarchy, that odious conclave of tumult, that frightful cathedral of discord, that poisonous garden of conspiracy, that hellish school of rebellion and opposition to all regular and well-balanced authority.
>
> *Xantippe* (1794) *Virginia Chronicle* July 17

The Federalists stood for social order and deference to one's societal betters. Political leadership was a burden that few were fitted to. Once the necessary authorisation from the people had been given on Election Day, the latter were supposed to vacate the political arena to the men of discernment and talent who formed the constituted authority, men who could be trusted to pursue that national good in a disinterested manner without a thought for their own material well-being. Sovereign power was spoken of as a possession, briefly held by the electorate on polling day and then returned to the constituted authority. Benjamin Rush spoke of the delegation of sovereignty to those 'freely appointed to administer (the) constitution, and by them alone can be rightly exercised, save at the stated period of election when the sovereignty is again at the disposal of the whole people'.[59]

As the 1790s unfolded, the political elite in Philadelphia[60] became increasingly concerned at the agitations of the working class. Governor Morris, the author of the Preamble to the US Constitution and from wealthy landowning stock in

[57] Wood's *Newark Gazette* (1794) March 12 and cited in Link ibid.
[58] L Kramer, *The People Themselves – Popular Constitutionalism and Judicial Review* at 109.
[59] B Rush, 'Order' *Columbian Centinel* 1 (3 September 1794) and cited in Kramer ibid at 129.
[60] Congress only moved to Washington, DC in 1800.

New York denounced the popular mood thus '(D)emocracy! savage and wild. Thou who wouldst bring down the virtuous and wise to thy level of folly and guilt.'

The liberal/patrician republican defence of representative forms of democratic government where the citizens were to be largely excluded after election day from exercising political judgment is nicely instanced in the writings of Federalists such as Morris at this time. Federalism was, as Kramer notes, a reaction to the liberating, equalising and volatile style of politics that had earlier found its voice in revolutionary war against the British.[61]

Alexander Hamilton who had just stood down from his role as Secretary of the US Treasury experienced a particularly hostile reception in 1795 when speaking publicly to a 5,000 strong audience in favour of the unpopular Jay Treaty with Great Britain. The *New York Argus* recorded vocal opposition from members of the audience which forced him to abandon his speech. Another speaker read out Hamilton's resolutions to the meeting. When the speaker read Hamilton's proposal that the people were not required to give an opinion on the treaty, several witnesses reported that a 'volley of stones' were launched from the crowd, one of which grazed Hamilton's head.[62] Hamilton later complained that the organisers of the meetings in Boston and New York had produced handbills 'full of invectives against the treaty as absurd as they were inflammatory, and manifestly designed to induce the citizens to surrender their reason to the empire of their passions.'[63]

The widespread opposition to the Jay Treaty with Great Britain was linked by Federalist supporting newspapers to the Jacobins in revolutionary France. The Boston-based *Columbian Centinel* compared protestors to 'Jacobins' and 'terrorists' who were intent on fomenting mobs and factions that would silence 'good citizens' of a contrary viewpoint.[64]

Hamilton, the arch-Federalist, had a barely concealed contempt for the political views of ordinary citizens.[65] He had previously asserted that once a law had been passed by Congress, all opposition to it should desist. Obedience to enacted law was the 'first principle' of the Constitution.[66] Hamilton wrote to Washington in 1794 that he had 'long since … learnt to hold popular opinion of no value.'[67]

[61] L Kramer, *The People Themselves: Popular Constitutionalism and Judicial Review* at ch 5.

[62] The Defence No 1 (22 July 1795) https://founders.archives.gov/documents/Hamilton/01-18-02-0305-0002#ARHN-01-18-02-0305-0002-fn-0031 at para 33. See further R Martin *Government by Dissent, Protest, Resistance & Radical Democratic Thought in the Early American Republic* at 147.

[63] The Defence No I (22 July 1795) available electronically at https://founders.archives.gov/documents/Hamilton/01-18-02-0305-0002#ARHN-01-18-02-0305-0002-fn-0031.

[64] *Columbian Centinel* 31 October 1795 and cited in R Martin *Government by Dissent: Protest, Resistance and Radical Democratic Thought in the Early American Republic* at 148–49.

[65] Hamilton's admiration for Julius Caesar as the 'greatest man that ever lived' tends if anything to corroborate this view of the first Secretary of the US Treasury. Quoted in J Meacham, *Thomas Jefferson – The Art of Power* at 260.

[66] Letter from Alexander Hamilton to George Washington, 2 September 1794 *The Papers of Alexander Hamilton*, Vol 17, *August 1794–December 1794* (ed Harold C Syrett. New York: Columbia University Press, 1972) at 180–90.

[67] Letter from Alexander Hamilton to George Washington 11 November, 1794 *The Papers of Alexander Hamilton*, ibid at 366–67. Thus put, Hamilton fits squarely within Madison's description of

His disdain for public opinion and its audacious questioning of government policy in the public sphere was typical of Federalist thinking at the time. Abigail Adams, the wife of President Adams, excoriated the republican newspapers as 'the offspring of faction and nursed by sedition'.[68] Her husband had expressed similar sentiments earlier in the same year 1798 but went somewhat further in May of that year. The Republican press had gone to 'all lengths of profligacy, falsehood and malignity in defaming our government … (the) misrepresentations which have misled so many citizens must be discountenanced by authority'.[69]

The precise form in which 'authority' would step in to rescue the government from falsehood and malignity would become apparent in that same year.

The target of Federalist opprobrium from Hamilton and the Adams included papers like the *Aurora* which was printed in Philadelphia and edited by Benjamin Franklin Bache. His personal attacks on President George Washington ('apish', 'monarchical' and 'the source of all the misfortunes of our country') and John Adams ('blind, bald, crippled, toothless, querulous')[70] certainly reflected a type of personal abuse that went well beyond strong political disagreement. Invective of this kind formed the essential context for the Federalist take-down of the Republican presses in the Sedition Act 1798.[71]

'The Reign of Witches' – Legislative and Judicial Restraints on Popular Expression

As support for Jefferson's Democratic Republicans grew, so commensurately did Federalist fears of a descent into factionalism and constitutional disorder. The hope that a geographically expansive and diverse republic would blunt the forces of narrow parochialism and lead to non-partisan, political leadership was coming under increasing strain. Senate and House seats were captured by Jeffersonian supporters in the early 1790s. By 1792, the Democratic Republicans had gained a small overall majority in the House of Representatives. In the Senate, overall Federalist majorities were reduced at successive elections.[72] By 1798 however

anti-Republicans who believed the people to be 'stupid, suspicious, licentious. They cannot safely trust themselves. When they have established government, they should think of nothing but obedience, leaving care of their liberties to their wiser rulers', in 'Who are the Best Keepers of the People's Liberties' in *Papers of James Madison* Vol 14 at 426–27.

[68] Cited in G Stone, *Perilous Times – Free Speech in Wartime* (New York, WW Norton, 2004) at 34.

[69] John Adams, *Answer to the Citizens of Newark in the State of Jersey* Gazette of the United States (2 May 1798).

[70] Cited in G Stone, *Perilous Times – Free Speech in Wartime* at 35.

[71] As Stone ibid points out, however, inflamed invective was not solely confined to the Republican side. On the Federal side, the editor of the *United States Gazette* derided Republican opponents as 'dismal cacklers' and the 'worst and basest of men'. Stone reports additionally William Cobbett's remarks in *Porcupine's Works* that Bache was an 'abandoned liar' and ought to be dealt with like 'a Turk, a Jew, a Jacobin or a Dog'.

[72] Senators at this time were elected by votes in state legislatures. This remained the position until the passing of the 17th Amendment in 1913.

the Federalists had regained overall control of both the House and the Senate. The Sedition Act 1798 passed its congressional stages and was signed into law by President Adams in July that year. By section 2 of the Act, offenders could be fined up to $2,000 and/or imprisoned for up to two years for writing, printing, uttering or publishing

> any false, scandalous, and malicious writing … against the government of the United States, or either House of the Congress of the United States, or the President, with intent to defame (them), or to bring them (into) contempt or disrepute, or to excite against them (the) hatred of the good people of the United States …'[73]

Secretary of State Timothy Pickering then pursued high-profile prosecutions against what he called the 'pests of society and disturbers of order and tranquility'.[74] Federalist-appointed judges such as Samuel Chase presided in partisan trials of Republican journalists and editors in which the result was hardly ever in doubt.[75] The extensive breadth of the new law was vividly illustrated in its very first recorded prosecutions. Three inebriated drinkers in a Newark bar were arrested, charged and convicted when one of them, Luther Baldwin, made a vulgar comment about President Adams' posterior as the Presidential stage coach passed through the city.[76]

Republican-controlled state legislatures in Kentucky and Virginia declared the Sedition Act to be 'void and of no force'. The resolution of the Virginia State Legislature drafted by James Madison asserted that the 1798 Act violated the First Amendment on the basis that the right of 'freely examining public characters and measures' was the necessary foundation of every other right.[77] Jefferson had previously moved in June 1798 to reassure his Republican supporters telling them that with 'a little patience and we shall see the reign of witches pass over, their spells dissolve, and the people, recovering their true sight, restore their government to its true principles'.[78]

The Sedition Act had a sunset clause which meant the statute lapsed in March 1801 just as President John Adams' term of office was ending and that of his successor Thomas Jefferson commencing. Later, however, as if to demonstrate the

[73] For a valuable account of the congressional debates leading up to enactment, see G Stone *Perilous Times – Free Speech in Wartime* at 36–41.

[74] CW Upham, *Life of Timothy Pickering Vol 3* (France, Ulan Press, 2012) at 475–76, and see for commentary M Farrell and M Cupito, *Newspapers: A Complete Guide to the Industry* (New York, Peter Lang, 2010) at 54 et seq; G Stone ibid 46–66.

[75] See Farrell and Cupito, and Stone ibid for discussion of the high-profile trials of Matthew Lyon, James Callender and Thomas Cooper.

[76] *Newark Gazette* (1799) 29 January and discussed in P Blumberg, *Repressive Jurisprudence in the Early American Republic* (New York, CUP, 2010) at 99–101. A useful resource here is F Wharton, *State Trials of Washington and Adams* (Philadelphia, Carey & Hart, 1849).

[77] Madison's Report on the Sedition Act to the Virginia Legislature is available here https://press-pubs.uchicago.edu/founders/documents/amendI_speechs24.html.

[78] Letter to John Taylor 4 June 1798 republished in https://thefederalistpapers.org/wp-content/uploads/2012/08/The-Essential-Thomas-Jefferson.pdf.

bipartisan allure of penal laws designed to shore up confidence in public administration, federal and state criminal libel laws would be deployed by Republican office holders to silence their Federalist critics in the local presses.[79]

Federalist attempts to rein in the 'unruly mobs' and partisan opinion that gained in public support did not wholly rest upon the enactment of widely drafted legislation of a sort that would not have been out of place across the Atlantic in Hanoverian England. Their palpable alarm during the 1790s that partisan Republican majorities in Congress or state legislatures would threaten aspects of the hard-won constitutional settlement of 1787–91 by repealing or amending key statutes spurred federalist interest in other 'constitutional' checks on legislative power. The constitutionality of Republican laws might be tested in judicial review actions before the courts. Accordingly Federalist thinking about the role of the judiciary in a written constitution evolved and an entirely new conception of the role of the courts emerged in federalist tracts as a possible counter-majoritarian check on legislative power. From this time onwards in federalist circles, judicial review was seen less as a device that protected the citizens from their rulers. Its principal function, Federalist writers such as the hitherto obscure law teacher at Columbia University James Kent argued, would be to secure the Constitution from the ill-considered legislative policies of the people's representatives'[80] Federalist judges began to articulate the novel idea that the judicial branch might be the 'only proper and competent authority to decide whether any Law made by Congress; or any of the State Legislatures is contrary to … the federal Constitution'.[81] The savagery and oppressive short-termism of popular opinion could be safeguarded against by layers of intermediate institutions. Where legislatures themselves temporarily succumbed to the impassioned folly of crowds, the courts would step in to save the people from themselves. The fact that the courts in general and the bench of the Supreme Court in particular were then staffed by Federalist judges lent considerable security to the latter proposition.[82] There could be some assurance that anti-federalist law-making would not pass constitutional muster.

[79] See further P Blumberg, *Repressive Jurisprudence in the Early American Republic* at ch 6 who observes 'Notwithstanding their pious, psalm-singing abhorrence of the doctrines when used by Federalists, Republicans seized on their political usefulness as they moved into power. Indeed, they went beyond targeting Federalists and used them against dissident factions in their own party in two of the country's most important states' at 187.

[80] See L Kramer, *The People Themselves: Popular Constitutionalism and Judicial Review* at 132 who credits Kent for having played a key role in developing Federalist thought in this way.

[81] These are the words of Judge Samuel Chase in his charge to the Grand Jury of the Circuit Court for the District of Pennsylvania on 12 April 1800 reported in M Marcus, *Documentary History of the United States Supreme Court 1789–1800* (New York, Columbia University Press, 1990) Vol 3 at 408–12. See further Justice William Paterson who informed a jury hearing a dispute over statutory land confiscation in October 1798 that legislatures did not have the power to enact unconstitutional laws. Such statutes were not binding on juries and courts who were the 'proper bodies' to pronounce on constitutional conformity, M Marcus ibid at 236.

[82] Stone writes '(b)ecause the Supreme Court was composed entirely of Federalist justices, Republicans had no incentive to seek review in the Supreme Court', *Perilous Times – Free Speech in Wartime* at 68.

On the Republican side, 'Brutus', in a prescient paper published in March 1788 some 15 years before Chief Justice Marshall's ruling in *Marbury v Madison*[83] set out the dangers of judicially determined constitutions. He compared the English position – where the legislature controlled the laws that were subsequently merely interpreted by the courts – with that pertaining at home where he predicted the judges under the Federal Constitution would come in time to 'control the legislature'.[84] This arrogation transcended any power given to the judges by 'any free government under heaven'.[85] So situated, there would be no power that could remove them. Independent of elected representatives and the citizens, men 'placed in this situation will generally soon feel themselves independent of heaven itself'.[86] Legislatures on the other hand were directly accountable to the people and could be removed by them if representatives exceeded their authority to act or otherwise pursued an erroneous interpretation of the Constitution.

Republican thinking at this time tended to endorse ideas of departmentalism in which no single branch ('department') of the Constitution could impose its preferred meaning of the Constitution upon the other branches.[87] The obvious difficulty that arose in cases where the different branches adopted mutually exclusive accounts of their respective competencies was not, however, simply ignored. In the first instance, the constitutional commitment to the notion of checks and balances would encourage efforts to find a compromise between the opposing positions. Where no accommodation was forthcoming, Madison, Jefferson and their adherents believed that sovereign power to resolve the matter one way or another lay with the people themselves.[88] The existence of the institutions of governmental power depended, as Senator Mason from Virginia stated, upon the enduring affection of the people.[89] Popular involvement in politics was not confined to the act of consenting to a proposed constitution or periodically renewing/refusing to renew the mandate of existing office holders. It could be resorted to in cases of an impasse between the legislature and the courts.

[83] 5 US 103 (1803).

[84] XV 20 March 1788, as reprinted in (ed R Ketcham) *Tne Anti-Federalist Papers* at 322.

[85] ibid at 323.

[86] ibid.

[87] Jefferson expressed departmentalism thus: 'each of the three departments has equally the right to decide for itself what is its duty under the constitution, without regard to what the others may have decided for themselves under a similar question'. *The Writings of Thomas Jefferson* Vol 10 at 142. This was in essence his objection to CJ Marshall's ruling in *Marbury v Madison* 5 US (1 Cranch) 137 (1803) which Jefferson famously denounced as making the judiciary a 'despotic branch'.

[88] Madison regularly invoked public opinion as setting the bounds of all legitimate governmental authority, see for example 'Public Opinion' in (ed W Hutchinson) *The Papers of James Madison* (Chicago & Charlottesville, University of Chicago and University Press of Virginia, 1962) Vol 14 at 170. For Jefferson the idea of popular sovereignty was central to his political thinking. See among numerous examples 'Opinion on French Treaties', *Letter to William Charles Jarvis* 28 September 1820; *Letter to Henry Lee* August 10, 1824; *Letter to John Adams* 27 June 1813. All the foregoing are reproduced in (ed P Foner) *Thomas Jefferson: Selections from His Writings* (US, International Publishers, 1943) at 52–54.

[89] Senator Mason *11 Annals of Congress 1798–1800* at 59 and cited in L Kramer *The People Themselves: Popular Constitutionalism and Judicial Review* at 107.

Nonetheless, a major qualification of the Republican Party leadership's enthusiasm for the popular resolution of constitutional disputes must be conceded. Sheehan has shown that Madison's endorsement of ongoing participation was nuanced. He did not defend public opinion in its raw, aggregated state as a determinant of public policy. He expected that the citizens when they came to act politically would do so responsibly and for constitutional design to facilitate such responsible law making.[90] His Enlightenment credentials are thus in plain sight when he decried the dangers attendant on the impassioned expression of political opinion at large gatherings. In *Federalist 55*, Madison maintained that, in assemblies composed of many persons, passion would always 'wrest the sceptre from reason'.[91] It would not matter that every assembly member had the intellectual rigour of Socrates, in the end impassioned, unreasoned debate would prevail and the republic jeopardised. Public reason ought to rule. Madison believed his constitutional design with its federal form, bicameral representative structure and accompanying separation of powers/checking components would 'remedy the vices of popular government and at the same time preserve its spirit and form'.[92] The patrician strand in Madison expected that the great and good would circulate their elevated ideas to the populace in newspaper articles.[93] In this way popular thinking would become more sophisticated as 'cultivators of the human mind and the manufacturers of useful knowledge'[94] shaped public discourse. Madison's Majority Report, which was appended to the Virginia Resolution (criticising the Alien and Sedition Acts), may have talked up the fundamental importance of being able to examine public figures freely and to communicate likewise freely on this topic.[95] However, given his insistence in other published writings upon reasoned discourse, it may be surmised that the 'free' examination of and communication regarding public figures was not intended to extend very far beyond the measured pronouncements of the enlightened men in whose company Madison circulated. It is true that he did defend the rights of Democratic Republican societies to political participation. Martin notes however that Madison did not 'actively encourage' such societies to theorise about the place of such counter-publics and the political role of citizens in a system of popular government.[96] Madison's position might in truth be put more starkly than that suggested by Martin's account.

[90] C Sheehan, *James Madison and the Spirit of Republican Self-Government* (New York, CUP, 2009) at 83.

[91] *Federalist 55* where the author goes on to claim, 'Had every Athenian citizen been a Socrates, every Athenian assembly would still have been a mob.' NB some repositories decline to attribute *Federalist 55* unequivocally to Madison, see, for example, the Avalon Project hosted by Yale Law School which credits 'Hamilton or Madison' with authorship at https://avalon.law.yale.edu/18th_century/fed55.asp.

[92] C Sheehan, *James Madison and the Spirit of Republican Self-Government* at 85.

[93] Sheehan remarks that 'the literati are … (the) civic educators in Madison's republic' ibid at 104.

[94] 'Notes on Government' in (ed W Hutchinson) *The Papers of James Madison* Vol 14 at 168.

[95] Available electronically at https://press-pubs.uchicago.edu/founders/documents/amendI_speechs24.html.

[96] R Martin, *Government by Dissent: Protest, Resistance and Radical Democratic Thought in the Early American Republic* at 146.

Madison believed that factional opinion was something to be overcome. It is extremely doubtful, for example, that Madison would have wanted to extend the right of free examination to the *Aurora's* crude personal attacks on Washington and Adams. In a letter to Jefferson, he worried that poisonous 'sophistries' would come to be accepted for the truth unless antidotes were applied quickly.[97] What form those antidotes would take may only be speculated. If Madison considered that the 'sophistries' were seriously corrosive of public confidence in the great men of the new Republic, we cannot rule out that he would have given active consideration to a combination of penal and civil restraints on publications.

As regards Jefferson, there is evidence not only that he shared Madison's belief in the importance of 'reasonable' public opinion in shaping public policy,[98] but also that he was not above acquiescing to/encouraging the use of federal and state criminal libel laws to silence political opponents.[99] Jefferson may have been *ad idem* with Madison on the unconstitutionality of the Sedition Act under the Federal Constitution but this did not prevent him defending the position of the states to determine for themselves the circumstances in which the 'licentiousness of speech and of the press may be abridged without lessening their useful freedom'.[100] Support for this speech-restrictive view of Jefferson is found in Levy.[101] Jefferson was particularly exercised by the danger posed by 'false facts' to the successful conclusion of foreign treaty negotiations and urged accordingly a narrowing of free speech protection. Levy contends that, were Jefferson's view to have prevailed, it could have had 'suppressive effects' on public discussion of the Jay Treaty with Great Britain.[102]

Popular Participation – Underlying Political Theory Rationales in Anti-Federalist Thinking

As Federalist judges were only too happy to point out, one obvious way for the emerging class of non-elite republican speakers to avoid the harsh penalties of the Sedition Act 1798 was to avoid 'false' utterances published maliciously. One of the prosecutions overseen by Secretary of State Pickering was that of Thomas Cooper.

[97] *Letter to Thomas Jefferson* (1798) February 12, *Papers of James Madison* Vol 17 at 79.

[98] eg see the text of Jefferson's first inaugural address as President on 4 March 1801 available at https://avalon.law.yale.edu/19th_century/jefinau1.asp.

[99] See thus P Blumberg, *Repressive Jurisprudence in the Early American Republic* especially at chs 5 and 6, where the author instances a series of partisan deployments of federal and state criminal laws by Republicans against their Federalist opponents especially in Pennsylvania. Indeed, as Blumberg reveals, Republicans even used these laws against opposing factions within the Republican Party.

[100] Jefferson, 'Draft of the Kentucky Resolution' in *The Papers of Thomas Jefferson* (2003, Princeton University Press Vol 30 at 536–43 at para.3). And see Blumberg ibid at 87.

[101] L Levy, 'On the Origins of the Free Speech Clause' (1984–85) 32 *UCLA L. Rev* 177, 205.

[102] ibid.

An Oxford graduate, lawyer and chemist, Cooper had produced a leaflet in which he described President Adams upon assuming office in 1796 as

> hardly in the infancy of political mistake: even those who doubted his capacity thought well of his intentions. Nor yet were we saddled with the expense of a permanent navy, or threatened, under his auspices with the existence of a standing army.[103]

Summing up, Justice Samuel Chase told the jury that if they were satisfied that Cooper had published without malice *and* had proved the truth of his claims, then they must acquit him.[104] The result was not in doubt however. In his sentencing remarks following the jury's guilty verdict, Justice Chase highlighted Cooper's capacity to 'mislead the ignorant'. The court was determined to restrain 'all such licentious attacks on the government of the country'.[105] Cooper was sentenced to six months' imprisonment and fined $400. Upon completing his sentence, he was required to enter sureties guaranteeing good behaviour totalling a further $2,000.

The state's demand in sedition trials that the defendant speaker establish the 'truth' of a claim made as part of political discourse was then (and remains today) hugely problematic for a society committed to the idea of pluralist politics. Yet, Republican leaders could not easily assert that the law's standard of 'political truth' was misconceived. They were after all committed to reasoned public discourse led by learned gentlemen. As such Republicans including Madison could hardly be heard to argue that enlightened self-rule was advanced by the false representations from poorly educated journeymen pamphleteers. *A fortiori* when these were levelled at the very class of men upon whose disinterested and enlightened judgment the future of the nation's affairs depended. As noted above, Madison's vision was that newspapers would ensure a one-directional flow of ideas from the *literati* to the people. This would help establish a republic of enlightened opinion as the people would come to gauge not only how ideas might be expressed in the public sphere but also in what those ideas might consist. In contrast, it is in more local expressions of republican opinion within the Democratic Republican societies that a more radical account of the basis of political participation is to be found. Far removed from Madisonian condemnations of factious disagreement, the speeches and writings of artisans and labouring men demonstrated the very embodiment of plural political discourse where dissent was a valued feature. In stressing the benefits of allowing opinions considered erroneous to be published, these writers were some 60 years ahead of John Stuart Mill's defence in *On Liberty*. What is more, unlike the epistocratic Mill, they were committed to the political equality of all citizens.[106] The isonomia these writers embraced entailed active political authorship of laws and policies.

[103] A report of the trial is to be found in Wharton, *State Trials of the United States During the Administrations of Washington and Adams* (Philadelphia, Carey & Hart, 1848) at 660–78.

[104] ibid at 676–67.

[105] ibid at 678.

[106] Mill proposed that those with greater levels of education be entitled to plural votes in order to secure optimal political decision-making in representative systems of government. For discussion see

As such they offered a radical challenge to passive notions of the represented citizen. The core and overlapping themes of four leading exemplars of radical democratic thought – Numa, Tunis Wortman, Thomas Cooper and John Thomson – can now be set out.[107]

Numa – Pseudonymous Newspaper Essayist

The chief relevance of Numa's writings for this chapter lie in their scepticism about ideas of truth in political discourse. He disputed the application of the scientific method to enquiries about society. Claims to political truth were simply not like their counterparts in investigations into planetary movements, gravity or electricity. The former were not capable of demonstration in the way that scientific truths were. Instead, they were the result of 'probable reasoning' only. This necessarily implied some degree of doubt. Men were prone to error in such matters. Should the judgments of one set of fallible men be trusted to determine political 'truths' in the opinions of others? This would amount to the creation of another Inquisition 'to serve the ends of political bigotry'.[108] Criminalising speech on account of alleged falseness would make citizens 'suspicious of their rulers … and poison the springs of public confidence …'[109] Numa is far removed from Madison's distaste for 'factious disagreement'. Political differences between people was an irrevocable fact of life. Consensus on matters of the public good could not be guaranteed. Numa perceptively identified the threat to the spirit of free public inquiry by 'obliging men to conceal their sentiments' to prevent them exercising the 'privileges of citizenship'. The chances of proper characters being elected to public office were correspondingly diminished. Numa's acceptance of inevitable difference and expressive discord marks out his contributions as one of the earliest endorsements of the importance of clashing opinions in public discourse.

Tunis Wortman – Treatise Concerning Political Enquiry and the Liberty of the Press

The contributions of Tunis Wortman offered a pre-Millian defence of the instrumental value of political speech. Public dissent and disagreement were conceived of as central means of improving the quality of debate and hence the quality of government. Wortman's publications themselves were careful to set out the

D Miller, 'The Place of Plural Voting in Mill's Conception of Representative Government' (2015) 77 *The Review of Politics* 399.

[107] Robert Martin's excellent *Government by Dissent* first alerted me to the rich body of writings in this early period of the American republic. I am heavily indebted to chs 5 and 6 of that work in the section of writing that follows.

[108] 'For the New York Journal' (1796) 15 November.

[109] ibid.

opposing case for maintaining the status quo alongside his arguments for reform. He disputed the idea found in patrician Federalist and Republican writings that speakers needed to be 'disinterested' contributors. Wortman's rejection of the merits of abstracted political discourse of the sort favoured by the patrician elite is significant.[110] On his view, it is our background lives and the events in them that shape how we come to acquire diverse viewpoints and legitimately animate our contributions in public speech. He was also comfortable with the fact that public debate might not conclude with unanimous agreement. Governments and majorities must not force dissenting voices into alignment with majority sentiment. Such was Wortman's commitment to the principle of free dissent that he directed this advice not only at Federalist opponents but at more sympathetic figures like Jefferson whose inauguration he supported.[111] Executive office holders would always be tempted to advance broad interpretations of their powers to crush opinions considered to be harmful. Each encroachment on public liberty would embolden subsequent curtailments.[112] Conversely, a political culture in which dissent was not silenced would over time induce greater powers of independent reflection on the part of the people. In a passage that predates John Stuart Mill's *On Liberty* by over a half a century Wortman argues that

> diversity of sentiment … is far from being unfavorable to the eventual reception of Truth. It produces Collision, engenders Argument and affords exercise and energy to the intellectual powers; it corrects our errors, removes our prejudices and strengthens our perceptions.[113]

Wortman also tapped into a recurring theme in republican political thought when he stressed the importance of state-funded education in securing independent reflection. Ordinary citizens needed a basic threshold competence in literacy and numeracy skills if they were going to be able to fulfil their sovereign role in holding governments to account and resisting unjustified encroachments on liberty that the Executive was liable to attempt. Wortman pointed out the circular reasoning of those who opposed the active participation of the 'ignorant masses' in affairs of state. Having decided that there would be no taxation to support the public education of children, the governing class of representative politicians then insisted that excluded ordinary citizens should defer to the political judgments of their representatives since the lack of general education in the population at large made reasoned accountability on their part impossible!

[110] See further R Martin, *Government by Dissent: Protest, Resistance and Radical Democratic Thought in the Early American Republic* (2013, NYU Press, New York) at 163.

[111] *A Solemn Address to Christians and Patriots* (1800) www.consource.org/document/a-solemn-address-to-christians-and-patriots-by-tunis-wortman-1800/.

[112] 'Every violation will increase the appetite for power; it will augment the danger by force of habit and the pretext of example. Encroachments always proceed with accelerated momentum …', ibid.

[113] Cited in Martin, *Government by Dissent* at 166.

Thomas Cooper – Propositions

Sharing with Numan and Wortman a belief in the centrality of dissent to self-government, the works of Thomas Cooper emphasise a contestatory and inclusive form of popular participation in political debate. In *Propositions* he defends a very broad account of free speech that extends to communication of ideas and opinions considered false[114] on the basis that would later also come to be associated with Mill, namely that the truth was more likely to emerge from its contact with erroneous opinion. Cooper believed that the discovery of truth was more likely to be accelerated by the clash with error than when, with erroneous viewpoints being suppressed, truthful claims were 'advanced absurdly or defended weakly'. Unlike Cooper however, Mill was unwilling to deem every citizen's opinions as worthy of equal respect. He advocated a system of plural voting entitlements in which the more intelligent would count for more at elections than those with lesser educational attainments. Whether Mill meant this epistocratic form of governance to be a permanent feature of representative systems of government is a matter of some academic debate.[115]

John Thomson – An Enquiry Concerning the Liberty and Licentiousness of the Press[116]

The full title of Thomson's work extends after the title immediately above to read 'and the Uncontroulable Nature of the Human Mind containing An Investigation of the Right which Government have to controul the free expression of Public Opinion'. Completed in March 1801 shortly after the expiry of the Sedition Law, Thomson's *Enquiry* is aimed at guarding against the possibility of future fettering by sedition laws. Remarkably for its time, it does so by advancing an absolutist defence of free speech in matters of politics, one founded on the idea of sovereign people. Thomson commenced his tract by noting the slipperiness of the language used by the opponents of press freedom. The 'licentiousness of the Press', Thomson

[114] In his comments on the Sedition Act 1798, Cooper doubted whether the 'truth' of an opinion (as opposed to a fact) could be proved. See T Cooper, 'Extract from a Speech of Mr Erksine on the Doctrine of Libel' text available at www.law.nyu.edu/sites/default/files/ECM_PRO_062717.pdf.

[115] D Miller, 'The Place of Plural Voting in Mill's Conception of Representative Government' (2015) 77 *The Review of Politics* 399. Some academic opinion now favours a return to an epistocratic system of voting in which presumably academic opinion gets to weigh more heavily in the ballot box than the rest of the population. See, for example, T Mulligan who asserts 'Recent events have cast doubt on the wisdom of democratic decision-making. Brexit, the Columbian people's (initial) rejection of peace with FARC and the election of Donald Trump suggest that the time is right to explore alternatives to democracy' in 'Plural Voting for the Twenty-First Century' (2018) 68 *Philosophical Quarterly* 286. The idea that optimal decision-making is best served by allowing intellectual elites to determine policy programmes denies the value of isonomy, a point made by Urbinati in *Democracy Disfigured – Opinion, Truth and the People* (Massachusetts, Harvard University Press, 2014) and explored in ch 2.

[116] 1801, New York. The reprinted version consulted here was published as J Thomson, *An Enquiry Concerning the Liberty and Licentiousness of the Press* (New York, Da Capo Press, 1970).

railed, was a term 'destitute of any meaning'.[117] The men that deployed it 'evidently wished nobody to enjoy Liberty of the Press, but such as were of their opinion'.[118] Thomson employed an analogy with scientific reasoning to endorse unrestrained freedom in political discourse. 'Men of science' had differed (and still differed) sometimes vehemently among themselves about the causes and effects of phenomena in the natural world. Yet, out of these very differences greater understanding about the natural world and 'superlative scientific advantages' had been gained.[119] So too in the political realm where advances in self-government would follow from unrestrained discourse.

Thomson observed that Article 1 Section 6 of the Federal Constitution conferred complete protection for speech and debates in the Senate and House of Representatives. If elected representatives were free to say what they wished in Congress, why should they be able to abridge this right in the people in statutes such as the Sedition Act 1798? At bottom, Thomson's argument was that the authority enjoyed by members of Congress derived solely from having been empowered by the people to act as the latter's agents. The people were the sole sovereign constituting authority. There could be no basis on which the agents might act to restrict the words and writings of their sovereign principals. The constituted powers were the 'creature of the people'. It was, he claimed, 'absurd to suppose the people divested of that which their public agents enjoy'.[120] Even in the absence of sedition laws, governments enjoyed very considerable powers to shape public opinion towards their own position.

Like Numa, Thomson concluded that the provision of a truth defence in the 1798 Act was worthless. The 'truth' of a political opinion would rarely if ever be capable of being proved to the satisfaction of a court of law. Moreover, the fact that federal prosecutors charged only those considered to utter 'disagreeable' claims and not the sycophantic flatterers who lavished unfounded praise upon the Federalist regime showed that the Act was not actually intended to suppress mere falsehood/promote truth on matters regarding the conduct of public affairs.[121] It was to silence those who had the courage to dispute the wisdom of public officials.

Conclusion

The demise of the Democratic Republican societies in the early part of the nineteenth century occurred at a time when the Republicans became the party of

[117] ibid at 7.
[118] ibid.
[119] ibid at 15.
[120] ibid at 77.
[121] ibid at 67–69.

government, capturing the Presidency at successive elections.[122] This undoubtedly contributed to some degree to the mainstreaming of republican energies that had previously found more radical outlets in the local clubs and societies that mushroomed in the 1790s.[123] Federalist claims that the societies were hotbeds of Jacobin radicalism that threatened the stability of the Republic have also been credited with diminishing their attractiveness to ordinary American citizens and hence their influence in national and state politics.[124] Nonetheless, Martin's study of the origins and political contributions of the Democratic Republican societies has allowed us to gain new insights into the dissentient energies that existed in the early days of the new Republic. Martin's broader normative defence of this period is that an invigorated dissentient tradition is vital to democratic society. It is required to be a permanent feature of the political landscape. If dissent emerges on an intermittent basis only, this necessarily means that, outside of those times, the status quo as presided over by elite office holders is left unchallenged. Arendt's observations concerning the absence of constitutional structures that might have captured and sustained the revolutionary spirit in the new Republic had the effect of requiring politically active citizens who wished to debate public policy and scrutinise the activities of their representatives to create their own fora and organise their own events.

The open accessible spaces needed to preserve the public freedoms to debate, discuss and disagree were not provided for in the constitutional settlement of the post-colonial era. It may be assumed that this was no accidental oversight. After the turmoil of the revolutionary period, the claim that the new constitutional arrangements needed to be given time to settle would have had an obvious appeal. In laying an exclusive emphasis upon the representative features of the Constitution and the disinterested wisdom of the men elected to hold public office, the Federalists wanted to minimise opportunities for popular forms of political expression. Arendt's view of human nature commits her to the opposing position where political action is a constant human need and the ability to create something new in the political sphere in association with others is the highest form of activity that humans can aspire to. This explains her enthusiasm for Jefferson's ideas of vigilant ward republics.

In contradistinction to the overall argument made in this book, Martin situates dissenting expression (at least in the US) within an overall linear progression towards a better society. In this way he is faithful to a commonly articulated core

[122] Candidates standing on the Republican ticket succeeded to the Presidency from the time of Jefferson (1801–09); through Madison (1809–17); James Monroe (1817–25) and John Quincy Adams (1825–29).

[123] R Martin, *Government by Dissent: Protest, Resistance and Radical Democratic Thought in the Early American Republic* at 198–99.

[124] See thus J Miller, *The Federalist Era 1789–1801* (London, Hamish Hamilton, 1960) who attributes the decline of the Democratic Republican societies to the 'increasingly critical attitude adopted by Americans toward the French Revolution', at 162.

strand in the writings of Tunis Wortman and John Thomson. Martin himself draws upon Habermas' defence of deliberative democracy within a liberal constitutionalist frame which he sees as facilitating a 'self-correcting learning process'.[125] As such, however, Martin's position is vulnerable to the criticism (as is likewise levelled at Habermas) that the democratic agency of the people is forever bound to operate and unfold within the horizons of liberal democracy and its central commitment to possessive individualism. The task of the dissenters, according to Martin, is to help propel society towards a more perfectly realised model of constitutionalism. Conversely, they are not to consider themselves engaged in the revolutionary mode whereby dissenting opinion helps usher new worlds into being. The worth of dissenting speech will be gauged in terms of the contribution made towards the further elaboration of the basic societal framework that has already been laid down. As was shown in chapter two, this teleological conception of democratic agency is at odds with an agonist view of the constitutive power of the people. It does not speak to what Honig has called the 'risky tumult of *a*constitutionalism'[126] that is associated with unsettling, disruptive contributions to public discourse.

Moreover, if Martin is to be entirely faithful to the precepts of deliberative democracy, his position requires a pre-commitment to respectful, empathetic, reason-giving and reasonable conduct by all participants in the public domain. These constraints invariably screen out of public discourse a number of contributions, more than a fair few of which may be surmised to emanate from non-elite speakers. Those excluded on these terms would have included a number of the pamphleteers active in the Democratic Republican societies that Martin celebrates as having kept the spirit of political dissent alive in the Federalist era. In the present era, the inability/failure to adapt to the current debating style of the university seminar entails severe costs to the political agency of certain speakers. Ironically, those excluded on these grounds are at no point given the chance to discuss whether they accept the set of public reason precommitments deemed appropriate by deliberative democrats. The discrete ways in which state and corporate elites transmit and enforce these demands to the detriment of an active and contestatory democracy is the subject of chapter six.

[125] Martin, *Government by Dissent* at n 117 at 201 citing J Habermas, 'Constitutional Democracy: A Paradoxical Union of Contradictory Principles?' (2001) 29 *Pol. Theory* 774.

[126] B Honig, 'Dead Rights, Live Futures: A Reply to Habermas' "Constitutional Democracy"' (2001) 29 *Pol. Theory* 792.

6

Official and Corporate Gatekeeping of Online Expression with Special Reference to False Statements on Public Affairs

Introduction

Earlier chapters in this book have looked at the impact of liberal constitutionalist theory and practice on opportunities for popular participation in political life. Chapters two and three showed how Enlightenment concerns with a rational public sphere connect to overarching themes in deliberative democracy scholarship and how this connection serves to narrow political pluralism in significant respects. Against that background, chapter four then considered current denouncements of popular participation and populism in public discourse. Exploiting a privileged degree of access to mainstream media, socio-economic elites and an overlapping class of public office holders/public intellectuals denounce popular participation in politics by talking up fears of majority tyranny and majority irrationality.

Using the language of 'post-truth' politics to denounce the outcomes of recent elections and referenda, some commentators point to a very recent crisis for democracy starting in 2016 with the outcome of the EU referendum in the UK and the election of Donald Trump to the US Presidency.[1] For example, in *Post-Truth The New War on Truth and How to Fight Back* D'Ancona argues that we entered an era of 'ugly populism' in 2016 in which the 'honesty' and 'accuracy' of an earlier era of decent and intellectually rigorous political discourse were abandoned. The book's narrow domestic focus falls on the Leave campaign whose leading members, the author argues, told repeated lies about what departure from the EU would mean. This has caused a serious erosion in voters' trust in our system of politics. Curiously, the exaggerated and unverifiable claims about an imminent economic collapse regularly aired by Prime Minister Cameron, Chancellor of the Exchequer Osborne and the leaders of the Liberal Democrat and Nationalist parties during the 2016 referendum are absent from the analysis. Conveniently

[1] M D'Ancona, *Post-Truth: The New War on Truth and How to Fight Back* (London, Ebury Press, 2017).

for the D'Ancona time frame, neither the 'dodgy dossier' of inaccurate intelligence about Iraqi weapons capability relied upon by Prime Minister Blair in 2003, nor the former PM's claims about the Iraqi war having essentially benign effects occurred before the Ancona era of *post-truth* politics. Neither set of claims can thus be attributed any contributory role in the story of how politics descended into 'fake news' soundbites and brazen lie-telling. A more rounded analysis would, however, have included these and other official statements to conclude that liberals are also prone to misinform and mislead like their populist bêtes noires, except in the case of UK and European liberals this has usually been done whilst holding the highest of public offices.[2] Might we then justifiably attribute the loss of trust in politics in some part at least to the untruths told by the leaders and prominent politicians in our mainstream political parties?

The D'Ancona view of an electorate led towards irrational policy choices by 'post-truth' speakers who peddle 'fake news' to gullible electorates raises some difficult questions about popular participation in politics that the author glides past. Although he calls for the people themselves to will the end of post-truth politics,[3] it seems that he favours a combination of the charismatic leader much like the 'ugly' populism he decries (Lincoln, Franklin Roosevelt, Churchill, Martin Luther King are all mentioned in the book's closing pages) and nudge-style government to 'steer citizens away from 'misinformation and towards fact-based decisions'.[4] Without any open acknowledgement of the dangers to political pluralism of official clampdowns on 'fake news' – incidentally a term used by D'Ancona without quote marks indicating that he finds it unproblematic – the author's hope is that the scourge of uninformed opinion can be brought to heel without the need for the 'blunt instruments of law and regulation'.[5] Apart from the obvious criticism that nudge-style government *is* regulation (albeit of a subtle kind) by government, one wonders whether D'Ancona would ultimately demur from calls for the criminalisation of 'fake news' in certain contexts such as those made by the UK Labour Party during the COVID-19 pandemic in respect of anti-vaccination expression.[6] D'Ancona's unqualified praise for the House of Commons Digital, Culture, Media and Sport Select Committee's inquiry into 'fake news' and the practice of democracy shows no awareness of the dangers to democratic self-government of permitting socio-political elites control over 'truth-telling'. Logically, if the search for truth is the ultimate raison d'être of democratic politics, it makes sense to deny those who possess the truth the power to sanction and deter through law those who peddle the lies and mistruths that deform democracy. D'Ancona wholly misses the fundamental point that so many contested political debates implicate

[2] J Gray, Book Review (2017) *The Guardian* 19 May.

[3] Although the book has very little to say about how this 'will' is to be made manifest.

[4] M D'Ancona, *Post-Truth: The New War on Truth and How to Fight Back* at 142.

[5] ibid.

[6] See https://labour.org.uk/press/labour-calls-for-emergency-legislation-to-stamp-out-dangerous-anti-vax-content/.

moral and philosophical questions where no truthful single correct answer exists. He also shows no awareness of the vital First Amendment insight that an insistence upon the truth in public discourse will likely result in acts of self-censorship by those who are unable to satisfy the state of the evidential standard. This will lead to a diminution in the sorts of claims and types of speaker that are heard in public spaces. In this sense, his strike against 'ugly populism' cannot avoid tamping down political expression by non-elites. It is perhaps correct to read the author as wishing to return to a mythical, halcyon era of objective journalism funded by public-spirited news proprietors whose journalists only ever produced empirically verified copy.

As chapter four was at pains to argue, commentators and scholars in the liberal tradition who argue for some sort of fightback against populist political forces exhibit some common blindspots. Their chief omission is the neglect to consider the very significant ways in which liberalism *already* closes down opportunities for the effective contestation of politics among ordinary citizens. This is a serious criticism when it is recalled just how frequently elected elites fail to implement majority-backed policy programmes and (what is worse) implement policies not endorsed by the electorate that have damaging outcomes for ordinary citizens. When we add proven instances of corrupt and unlawful behaviour by the same elites, the case for a broad freedom of meaningful political participation becomes more, not less, compelling.

This chapter describes and evaluates how opportunities for popular participation in online forms of political debate are closed down, with particular reference to UK law and regulatory policy. As chapter four showed, elite attacks on popular self rule have been very successful. That 'populism' has become a term of denigration tells much. Liberals' distrust of ordinary citizens' participation in politics is *de rigueur*. As D'Ancona and others would observe, the voters' susceptibility to choose 'self-harming' policies is well established by recent election/referendum results.[7] It is a leitmotif of many in the mainstream media commentariat and academia. The tendency of the citizens to misunderstand their true interests even figures in aristocratic forms of purportedly republican political thought where concerns about the unruly passions of ordinary citizens' political contributions are centre stage and where, by contrast, lip service only is paid to the skewing impacts of elite wealth and corporate power upon political discourse.

The aim of this chapter is to ground more firmly in current (mainly though not exclusively UK) legal practice and policy the idea of the unreliable citizen speaker in the Web 2.0 era. I intend to flesh out this notion in the following manner. The following part describes key issues of principle that are engaged by official (via criminal laws and state regulators) and corporate censoring/modification of purportedly 'false' digital expression. Then attention is directed at the nature of some of those penal and regulatory interventions. In recent times, some

[7] Although curiously when the wealthier sections of society vote for tax-raising parties, this is seen as noble and selfless rather than self-harming.

of the major instances of state and corporate interference have occurred in the context of expression concerning COVID-19 and vaccination programmes. The work of the low-profile Coronavirus Disinformation Unit is analysed here (including what is known about its relations with social media platforms), as well as the role played by OFCOM. Other state agencies involved in questionable attempts to curtail online expression include the Metropolitan Police who are reported in *The Economist* to have approached social media platforms with 'requests' to remove lawful posts?[8] Moving across to the corporate sector where shareholder interests in ever greater profitability are determinative of company policy, the recent track records of Google, YouTube, Facebook and Twitter in censoring/acting on the censoring demands of others under their respective in-house policies are considered. Should we be concerned that a select band of UK civil servants have 'trusted flagger' status with social media corporations that give priority to official concerns and complaints about online content? Does the 'blue badge' status accorded by Twitter to certain prominent activists and influential individuals confer an even higher profile status to existing elite (and centrist) opinion formers at the expense of a more democratised public sphere? The picture that is developed here reveals a multi-pronged and inter-linked set of responses to instances of online expression considered by political and corporate elites to be problematic.

If, as seems to be increasingly the case, social media platforms now take it upon themselves to regulate otherwise lawful expression according to viewpoint, ought this to be a matter of concern? Have the platforms become editors and publishers in the same way that the print and broadcast media are? What should follow in policy terms from this change of status from mere conduit to active editor? Might a democratic republican analysis direct us to re-affirm the common carrier status of social media platforms and demand as part of a foundational commitment to ongoing, active self-government that those platforms be (i) prevented from viewpoint discrimination and (ii) publish the algorithms that determine the political content that is pushed towards individual users? What of the more clunky (but more democratically legitimate) forms of domestic statutory regulation that create criminal and civil liability for speakers and their host platforms? The UK's Online Safety Bill is currently working its way through Parliament and is drafted in broad enough terms for its provisions to be used (or threatened to be used) against political expression. Does the proposed 'duty of care' imposed on websites to make risk assessments for harms to adults (as well as children) caused by online speech incentivise the removal of a range of valuable political expression including truthful claims that are somewhat speculatively said to cause psychological harm (such as reporting scenes from criminal activity or conflict zones)? Is there, in addition, a danger that the flawed characters of some of our politicians will be placed away from sight and accompanying criticism as an enforced silence is imposed on the public sphere? Prior to the proposals contained in the Online Safety Bill, a clutch

[8] 'Who Controls the Conversation?' (2020) *The Economist* 24 October.

of UK statutes already outlawed false and misleading speech (both online and offline),[9] and grossly offensive online speech in terms that remain broad enough to capture many diverse contributions to political discourse.[10] An analysis of these existing restrictions is offered below.

Protecting False Statements in Political Discourse – Some Principled Arguments

> But in the midst of this envied situation, we have heard the government as grossly abused as if it had been guilty of the vilest tyranny; as if common sense or common virtue had fled from our country … can it be tolerated in any civilised society that any should be permitted with impunity to tell falsehoods to the people, with an intention to deceive them, and lead them into discontent, if not insurrection, which is apt to follow?
>
> Justice Iredell, Case of Fries (1799) 9 F. Cas. 826, at 827 and 838
>
> The difficulty is that government control over factual truth is in tension with the value of democratic legitimation. Citizens who seek to participate in public discourse, and who are penalized because they disagree with official versions of factual truth, are excluded from the possibility of influencing public opinion.
>
> Robert Post, *Democracy, Expertise, Academic Freedom* (2012)[11]

David Kaye, the UN Special Rapporteur on the Promotion and Protection of the Right to Freedom of Expression, has expressed strong criticism of 'fake news' laws. In a Joint Declaration with the Organisation for Security and Co-operation in Europe, Kaye stated that vague and ambiguous references to 'false news' and 'non-objective information' were 'incompatible with international standards … and should be abolished'.[12] In his report 'Elections in the Digital Age', Kaye criticised a provision of Italian criminal law that prohibited 'unfounded', 'biased, 'false' and 'fake' information on grounds of vagueness that would both inhibit individual speakers and leave government officials unclear regarding what was permitted and what was forbidden.[13] At the same time, difficult issues can arise where a deliberately misleading political expression is said to threaten the integrity of the election process. Think here about a knowingly false statement in the evening of Election

[9] Communications Act 2003, s 127(2).

[10] Communications Act 2003, s 127(1). For discussion, see J Horder, 'Criminal Law at the Limit: Countering False Claims in Elections and Referendums' (2021) 84 *M.L.R.* 429 who notes that in 2017 there were 254 charges under s 127(1) and (2).

[11] R Post, *Democracy, Expertise, Academic Freedom – A First Amendment Jurisprudence for the Modern State* (New Haven, Yale University Press, 2012) at 29.

[12] See www.ohchr.org/Documents/Issues/Opinion/ElectionsReportDigitalAge.pdf at 9.

[13] *Freedom of Expression and the Elections in the Digital Age* UN Research Paper 1/2019 (June 2019) at 9. See further for analysis E Aswad, 'In a World of "Fake News," What's a Social Media Platform to Do?' (2020) 4 *Utah L. Rev.*1009, at 1014–17.

Day to the effect that the local polling station is no longer open.[14] A later section of this chapter returns to the hard questions thrown up by speech that is considered to threaten specifically the integrity of the electoral process.

Beyond this specific limitation on free political expression, some argue that the dissemination of known falsehoods about public affairs in general has no claim to protection. We may have moved on from Justice Iredell's application of penal sedition laws to false speech about the government, but the general idea that a self-governing republic needs truthful information to sustain confidence in the institutions of government continues to exercise its grip on much official thinking. Justice Brandeis' famous argument for freedom of political expression in *Whitney v California* (1927) was, after all, couched in terms of finding the 'truth' in political disputes. False statements can make no claim to constitutional protection on this rationale. The citizens were more likely to choose policies and politicians that offered rationally better solutions to society's problems if presented solely with truthful pieces of information. 'Men feared witches and burnt women. It is the function of speech to free men from the bondage of irrationality.'[15] Where false assertions of fact obstruct the rational discussion of political policy, Brandeis supplies a justification for their removal from the public sphere.[16] Unfortunately, his formulation overlooks the potential danger of elected office holders using their control over law enactment to abuse this power to favour incumbent office holders by prohibiting the 'untruthful' claims of political opponents. Madison was correct to warn of the dangers to self-government that arise when the censorial power vests in public office holders rather than the citizens on whose behalf political elites are supposed to act. A more authentically republican analysis of the regulation of purportedly false political claims would accordingly entail a much more searching look inter alia at the nature and extent of any restriction on political participation; the imminence and seriousness of the harm(s) caused/likely to be caused by the false statement; the potential dangers of official misuse of those powers to protect incumbent office holders and their policies from criticism; and the practical availability of counter-speech alternatives to overcome the intended deception. A republican analysis would also be alive to the potential for the state itself (and for-profit private corporations) to be the active, dominating *sources* of disinformation and falsehoods. State disinformation might after all serve a useful purpose in conditioning citizens to acquiesce to new governmental restrictions on individual freedom. Private corporations' skewing of public discourse might target and narrow the reach of radical, anti-capitalist expression. Acting in concert, these two dominating sets of forces have the clear potential to truncate disruptive, dissenting expression.

[14] J Horder, 'Criminal Law at the Limit: Countering False Claims in Elections and Referendums' (2021) 84 *M.L.R.* 429; I Cram, 'Keeping the Demos out of Liberal Democracy?: Participatory Politics, "Fake News" and the Online Speaker' (2019) 11 *J.M.L.* 113.

[15] *Whitney v California* 274 US 357 (1927) at 376.

[16] This view would deny free speech protection to Holocaust denial, see S Gey, 'The First Amendment and the Dissemination of Socially Worthless Untruths' (2008) 36 *Fla. St. U.L. Rev.* 1, 10.

An initial sense – borne out by the experience of the linked state and social media censorship witnessed during the COVID-19 public health crisis – is that we move in the UK too quickly to call for the removal of purportedly false materials concerning political and scientific disagreements. This may be attributable in part to an under-developed awareness in our domestic politics of the dangers of conferring on the state/corporate platforms the power to remove 'fake' news. Somewhat belatedly though nonetheless welcome, the House of Lords' Communications and Digital Select Committee raised the dangers of content regulation by social media platforms in 2021.[17] In general, however, few are willing to make the important argument that even demonstrably false speech about politics and public affairs might be worth defending under a free speech principle. Conversely, in our political culture there is considerable support for the idea that false statements on matters of public interest are likely to be *prima facie* unhelpful to informed democratic debate where the false statement is believed and used in taking a political stance. Few, I imagine, would disagree with Lord Hobhouse's trenchant statement in *Reynolds v Times Newspapers* concerning the publication of false statements on matters of public interest:

> There is no human right to disseminate information that is not true. No public interest is served by publishing or communicating misinformation. The working of a democratic society depends on the members of that society being informed not misinformed. Misleading people and the purveying as facts statements which are not true is destructive of the democratic society and should form no part of such a society.[18]

In the specific case of false statements about the transmission of viruses and their treatment, it seems clear that certain false statements where acted upon by others may tragically lead to higher levels of illness/death and place scarce public resources (healthcare) under severe strain. At the time of writing, the unfolding COVID-19 pandemic has seen calls from some for the denial of platforms to and/or prosecutions of those who disseminate untrue claims about the virus or who 'discredit' mainstream opinion.[19] The Labour Party has taken such an anti-pluralist stance.[20] In November 2020 it even called for criminal penalties to be inserted into emergency legislation and applied to social media companies who 'fail to stamp out dangerous anti-vaccination content'.[21] Epistemic democrats looking on

[17] HL Communications and Digital Select Committee, *Free for All? Freedom of Expression in the Digital Age* (2021–22) HL Paper 54, at para 111. The Committee's report will be picked up later in the chapter.

[18] [2001] 2 AC 127, 238.

[19] See, for example, prominent social media commentator Owen Jones, 'Giving people false hope about the pandemic isn't "balanced" – it's dangerous' at www.theguardian.com/commentisfree/2021/jan/01/false-hope-pandemic-dangerous-disinformation calling for the de-platforming of Professor Karol Sikora who criticised lockdown measures on account of their neglect of cancer patients.

[20] See https://labour.org.uk/press/labour-calls-for-action-to-tackle-coronavirus-disinformation-on-social-media-platforms/ Press Release (2020) 4 June.

[21] See https://labour.org.uk/press/labour-calls-for-emergency-legislation-to-stamp-out-dangerous-anti-vax-content/ Press Release (2020) 14 November. It is not clear if Labour believes the

would doubtless approve. As was argued in chapter two, the primacy accorded to truth-seeking and reliable outcomes in epistemic accounts means that the pursuit of truth and rational policy-making trump concerns about participatory inclusiveness, especially where some speech contributions would be said to hinder the search for truth and rational policy formulation. The COVID-19 crisis is plainly a difficult time to make free speech arguments that tackle the censoring impulses described above but this seems to be an opportune moment *precisely because* the arguments for censorship look strong. So how might a defender of republican self-government respond to such calls and to arguments for suppressing false claims about politics and societal affairs more generally?

A starting point is to recognise that the use of criminal and civil law sanctions to suppress speakers and/or disseminators will likely have harmful consequences of their own. An obvious harm caused by 'false speech' laws to the notion of self-government is that of reducing the flow of truthful claims into public discourse. The risks that speakers will self-censor and that some truthful claims will never see the light of day is ever present under such a prohibition. A bold speaker might be prepared to take a risk but the uncertainties that arise from not knowing how the respective ideological persuasions of prosecutors, judges and juries might combine and play out makes the decision to speak a hazardous one. Moreover, a criminal or civil law sanction for false statements relieves supporters of the relevant true statement from the civic responsibility from showing why the first speaker's statement is mistaken. Here we can recall Mill's claim that the collision between truth and error produces a 'clearer and livelier impression of truth'.[22] This holds I believe for statements about scientific matters, historical claims as well as for topics of political debate.

In this regard, Richard Feynman's point about the importance of doubt and uncertainty in science has become obscured. In *The Pleasure of Finding Things Out* Feynman maintained that

> when we know that we do actually live in uncertainty, then we ought to admit it; it is of great value to admit that we do not know the answers to certain questions. This attitude of mind – this attitude of uncertainty – is vital to the scientist, and it is this attitude of mind which the student must first acquire. It becomes a habit of thought. Once acquired, one cannot retreat from it anymore.[23]

The current dominant scientific explanation for a particular phenomenon is only provisionally valid until/unless a more convincing one comes along. This requires that sceptical scientists remain free to enquire and publish their doubts

criminal sanction should apply to statements questioning (i) whether compulsory vaccination should be introduced or (ii) whether all young people should be vaccinated before being allowed back into school. The extent of Labour's proposed prohibition has largely escaped critical commentary and shows no understanding of the dangers of viewpoint suppression by the state.

[22] *On Liberty* (London, Watts & Co., 1941) at 20, although it is entirely fair to remark that Mill does not have a popularly participative sphere in mind, but rather a form of intellectual jousting among educated elites.

[23] New York, Basic Books, 1999, at 248.

and advance their alternative explanations that get tested in their turn. Volokh makes the separate argument that the reason we endorse conventional viewpoints when the vast majority of us are non-experts in the matter under discussion is that we do so in the knowledge that others wishing to challenge the conventional viewpoint have been free to do so. Where, by contrast, orthodox viewpoints are shielded from challenge by criminal and civil laws, this assurance is absent and consequently public confidence in the orthodoxy may be shaken by the charge that the accepted account has not been opened up to the criticism of rival perspectives. Unifying these objections to governmental regulation of false statements is the republican argument that for popular control over the constituted authorities to be meaningful, governments must not be allowed to instill in the citizens a particular ideological viewpoint. If the state is permitted to do this, it can construct a citizen body in its own image. Such a construction would make it considerably easier for the present office holders and their ideological successors to remain in power in perpetuity.[24]

Some of the above concerns were apparent in the US Supreme Court ruling in *Alvarez v United States* where the Stolen Valor Act's prohibition on false speech concerning military honours was held on a 6–3 split to violate the First Amendment.[25] The Act made it a criminal offence to make false claims about the receipt of false military honours and set out an enhanced penalty for making false claims about the 'Congressional Medal of Honor'. Xavier Alvarez was attending his first public meeting of the Three Valley Water District Board (a state body) when he falsely claimed that he had received the Congressional Medal of Honor after being wounded 'many times by the same guy' whilst serving in the US Marines. As the Court report notes, Alvarez's lie was not designed to secure financial gain or improve his employment prospects. Rather it was told in order to bolster his credibility and status at meetings of the Board. He was charged and pleaded guilty to the offence of 'falsely represent(ing) himself … verbally or in writing, to have been awarded any decoration or medal authorized by Congress for the Armed Forces of the United States …' The Court's opinion was given by Kennedy J who observed that the Act had failed to specify the distinct harms that flowed from allowing people to make deliberately false claims about their military records. The prohibition applied at all times and to all contexts in which people spoke to each other, including whispered conversations at the dinner table among family or friends Furthermore, the evidential record failed to show any lowering of the public esteem in which actual recipients of the Medal of Honor were held as a consequence of Alvarez's lies. There were no identifiable victims of Alvarez's speech unlike cases of (i) fraudulent speech where the person to whom the lie is addressed suffers a financial loss

[24] See S Gey 'The First Amendment and the Dissemination of Socially Worthless Untruths' (2008) 36 *Fla. St. U.L. Rev.* 1 at 19 'In a democracy, government cannot be allowed to systematically indoctrinate its citizenry or instill in citizens a particular ideological bias, because to do so would essentially allow the government to undermine popular control by manufacturing its own consent.'

[25] 567 US 709 (2012).

after acting on the speaker's deliberate falsehood; or (ii) a lie told to secure an offer of employment where the employer makes an offer of employment on the basis of that deliberate falsehood. The state's legitimate interest in maintaining the integrity of the system of military honours could have been advanced through counterspeech and refutation of Alvarez's lies. The state could, for example, have maintained a publicly searchable database of Medal winners. It could have publicly called out Alvarez as a liar in this matter. Indeed, Alvarez had been ridiculed as a liar in a local newspaper. The criminal law response to Alvarez's lies was thus not narrowly tailored to intrude minimally on First Amendment freedoms. Were the statute upheld, the Court would be permitting the state to compile a list of topics about which the making of a false statement was a criminal offence. Kennedy was adamant that this Orwellian interpretation of state power was entirely alien to the First Amendment. 'Our constitutional tradition' he declared, 'stands against the idea that we need Oceania's Ministry of Truth'.[26]

The joint concurrence (Breyer and Kagan JJ) and the dissent (Alito J joined by Scalia and Thomas JJ) both stressed the importance of protecting more valuable speech by insulating certain types of false statement from criminal liability.[27] This is an argument that may be traced back to the seminal libel ruling in *New York Times v Sullivan*.[28] The idea in *New York Times v Sullivan* is that honest speakers on matters of public concern need the reassurance of a 'breathing space' in order to contribute to public discourse.[29] This is secured by setting exacting proof requirements on the plaintiff seeking redress for a defamatory statement, namely evidence of the speaker's knowing or reckless disregard for the falsity of his/her statement. The breathing space is achieved in the knowledge that some false claims will enter the public sphere purporting to be the truth. Conversely, failure to provide a breathing space makes it much more likely that truthful speakers will self-censor for fear of incurring liability upon speaking. Being the narrowest statement of First Amendment protection to issue from the Court, Alito's dissent is especially interesting especially to a non-US audience for its instrumental defence of the constitutional freedom to speak falsely about matters of public concern.

[26] ibid at 720.

[27] Or to put it another way, the falsity of a statement by itself could not be determinative of the question of constitutional protection for the statement. The concurrence applied an intermediate scrutiny standard and found that the Government had failed to show why a more narrowly defined Stolen Valor Act would not have equally safeguarded the legitimate state interest at issue.

[28] 376 US 254 (1964).

[29] For the dissent, Alvarez's lie did not pose a risk that more valuable speech about history, politics or science would be suppressed by the state (567 US 709 (2012) at 531–40). Accordingly the Stolen Valor Act did not intrude impermissibly into speech on matters of public concern protected under the First Amendment, see ibid at 755. I disagree with Alito's analysis on this point. It can be argued that regulating a speaker (who is a board member of a public authority and speaks at the public meeting in ways that seek to boost his/her credibility to other board/audience members) by outlawing false statements about his/her military record or other aspects of personal character *does* pose a risk to self-government. Such a speaker may feel constrained not to refer to matters of personal character that could be considered valuable to an audience assessment about the proper weight to attach to the speaker's arguments but in respect of which the speaker lacks convincing proof.

Reading domestic debates here in the UK leads one to conclude that this more circumspect defence of false speech has been overlooked, especially in the context of purportedly false statements about COVID-19.

Justice Alito's strategic defence of false speech is expressed to apply in matters of 'philosophy, religion, history, the social sciences, the arts and other matters of public concern'.[30] To penalise purportedly false speech in these areas would pose a 'grave and unacceptable risk' of censoring truthful statements.[31] One reason Alito gives why the Court should be alert to the suppression of such speech is quite simply that it is 'perilous to permit the state to be the arbiter of truth'.[32] Even where a broad scholarly consensus exists, extending constitutional protection to speech that challenges the consensus is valuable on account of the fact that today's accepted wisdom may turn out to be mistaken tomorrow. My own example in support of Alito's point relates to scientific theories about the spread of cholera in London in the mid-nineteenth century. The dominant account of the disease's progression in certain parts of the city asserted that foul-smelling particles of decaying matter that hung suspended in the air were responsible.[33] The airborne or miasma theory of infection continued to command official support through second and third waves of cholera deaths in 1848–49 and 1854.[34] In 1849 John Snow, a London physician, published a paper entitled *On the Mode of Communication of Cholera* which challenged the accepted account by arguing that the disease was in fact water-borne. His paper was largely ignored. Snow subsequently collected empirical data from a street in Soho which showed that a majority of cholera deaths occurred in houses where the inhabitants drew their water from the same water pump. When the handle of the pump was removed, it was revealed that a leaking sewer was contaminating the water supply. Tragically, it took more than a decade for the medical and scientific establishment to accept the water-borne theory of cholera transmission after a further deadly outbreak of the disease among people who drew their water from the Old Ford Reservoir at Bow Bridge, East London in 1866.

A further reason offered by Alito for denying the state the power to prescribe false statements goes to the core of the republican case for broad freedom of political expression. It relates to the temptation put before the state (ie current office holders) to use its powers for partisan political ends. Alito here is alluding to the possibility of viewpoint-motivated prosecutions or partisan executive enforcements of laws outlawing false statements:

> Statements about history illustrate this point. If some false statements about historical events may be banned, how certain must it be that a statement is false before the ban

[30] The list is extended to include 'science' at 755.
[31] ibid at 753.
[32] ibid.
[33] See further S Hempel, *The Medical Detective: John Snow, Cholera and the Mystery of the Broad Street Pump* (London, Granta, 2007), S Johnson, *The Ghost Map: The Story of London's Most Terrifying Epidemic* (US, Riverhead Books, 2006).
[34] For an account see the British Science Museum website at www.sciencemuseum.org.uk/objects-and-stories/medicine/cholera-victorian-london.

> may be upheld? And who should make that calculation? … the potential for abuse of power in these areas is simply too great.[35]

Wisely, an attempt to persuade the UK courts to arbitrate the truthfulness of contested claims regarding the public finances made during 2016 EU referendum campaign via the tort of misuse of public office was dismissed by the High Court in *Johnson v Westminster Magistrates Court* in 2019.[36] The clumsiness of the tort as a remedial mechanism for penalising untruthful political claims is fairly obvious. Interestingly, however, the court cited with approval the Electoral Commission's more principled view that

> In a referendum there are at least two sides of competing arguments, both of which are highly likely to be contested to some degree. Even official data can and will be presented by campaigners in a way that favours their argument – that is the nature of political campaigns. It will not always be possible to establish the truth about campaign claims in an independent truly objective sense.[37]

Viewpoint suppression, whether by elected office holders, state regulatory bodies, courts or, as is increasingly common, for-profit media platforms, should always send out the loudest of alarm signals. Yet, in today's political culture where ill-defined, speculative and sometimes entirely spurious claims of 'harmful speech' are often accepted at face-value during digital moral panics, the dangers posed by official or corporate viewpoint suppression to self-government are rarely flagged. I take Sunstein to concur with the seriousness of the threat to the republic posed by viewpoint suppression when he states in *#Republic*:

> Government should not be allowed to censor arguments and positions merely because it fears or disapproves of them. If officials are banning a disfavored viewpoint, they ought to be required to show, at the very least, that the viewpoint really creates serious risks that cannot be adequately combated with more speech. Officials ought also be required to explain, in convincing terms, why they are punishing one viewpoint and not its opposite.[38]

This seems to set out the case for a broadly inclusive freedom of political expression that would reassure dissenters and defenders of political pluralism alike. Sunstein's *Afterword* in the paperback edition of *#Republic* strikes a different tone however. There, the limits of popular participation in digitalised political debate emerge. Sunstein's overall aim is to stimulate thinking about how we overcome

[35] ibid at 754–55.

[36] See www.judiciary.uk/wp-content/uploads/2019/07/2019ewhc-1709-admin-johnson-v-westminster-mags-final.pdf (3 July) noting that Parliament had legislated to criminalise false statements of fact about a rival candidate's character or conduct but not, as here, in respect of statistical claims about savings to the Exchequer following a decision to leave the European Union.

[37] See www.electoralcommission.org.uk/sites/default/files/pdf_file/2016-EU-referendum-report.pdf at para 3.99 (2016). For commentary see J Horder, 'Criminal Law at the Limit: Countering False Claims in Elections and Referendums' (2021) 84 *M.L.R.* 429.

[38] *#Republic – Divided Democracy in the Age of Social Media* (2018, New Jersey, Princeton University Press) at 208–09.

the tendency of social media to further fragment the already polarised state of public spaces where different sets of users confine their interactions to sites and enclaves where they know they will find those who hold like-minded opinions. This is the so-called problem of 'echo chambers', where little or no meaningful interaction among people with different world views occurs.[39] What is needed in Sunstein's view is something that will force people to re-examine and challenge their own beliefs and views by nudging them towards an encounter with competing accounts. He applauds efforts by Facebook to reduce the possibility that users will believe falsehoods. The company's use of 'independent' fact checkers in flagging up that the veracity of certain content has been disputed and is likely to contain false statements enables

> users to learn that certain alleged facts have been disputed (and are likely falsehoods). Facebook also reworked its News Feed in positive ways, not by eliminating freedom of choice, but by giving people a better sense, with 'Related Articles,' of what is out there … They are steps in the right direction, both for individual lives and self-government.[40]

So far, this looks like a gentle shift towards a 'more speech' solution that avoids the censorship difficulties of outright bans on false statements.[41] There are, however, significant downsides from a democratic republican perspective with fact checking by Facebook. Chief among these is the absence of any connection to ideas of democratic accountability. None of us have had any say in the appointment of people to fact-checker positions in Facebook. None of us (and none of our elected representatives it would seem) have any direct role in the oversight of the actual performance of these fact checkers. Horder reports the additional concern that fact-checking in general has a credibility problem, namely it is considered by some to be a 'predominantly "liberal" political enterprise' lacking in political neutrality.[42] Then there is the selection of stories by Facebook to give its users a 'better sense' of what else is out there. This suggested additional news content does of course have the capacity to widen users' engagement with different stories. From a democratic self-government perspective, the crucial questions concern who enjoys the power of suggesting content and which types of content are being suggested

[39] Though it should be noted that evidence in social science literature for the existence of online echo chambers is rather limited, see the review study by R Fletcher and J Jenkins of the Reuters Institute for the Study of Journalism, Oxford University, 'Polarisation and the news media in Europe' at https://reutersinstitute.politics.ox.ac.uk/our-research/polarisation-and-news-media-europe.

[40] ibid at 264.

[41] There are separate issues which arise with 'more speech' solutions that are explored later in the chapter.

[42] J Horder 'Criminal Law at the Limit: Countering False Claims in Elections and Referendums' (2021) 84 *M.L.R.* 429 at 439–40 citing C Robertson, R Mourao and E Thorson 'Who Uses Fact-Checking Sites? The Impact of Demographics, Political Antecedents, and Media Use on Fact-Checking Site Awareness, Attitudes and Behaviour' (2020) 5 *Int. Jo. of Press Politics* 217. For an allegation that a major political party was seeking to mislead members of the public by posing as independent 'fact-checkers' during a General Election campaign, see F Perraudin, 'Twitter accuses Tories of misleading public with "factcheck" foray' (2019) *The Guardian* 20 November.

(and which content users are being steered away from). It would be wrong to assume, as Sunstein does, that Facebook's sense of what you or I should be reading correlates well or even approximately well to the range of reading that a diverse range of politically interested and active citizens would select or be curious about.

The latter point links to a deeper level problem with #Republic which is revealed in a profoundly elitist and technocratic approach to policymaking in which ordinary citizens are kept at distance from the locus of real power. Recall from chapter two that Sunstein's normative defence of deliberative decision-making is properly considered to fall within the civic republican strand of liberal democracy. That is to say, it is committed to appropriately designed deliberative structures which will yield up progressive and rational policies. The latter will be recognised as such and command an unforced consensus among reasonable, reflective and empathetic participants. To ensure the rational component of policymaking, Sunstein contends that, since the government 'insistently' faces technical problems these deliberations 'should be handled with the aid of technical specialists'.[43] Working groups of scientists, economists and lawyers are needed to guide the search for viable policy options. In the past, these groups have shown their ability to reach consensus through substantive argument and evidence-based discussion. As an example he cites the outputs of the 2009–10 US interagency group on the social cost of carbon which produced documentation and advice that was 'reasonable and highly professional'.[44] Sunstein's close personal knowledge of this matter was derived from his membership of the group. His broader involvement in the Obama Administration around this time saw his appointment as the first ever Head of the Office of Information and Regulatory Affairs.

If it could not be guessed at before, the paradox that Sunstein endorses at the conclusion of *#Republic* is now revealed. The 'best way' to overcome the fragmented nature of online political expression and secure active, plural, democratic self-government is for the state to give '*real* authority to its own specialists – people who know what they are doing' (emphasis added). By 'specialists' Sunstein is presumably referring to people such as, well, Sunstein and other mainstream academics drawn from Ivy League universities and Washington, DC think-tanks who have long enjoyed regular and privileged access to inner governmental circles where policy formation occurs. Remember too that these policy advisers would be advising existing office holders how best to promote and sustain a vibrant online democracy, a core feature of which is that challenges to the status quo and dominant, conventional thought must freely circulate among politically active and engaged citizens. Authentic advocates of open democratic politics ought to be sceptical of entrusting to the 'ins' and their advisers a decision about how much freedom of political expression to allow the 'outs'. In the final analysis, Sunstein's preference for expert-led deliberation has the hallmarks of a *post*-politics elitist/

[43] *#Republic* at 265.
[44] ibid at 266–67.

centrist managerial account of democracy that closes down forms of political contestation emanating from beyond the usual locales and dissenting from the core of orthodox liberal constitutional thinking.[45] To be blunt, this is a #sham-republic in which the usual elites frame political choices and where citizens' primary and passive function is to give democratic cover to the same by selecting from a limited menu of options put before them.

The Long Reach of UK Criminal Law into Online Political Discourse and Selected Comparisons Across Western Liberal Democracies

This section discusses (i) false statements on political matters, and (ii) false, materially misleading statements on political matters at election time.

False Statements on Political Matters in General

One of the major legal impediments to the development of a broadly participative democracy in the UK can be traced to the absence in our jurisprudence of one precept that is intimately connected to active self-government. The precept holds that valuable forms of political speech may be better protected by immunising certain types of false statement from criminal liability, the laws of libel and regulatory censure/removal. This is the notion of a 'breathing space' for expression about societal affairs first articulated by the US Supreme Court in *Sullivan v New York Times*.[46] It was expressly rejected by the House of Lords in *Reynolds v Times Newspapers* when the claim for a generic privilege for speech about public affairs was given short shrift.[47] *Post*-Reynolds, the role of domestic libel law in curtailing political expression has been thoroughly explored elsewhere.[48] In passing, it is clear that the continuing relevance of the Nicholls checklist to the construction of the statutory publication on a matter of public interest defence

[45] Expert-led formation of public opinion and policy of the sort endorsed by Sunstein places him closer to epistemic accounts of liberal democracy where the pursuit of truth and reasoned policy trumps the democratic legitimacy of more broadly participative processes which are always at risk of producing 'wrong' answers. This is something that is returned to in the pages below.

[46] 376 US 254 (1964).

[47] [1999] 3 WLR 1010, 1045 (Lord Cooke).

[48] See, for example, E Barendt, 'Balancing Freedom of Expression and the Right to Reputation: Reflections on Reynolds and Reportage' (2012) 63 *N.I.Q.R.* 59, 74 who concludes that whilst *Reynolds* can be seen as a 'laudable attempt to enhance freedom of expression … it hardly removes the chilling effect of libel laws'. And H Young, *Reynolds v Times Newspapers* (2018) at https://papers.ssrn.com/sol3/papers.cfm?abstract_id=3128626 at 8 et seq.

has served to perpetuate rather than disambiguate the common law's previous uncertainties.[49]

Instead of a commitment to robust political exchanges with its attendant risks of falsehoods entering the public domain, our political/legal culture is captured by Lord Hobhouse's superficially attractive, though far-reaching assertion in *Reynolds v Times Newspapers* noted earlier, namely that there can be no legitimate public interest in the publication or dissemination of misinformation. What was crucial to the proper working of democratic society was that its members were 'informed not misinformed'.[50]

A rather overlooked part of section 127(2) of the Communications Act 2003 puts a different version of Lord Hobhouse's postulation into statutory form. This states:

> A person is guilty of an offence, if for the purpose of causing annoyance, inconvenience or needless anxiety to another, he
>
> (a) sends, by means of a public electronic communications network a message he knows to be false;
>
> (b) causes such a message to be sent
>
> (c) …

It should also be noted that some online expression (including political expression is caught by the preceding subsection (s 127(1)(a)) of the 2003 Act which makes it an offence to 'send by means of a public electronic communications network a message or other matter that is grossly offensive or of an indecent, obscene or menacing character'.[51]

Although the use of the criminal law to enforce in section 127(1)(a) majoritarian standards of propriety in the tone of political discourse (and the accompanying incarceration of offenders) is highly problematic on its own terms,[52] the focus in

[49] As the *Explanatory Notes* to the Defamation Act 2013, s 4, Publication on a matter of public interest state: 'This section creates a new defence to an action for defamation of publication on a matter of public interest. It is based on the existing common law defence established in *Reynolds v Times Newspapers* and is intended to reflect the principles established in that case and in subsequent case law.' See www.legislation.gov.uk/ukpga/2013/26/notes/division/5/4.

[50] [2001] 2 AC 127, 238.

[51] Section 127(1)(a) 'menace' is not present where the message does not create fear or apprehension in those who receive the message or where those that receive could reasonably be expected to see that the message lacks menace see *Chambers v DPP* [2012] EWHC 2157 (Admin). Lord Bingham observed obiter in *DPP v Collins* [2006] UKHL 40 at para 6 that the purpose of s 127(1)(a) was to prohibit the online transmission on public networks of communications that 'contravene the basic standards of society'. A truthful statement on political matters might contravene this subsection and incur criminal liability where the speaker affronts standards of civility. Here, in the absence of a defence of truth, is the coercive force of the criminal law being used to punish those who tweet or post in bad taste, as defined by transient, majoritarian sentiment.

[52] One presumes that in instances of political expression deemed 'uncouth' according to prevailing/majority sensibilities, the courts would be alive to their duty to read down' the offence in line with Article 10 ECHR. See in this regard *Scottow v Crown Prosecution Service* [2020] EWHC 3421 (Admin). For reasons that were outlined in ch 2, it is probably mistaken to expect significant additional scope to be afforded to robust contributions to political debate.

this chapter is on the prohibition on false statements in section 127(2) in general and specifically at election time.

The breadth of the prohibition is worth noting. A direct message say on Twitter or Facebook that is unseen by people other than the recipient is caught. Moreover section 127(2) treats political communications containing known falsehoods in the same way as false statements of a non-political nature. Neither need the prosecution show that the speaker intended to deceive another person.[53] The purpose of prohibited communications must be to cause 'annoyance, inconvenience or needless anxiety' to another who might (but need not necessarily) be the subject of the false statement. In the context of political communications, the lack of a clear meaning of these terms might reasonably be considered to induce a degree of self-censorship on the part of speakers who challenge the conduct of politicians who might complain subsequently that their lives were inconvenienced by a speaker's false claims. The absence of a qualifying adjective such as 'serious' or 'substantial' would appear to make the prosecution's task a little more straightforward. The listed purposes themselves reveal in any case that the rationale behind the criminalisation of the targeted digital expression is not the pursuit of a more truthful public sphere but rather the avoidance of annoyance and discomfort to another. Where the evidence falls short of proving beyond reasonable doubt an intention to cause annoyance etc, then a knowingly false statement does not by itself create liability. It follows that Lord Hobhouse's mischief of a misinformed public sphere is not fully addressed by section 127(2).

Some measure of protection for speakers is created by the requirement on the prosecution to establish the sending of a 'knowing falsehood'. This is to put matters on a similar footing to the civil law defamation cases in the US under the public figure doctrine from *New York Times v Sullivan* where the claimant faces the burden of showing that the defendant spoke with knowledge of the falsehood or at the very least, is reckless as to the truth or falsity of the impugned statement.[54] The speaker who mistakenly believes in the truth of his/her false statement is beyond the ambit of section 127(2) even if the effect of their digital expression is to cause annoyance etc and is believed by others.

A trawl through the legal databases in England and Wales using section 127(2) of the 2003 Act as search terms did not disclose a single ruling. It thus remains unclear how often, if at all, the offence is charged and prosecuted domestically.

[53] The element of deceit will be present where the speaker intends that the recipient acts on the knowingly false statement. In political communications, this could be satisfied where the false statement about politician A is made in order to lower the esteem in which citizens hold A.

[54] For an account of how the initial scope of the 'actual malice' rule in *New York Times v Sullivan* was extended in various significant ways post 1964, see D Anderson, 'The Promises of New York Times v Sullivan' (2015) 20 *Roger Williams Uni. L. Rev.* 1. Explaining the defendant-friendly features of the ruling, Anderson points in particular to the discretion given to judges to overturn jury findings as to 'actual malice'. This can be done on the basis that the trial judge or appellate court concludes that no 'clear and convincing' evidence of knowing falsehood/reckless disregard for the truth had been established before the court.

False, Materially Misleading Statements at Election Time

Arguments for the legal control of false statements gain particularly strong purchase at the time of electoral and referendum contests between opposing political viewpoints. High-quality information (understood as comprising in part having the attributes of accuracy, relevancy and balance) is especially prized at these times.[55] Some argue that better-quality information is 'owed' to the electorate as a matter of 'respect'.[56] This may include the claim that voters are entitled not to be manipulated by deliberate falsehoods.[57] Arguments for suppression of false statements invoke deeper level commitments to protecting the integrity of the electoral process. It could be argued that preserving the autonomous choices of voters is an essential component in that which makes up the integrity of democratic elections. Voters' autonomy (in the sense of being able to make unforced, rational political choices at the ballot box) is undermined when they are intentionally misled by speakers.[58] Others (epistemic democrats) would point to the systemic gains of better outcomes in terms of choosing on an informed basis the more 'rational' set of policies/referendum option.

UK law on this matter is found in a provision of a pre-Internet era statute. Section 106 of the Representation of the People Act 1983 makes it a criminal offence (termed an 'illegal practice') 'before or during an election' to publish a 'false statement of fact in relation to a candidate's personal character or conduct … unless he can show that he had reasonable grounds for believing and did believe the statement to be true'.[59]

The 1983 Act's scope in ensuring that voters do not cast their ballots or otherwise engage in political expression on the strength of a falsehood is thus quite limited. In its own terms, the actionable lie aimed at in section 106 is confined to factual statements about the personal character or conduct of a candidate, not about the candidate's political views or the political stances of the party he/she represents. Leaving aside some difficult definitional questions about the boundaries between (i) statements relating to the personal character or conduct and those that concern policy matters,[60] and (ii) statements of fact and those

[55] A Renwick and M Palese, *Doing Democracy Better: How Can Information and Discourse in Election and Referendum Campaigns in the UK Be Improved* (London, UCL Constitution Unit, 2019) ch 1 noting that false predictive statements were made by both Leave and Remain sides in the June 2016 EU Referendum.

[56] A Renwick and M Palese ibid at 7.

[57] J Rowbottom, 'Lies, Manipulation and Elections – Controlling False Campaign Statements' (2012) 32 *O.J.L.S.* 507 esp 512–16.

[58] ibid at 524.

[59] As Rowbottom points out, aside from a criminal penalty, additional civil law sanctions apply to convicted people. They are barred from standing for Parliament or holding elective office for three years after conviction, ss 160, 173. Most seriously of all, such people are unable to vote in parliamentary or local elections for a period of three years after being reported for an illegal practice.

[60] For an attempt to draw the distinction, see the leading case of *R (Woolas) v Parliamentary Election Court* [2010] EWHC 3169.

of opinion,[61] it is nonetheless hard to see how this section promotes electoral integrity. After all, it is clear that a deliberate lie about what the candidate's party has done whilst in government or what its current manifesto commits the party to doing if elected again evades the penal reach of section 106.[62] Yet, a commitment to voter autonomy would require this type of statement (where considered by some electors to be credible) to be proscribed. Indeed, voter autonomy is equally threatened by the honest but false speaker who inaccurately states (i) what a candidate's policy is on a particular topic, or (ii) that the character of a candidate is flawed in some respect.[63] Such a speaker commits no offence under section 106, but it is plain that the free unconstrained choice of the voters is undermined here if the false statement is believed just as much as in the case of the intentionally misleading and manipulative speaker.

If a concern for the integrity of the electoral process truly underpinned our system of prohibited statements, the intention of the speaker would be wholly irrelevant to the matter of liability. On this view, liability ought to turn instead upon the *effect* of the inaccurate statement on voters. The outcomes in a number of constituencies could be impacted by a series of honest though misleading statements about national party policy and/or candidates' policy stances.[64] Equally if the false statement carried little or no credibility, it might asked why the law should become involved at all? Here a thorny epistemological issue arises: how should the precise effect of erroneous statements on election outcomes be known? What sort of evidence might be needed to discharge the burden on the state to prove that the erroneous statement was acted upon? What also of predictive claims about what a candidate will/will not do if elected to office? Do such predictions constitute statements of fact or opinion?

The pursuit of electoral integrity (especially as it relates to electoral outcomes) takes us back to Lord Hobhouse's support for widely crafted restrictions on

[61] This is a difficulty with which libel law has wrestled unsatisfactorily in relation to the fair comment defence. The dividing line between factual statements and those of opinion remains disputed. See in this regard *Waterson v Lloyd and Carr* [2013] EWCA Civ 136 concerning claims made by Liberal Democrats in Eastbourne about the sitting Conservative MP during the 2010 General Election. The MP had been described as an 'expenses scandal MP'. There two of the three judges in the Court of Appeal held that the reference to a scandal was one of comment, since it was an opinion about how much public money the MP had claimed. The dissenting Court of Appeal judge and the High Court judge both ruled the impugned statement to be one of fact in respect of which the fair comment defence was not available. By way of comment, one can see all too easily the likelihood of self-censorship among speakers made nervous by this uncertain application of the law.

[62] It is difficult to know whether a predictive statement about what a candidate will/will not do if elected to office constitutes a statement of fact or opinion for the purposes of liability under s 106. Consider the claim that voters should think carefully before voting for X since she is unlikely to be able to devote 100% of her time to her elected duties.

[63] Here, of course, the burden of proof in s 106 shifts to the honest but mistaken speaker which may induce a degree of self-censorship among those speakers with an understanding of this shift.

[64] The misleading statement might even be craftily constructed in a way that avoids saying anything that is strictly false, see A Renwick, M Palese and J Sargeant, 'Information in Referendum Campaigns: How Can It Be Improved?' (2020) 56 *Representation* 521, 528.

statements which mislead or are untrue and which are, on his somewhat melodramatic view, 'destructive of the democratic society and should form no part of such a society'.[65] Supporters of the Hobhouse position (which it should be emphasised is so comprehensively framed as to extend outside election times to political discourse at all times) might claim that prohibitions on false statements of fact bite evenly across the political spectrum and do not favour one party or viewpoint more than a rival party/viewpoint. Whilst this is true as a matter of legal formality, it invites a potentially messy set of judicial interventions during political campaigns (and beyond) in a context where it is probable that expensively lawyered political organisations would fare better than their less well-endowed political rivals, at the very least in terms of access to the courts.[66] There is also a question of institutional competence that cautions against overzealous interventions by the judicial branch. Lord Hobhouse's enthusiasm for expunging false statements of fact from the public arena risks drawing the courts into difficult and politically contested matters that they have no especial expertise in assessing and where court rulings might tend to lower overall levels of confidence in judicial independence.

The wisdom of imposing criminal liability for negligent misstatement in such cases has been rightly doubted by the US Supreme Court.[67] In *Cantwell v Connecticut* a unanimous US Supreme Court indicated that, unlike Hobhouse, it had no wish to become embroiled in judging the accuracy of factual claims made in heated political discourse.

> In the realm of religious faith, and in that of political belief, sharp differences arise. In both fields the tenets of one man may seem the rankest error to his neighbor. To persuade others to his own point of view, the pleader, as we know, at times, resorts to exaggeration, to vilification of men who have been, or are, prominent in church or state, and even to false statement.[68]

Nonetheless it is true that other liberal democratic jurisdictions do confront the problem of political misinformation during election campaigns via the coercive force of the criminal law.[69] South Australia for example criminalises the making

[65] [2001] 2 AC 127, 238.

[66] eg a less well-resourced party without access to senior legal counsel might self censor in circumstances where a well-resourced rival might enjoy greater legal clarity about how to keep within the boundaries of the law.

[67] See thus J Rowbottom, 'Lies, Manipulation and Elections – Controlling False Campaign Statements' (2012) 32 *O.J.L.S.* 507 at 529 who rightly points to the chilling effect of such a rule in cases where the speaker considers that he/she may lack evidential proof to support the claim to a legal standard. In this scenario Rowbottom argues that a penal sanction would go 'beyond what is required to address harms to the electoral process'.

[68] 310 US 296 (1940) Roberts J at 310 and cited with approval by Brennan J in *New York Times v Sullivan* 376 US 254 (1964).

[69] In New Zealand, it is an offence punishable with a prison sentence of two years or a fine of $40,000 to commit a corrupt practice. Section 199A of the Electoral Act 1993 extended the definition of a corrupt practice to knowingly making a false and material statement in a 67-hour period that stretches from two days prior to the election and extends to the end of Election Day itself. Liability arises where the speaker intends that the false statement will influence the vote of any elector. The ambit of

of an inaccurate, materially misleading statement of purported fact in electoral advertisements. Section 113 of the Electoral Act 1985 (as amended) states:

> A person who authorises, causes or permits the publication of an election advertisement (an advertiser) is guilty of an offence if the advertisement contains a statement purporting to be a statement of fact that is inaccurate and misleading to a material extent.

The Electoral Commissioner is separately empowered under this statute to request removal of the advertisement or, where the request is ignored, can seek an order from the state Supreme Court requiring its removal and a published retraction. The Electoral Act 1985 applies to online and printed/broadcast statements. Here, unsurprisingly, the boundary between regulated statements of purported fact and unregulated statements of opinion has generated disagreement.[70] Fears also exist about the potential for strategic use of spurious complaints to the Electoral Commission to derail another candidate's campaign.[71] As for any perception of bias on the part of the Commission towards or against a party, Renwick and Palese's review of recent campaigns in South Australia found that the main Labour and Liberal Parties had no criticism of the Commission on this score.[72] What Renwick and Palese do not appear to have considered is how non-mainstream parties view the operation of the rules. No evidence is provided on the point. Non-mainstream parties might be anxious that their relatively low profiles and minority-peripheral status would lead regulators to have fewer qualms about taking a more robust approach to those parties' election statements. In the absence of supporting evidence however, this remains a matter of speculation only.

At the level of principle, allocating to appointed Commissioners and courts the task of deciding which statements in electoral contests are truthful and thus fit to be put before the sovereign electorate is impossible to reconcile with the republican commitment to popular self-government. This is especially so in respect of the regulation of statements made during the election about party policy. In South Australia, the Electoral Commissioner and the Deputy Electoral Commissioner are appointed by the Governor General after consultation with both a parliamentary committee and the political parties represented in the state legislature.[73]

s 199A was expanded by the High Court in *Peters v Electoral Commission* [2015] NZHC 394 when it ruled that statements published before the start of the 67-hour period would infringe s 199A where they remained available for reading/viewing within the 67-hour period. This poses a particular problem for previously published online content that needs to be taken down before the last two days of campaigning.

[70] See the opinion of the Attorney-General of South Australia as cited in A Renwick and M Palese, *Doing Democracy Better: How Can Information and Discourse in Election and Referendum Campaigns in the UK Be Improved?*, where he described the boundary as a 'fairly contested piece of turf' at 27.

[71] Fears that the system might be 'gamed' through spurious/speculative allegations of falsity would apply *a fortiori* in more populous and partisan democracies.

[72] ibid at 28 although the authors do note the isolated example in 2014 of former Liberal Party leader Isobel Redmond who described the then Electoral Commissioner as 'utterly corrupt'. The claim was later withdrawn.

[73] Electoral Act 1985, s 5 (South Australia).

Affirmatory resolutions from both houses of legislature recommending the candidates are also needed before the Governor-General is able to confirm the nominees. It is thus quite clear from the foregoing that existing public office holders in the Parliament enjoy control over the selection of the Commissioners who in turn decide to an important degree what kinds of political claim and counterclaim may be made in the heat of an election campaign. An observer might fairly conclude that the 'ins' are accorded the crucial role in determining how the speech of the 'outs' will be policed. This does not augur well for democratic openness as Ely and others understand the term.

Of course, the 'outs' may try to circumvent any such incumbency-favouring by forms of political advertising that steer clear of unambiguous factual claims. So instead of asserting that last year public debt levels were at x per cent of GDP or that the Government's response to COVID has caused the premature deaths of 135,000 people, an anti-government advertisement make confine itself to inviting the reader to agree with the opinion that 'public debt levels are unsustainable' or that 'the levels of premature Covid-related deaths is a morally damning indictment of the Government's public health programme'.[74] The law does not after all require the advertisement to make explicit the factual basis of the opinion. If the purpose of the South Australian prohibition on inaccurate and misleading advertisements is to facilitate more informed decision-making, the ongoing freedom to make statements of opinion without an explicit factual grounding may well undermine this objective. The matter becomes even more complicated when, as in the case of COVID-19 virus, the state of factual knowledge about many aspects of the virus has been developing as new empirical studies shed new light on/challenge previous assumptions about the virus.

Defenders of the South Australian system make a number of questionable claims regarding the impact of these draconian rules and reveal themselves to have a narrow conception of meaningful political participation. These claims are, however, valuable in shedding light on the sort of truncated, unrepublican polity that the current rules prop up. Jaensch, a strong supporter of false political advertising laws, believes that they promote informed voting on the basis of quality information. He conceives participation in political discourse on a par with consumers' selection of products in the world of commercial advertising. On his view, electors should enjoy the equivalent level of protection from false statements as consumers do when buying shoes or soap.[75] This is a model

[74] The close and complex interrelationship between the factual and normative content of statements has predictably led some Habermassian scholars to push for 'value-checking' alongside factual checking as a means of enriching the public sphere along 'epistemically friendly' Enlightenment lines. At the moment, there are no calls for a legally established and enforced system of value checking, See further for a troubling defence of value-checking D Yarrow, 'From Fact-checking to Value-checking: Normative Reasoning in the New Public Sphere' (2021) *Pol. Quarterly* 6 May at https://doi.org/10.1111/1467-923X.12999.

[75] Cited in A Renwick and M Palese, *Doing Democracy Better: How Can Information and Discourse in Election and Referendum Campaigns in the UK Be Improved?* at 28. The notion of the citizen as a *speaker* who might wish to communicate his/her own views to others is noticeably missing from this account.

of citizens as consumerist clients of the menu of options offered by the parties, exchanging their commodified votes in return for a promised set of benefits. The insistence on truthful advertising pitches is intended to safeguard an honest set of exchanges between patrons and clients. Another consultee cited by Renwick and Palese, journalist Tom Richardson, is quoted as saying that '(n)o one sees an issue' with the restrictions. Denying that the rules have a chilling effect on free speech, Richardson added confidently that the law 'forces people to be a bit less strident … the benefit is that politicians understand that they can't peddle blatant falsehoods'.[76] It is, of course, impossible to know whether the rules have actually inhibited all speakers from communicating via a political advertisement so Richardson's confidence lacks an evidential basis and looks somewhat misplaced.[77] As for the alleged benefit of reduced stridency, what if a section of the population has a legitimate grievance? Is this group not entitled to express itself forcefully about the lack of redress? Perhaps stridency is sometimes warranted in political disputes. Is Richardson advocating that political disputes in the public sphere be conducted as *per* the etiquette rules applicable in university seminars? Contrary to the positive endorsements just cited however, an overview by Renwick and Palese concluded that, whilst the rules were 'widely trusted and regarded as legitimate', they had only a 'limited impact on the quality of information or the wider debate'.[78] This conclusion cannot be considered a ringing endorsement of South Australia's criminal prohibition on false statements at election time.

What if, for the sake of argument, it is assumed in a sort of Panglossian way that the provisions enacted in South Australia did meet their objective of eliminating unverified, possibly false statements from public discourse.[79] At its most basic level, when the legal ability to communicate politically via advertisements is made conditional upon making verifiably true claims as judged by state officials, any pretense to have a self-governing democracy must be abandoned. Speakers in republican democracies have to remain free to make opinionated claims without being called upon to verify the truthfulness of any underlying premise. As Post argues on grounds of democratic legitimacy, the state cannot be allowed to construct the public sphere in terms that insist upon notions of reliability usually

[76] ibid at 29.

[77] This criticism also applies to Renwick and Palese who similarly claim that the South Australian rules 'constrain politicians from making claims that are demonstrably false', ibid. It is interesting that Renwick and Palese's conception of those constrained by s 113 of the Election Act 1985 is limited to 'politicians'. There seems no awareness that NGOs, community groups and private individuals might wish to place political advertisements during election time and be caught by the prohibition in that section. The passive notion of the 'voter' implicit in Renwick and Palese is antithetical to the idea of republican citizenship and sits more comfortably with liberal elitist accounts of democracy.

[78] *Doing Democracy Better: How Can Information and Discourse in Election and Referendum Campaigns in the UK Be Improved?* See specifically 22–30.

[79] On the view of Renwick et al, campaigners may well be able to express themselves in ways that deliberately create a misleading impression without saying anything that is strictly false, thereby circumventing existing legal controls. See A Renwick, M Palese and J Sargeant, 'Information in Referendum Campaigns: How Can It Be Improved?' (2020) 56 *Representation* 521 at 528–29.

associated with expert knowledge.[80] Democratic self-government (ie citizen authorship of the laws) does not presume to have attained any unalterable or uncontested truths. It exists as the permanent site of revisability and changing laws and policies. That yesterday's best policy is open to re-evaluation and replacement by today's citizens is what confers democratic legitimacy upon systems of self-government. Volokh accepts that lies will often be devoid of constitutional value but separately points to the dangers of overreach into more valuable expression where law prohibits deliberate falsehoods about current affairs, history and science. Where the state is able to bring prosecutions against speakers for making deliberately false statements, this could also inhibit the making of true statements and assertions of opinion.[81]

Fact Checkers as More Speech Solutions

Fact-checking organisations are now an established extra-legal feature of election/referendum campaigns in the UK and elsewhere. Fact-checking has also been deployed during the COVID-19 pandemic. The purpose of such checks is to examine the accuracy of statements made in the political realm and inform audiences of the check outcomes. It is hoped in this way to confront perceived instances of misinformation and disinformation. In 2019, Renwick and Palese stated that four out of the six UK fact-checking organisations had close ties to broadcast media such as the BBC, ITV and Channel 4.[82] The BBC set up Reality Check in 2010 to monitor statements made across social media platforms in the 2010 General Election. It continued to fact check in the subsequent General Elections and the EU referendum. ITV used the services of an independent organisation FullFact.org to check the accuracy of statements made by Boris Johnson and Jeremy Corbyn in the 2019 General Election. Reality Check now exists as a permanent feature of the BBC's online presence at www.bbc.co.uk/news/reality_check. A glance at the website on 15 September 2021 revealed fact-checking investigations into claims inter alia: (i) made by the candidates in the Californian Governorship race; (ii) the Delta variant of COVID-19; (iii) Boris Johnson's claims about numbers of police officers in active service. The stated aim of the Director of BBC News James Harding was to 'fact check the most popular outliers on Facebook, Instagram and other social media … Where we see deliberately misleading stories masquerading as news, we'll publish a *Reality Check* that says so'.[83]

Empirical research into the impact of fact-checking organisations is at an early stage at the present time and so it is difficult to know how effective they are singly

[80] R Post, *Democracy, Expertise, Academic Freedom* at 31.
[81] E Volokh, 'Fake News and the Law, from 1798 to Now' (2016) *Washington Post* 9 December.
[82] *Doing Democracy Better: How Can Information and Discourse in Election and Referendum Campaigns in the UK Be Improved?* at 42–43.
[83] J Jackson, 'BBC Sets up Team to Debunk Fake News', *The Guardian* (2017) 12 January.

or combined in achieving their raison d'être of nudging citizens towards better-quality information. As they function in the main to flag up rather than remove content considered to be misleading or inaccurate,[84] they cannot be said to directly narrow viewpoint diversity. However, judged by their stated goal of improving the quality of political information by undermining the credibility of unsubstantiated or factually disproven claims, some of the academic literature points to a possible 'backfire effect'. In the case of the BBC's Reality Check this might occur when the broadcaster tells its viewers that a particular politician or group is misleading the public. The 'backfire effect' refers to the likelihood not only that the fact check will be dismissed by those already disinclined to trust the BBC but also that such people will come to hold even more firmly to the views of the fact-checked speaker.[85]

Then there are the issues that go to the democratic legitimacy and transparency of fact-checking organisations. Foremost among them is Juvenal's *quis custodiet ipsos custodes* question. How and by whom are the performances of fact-checking organisations monitored and audited? What if fact checkers spend their time looking primarily for materials that tend to challenge official accounts with the consequence that untrue stories that bolster official narratives are less likely to be flagged? Are in-house fact checkers such as Reality Check at liberty to highlight factual errors in other BBC output? What level of democratic oversight of purportedly independent organisations exists in Parliament? What are the qualifications and backgrounds of those people who purport to be able to distinguish high-quality information from misleading, uncontextualised and deliberately inaccurate statements? How and by whom are such groups funded? Facebook's fact checkers have been accused of pursuing their own political agendas when reviewing and tagging certain news stories. A number of news organisations reported an admission by Nick Clegg, Facebook vice-chairman that the personal biases of fact checkers might have resulted in tagging of certain news stories as false or their relegation in the order of search results at the time of US Presidential Election in November 2020.[86] This suggests that some fact checkers may have ventured beyond merely pointing out perceived instances of misleading factual content and actually censored/rendered much less visible content considered by them to be misleading.

[84] See, however, the examples of removed or relegated content discussed below.

[85] B Nyhan and J Reifler, 'When Corrections Fail: The Persistence of Political Misperceptions' (2010) 32 *Pol. Behaviour* 303. Of course, BBC journalism has not always matched the high standards of honesty and accuracy that *Reality Check* claim to be monitoring in other sections of the media, see Lord Dyson's Report into the BBC's serious failings in the Martin Bashir/Princess Diana interview broadcast on *Panorama* in 1995 at http://downloads.bbc.co.uk/aboutthebbc/reports/reports/dyson-report-20-may-21.pdf. The report found that '(w)ithout justification, the BBC fell short of the high standards of integrity and transparency which are its hallmark …' at 5.

[86] See thus www.fr24news.com/a/2021/06/facebook-fact-checkers-could-be-politically-biased-nick-clegg-admits.html and https://thepinkreportnews.com/2021/06/15/report-facebook-vp-nick-clegg-admits-their-fact-checkers-possibly-politically-biased/.

State Regulation of Contentious Expression – OFCOM and the Coronavirus Disinformation Unit

State regulation of content and viewpoint expression in the broadcast media is entrusted to OFCOM – the Office for Communication.[87] The state agency has a duty under section 319 of the Communication Act 2003 to set standards in a Code of Practice that appear best calculated to ensure that news is presented with due impartiality and accuracy.[88] Members of the public must be given adequate protection from offensive and harmful material in broadcast services.[89] The requirement of due impartiality is explained further in section 320(2) of the same Act to apply to matters of political or industrial controversy and current public policy. This is intended to ensure that service providers are free from 'undue bias'.

During the COVID-19 pandemic OFCOM has created resources on its webpage to help people 'navigate news and information' about the virus so that 'common misconceptions and harmful claims' can be debunked.[90] Clicking on the link 'Fact checking and debunking' opens a page with further links to fact-checking organisations such as Full Fact in the UK and The Poynter Institute and CNN in the US. Full Fact, for example, warns users to be wary of anonymous online speakers and steers citizens towards official sources such as the World Health Organization, The European Centre for Disease Prevention and Control and Johns Hopkins University in the US. Full Fact reminds users that 'Covid-19 is still a new disease and there is a lot we don't yet know about it, and so be wary of anything that seems to be making a definite claim about the illness without clear evidence'.[91]

It also tells users to be aware that the purveyors of false news will try to manipulate users' feelings and try to provoke states of anger or worry. Users should resist the temptation to share the material with other users before assessing the credibility of a particular post/blog etc.

It is known that the UK Government set up a cross-departmental 'Coronavirus Disinformation Unit' in March 2020 that was pledged to identify and respond to instances of disinformation linked to the virus. The unit is based in the Department of Digital, Culture, Media and Sport and works closely with a rapid response unit based in the Cabinet Office and No 10 Downing Street.[92] The then Secretary of State Oliver Dowden was quoted as saying that 'defending the country from misinformation (sic) and digital interference is a top priority'.[93] Somewhat paradoxically,

[87] The BBC and Channel 4 are subject to additional content obligations laid down in respectively the Charter and Licence and Agreement (BBC) and (Channel 4).

[88] Section 319(2)(c).

[89] Section 319(2)(f).

[90] See www.ofcom.org.uk/research-and-data/media-literacy-research/coronavirus-resources.

[91] See https://fullfact.org/health/how-to-fact-check-coronavirus/.

[92] Press Release www.gov.uk/government/news/government-cracks-down-on-spread-of-false-coronavirus-information-online (2020) 30 March.

[93] A Scroxton, 'DCMS to Oversee Coronavirus Disinformation Unit' *Computer Weekly* (2020) 9 March at www.computerweekly.com/news/252479721/DCMS-to-oversee-coronavirus-disinformation-unit.

it is rather difficult to discover information about how the unit has been operating. A search through news databases on the BBC did not reveal any stories. A similar search on *The Guardian* database produced a handful of stories about the unit's creation but nothing subsequently by way of evaluation of its performance.[94] An article published in *The Guardian* within a month of the unit's inception stated that once the 'false narratives' were identified by unnamed experts drawn from government and the tech sector, the unit coordinated with other Whitehall departments to 'find a way to tackle the content if it cannot be taken down. This can include a direct rebuttal on social media and ensuring public health campaigns are promoted through reliable sources'.[95]

The ordering of responses is significant here. Removal and taking down of problematic content is the preferred option for by government officials, followed by consideration of 'more speech' options. In addition, the government's *Don't Feed the Beast* public information campaign encouraged social media users to question more pro-actively what they encountered online.

At the time of writing in early 2002, almost two years after its creation, the House of Commons Select Committee on Digital, Culture, Media and Sport was yet to make the Unit the subject of inquiry. It is known however that individual civil servants enjoy 'trusted flagger' status with Twitter and other social media platforms which means that, once raised, official concerns about false claims are prioritised for response.[96] From the perspective of democratic legitimacy, the absence of scrutiny of content removal requests and responses is deeply concerning. Unless some mechanisms of public oversight are trained on government, fact checkers and tech platforms, it cannot be known whether, in addition to preventing the dissemination of possibly harmful false claims about unproven treatments,[97] governments are self-interestedly removing from the public sphere other sorts of materials. It is disappointing too that academic research appears largely unconcerned by the potential for executive-prompted, tech company misuse of removal powers. Research is needed on the governmental structures (and regulatory agencies' structures such as OFCOM) through which problematic material is identified, removal requests made and decisions taken by social media platforms. This would provide greater insights into the relationship between government and the social media corporations. Currently there is no transparency in the form of readily-accessible data about how these inter-connected, speech-inhibiting actors variously function.

[94] K Proctor, 'UK Anti-fake News Unit Dealing with up to 10 False Coronavirus Articles a Day' (2020) *The Guardian* 30 March.

[95] ibid.

[96] For details and critical commentary of practices associated with the 'trusted flagger' category on YouTube see F Stjernfelt and A Lauritzen, *Your Post has Been Removed – Tech Giants and Freedom of Speech* (2020 Springer, Berlin) at 101–03.

[97] Even then, it would need to be shown that counter-speech solutions pointing out the absence of empirical evidence to support claims that gargling with water for 15 seconds or holding one's breath for a similar period will confer immunity from the virus.

It is known, however, that OFCOM issued a warning to ITV in respect of one of its broadcast programmes, *This Morning*, after receiving hundreds of complaints about an item that contained what it described as 'potentially harmful' comments.[98] The offending section of the broadcast in April 2020 concerned the dissemination of false statements about COVID-19, linking it to the roll-out of 5G technology. The programme's consumer editor referred to 'fake news that is travelling around at the moment … (that) the coronavirus is man-made … it is designed to cull the population, and the lock-down is just a device for the roll out of 5G'.

She went on to note recent acts of vandalism and arson against 5G masts that had occurred. The programme's main anchor Eamonn Holmes then responded:

> The only thing I would say, I totally agree with everything you are saying but what I don't accept is mainstream media slapping that down as not true when they do not know it's not true. No-one should attack or damage or do anything like that. But it is very easy to say it is not true because it suits the state narrative. That's all I would say as someone with an enquiring mind.[99]

OFCOM assessed the matter to see whether the broadcast had infringed Rule 2.1 of its Code, which requires 'adequate protection for members of the public from … harmful and/or offensive material'. It concluded that Holmes' statement had

> the potential to cause harm because it could have undermined people's trust in the views being expressed by the authorities on the Coronavirus and the advice of mainstream sources of public health information. In assessing the potential degree of harm, we took into account that Eamonn Holmes did also state that 'No-one should attack or damage' mobile phone masts. However, we considered that his statement overall potentially risked fuelling a volatile situation surrounding the 5G claims.[100]

This risk was exacerbated because Holmes was a well-known presenter. His comments, the regulator said, amounted to an 'ill-judged' intervention. However, when considered alongside the consumer editor's 'strong rejection' of the conspiracy, there had been adequate protection for viewers from Holmes' potentially harmful statements.[101] OFCOM's argument that a loss of trust in the views being expressed by the authorities carries with it the potential to cause harm is striking. Judged on its own terms, it is difficult to see why Holmes' statement merited this response. All Holmes actually said was that he was not sure whether the unevidenced claims made about the virus as reported by the programme's consumer editor were true or not. It turns out he was right to be unsure, at least as far as one of those claims was concerned. There is now a body of scientific opinion that is looking into the possibility that the virus was man-made and did leak from a laboratory in Wuhan.

[98] See www.ofcom.org.uk/__data/assets/pdf_file/0021/194403/assessment-decision-this-morning-itv-13-apr-2020.pdf.

[99] ibid at 2.

[100] ibid at 5.

[101] ibid at 6.

In May 2021, President Biden ordered US officials to investigate the possibility of a man-made virus having leaked from Wuhan.[102] I return to this matter below when discussing social media censorship of online expression.

A judicial review challenge brought against OFCOM's Code and accompanying Guidance Notes on freedom of expression grounds failed in December 2020.[103] Justice Fordham ruled that the proper meaning of the Guidance Notes accompanying the Code was that statements which challenged official narratives (including claims that were potentially harmful or inaccurate in the sense of reducing public compliance with public health) measures could still be aired. Paragraph 26 of the Guidance Notes states that broadcasters are 'strongly advised to take particular care' when broadcasting materials that challenge official narratives. From this provision Fordham J held that potentially harmful and inaccurate claims could still be broadcast, provided the broadcaster contextualised these claims and allowed them to be challenged.

At some level, the High Court's acknowledgment that claims at odds with official narratives may still be broadcast should be welcomed. Much less encouraging is the finding that the unambiguous steer in the Guidance away from broadcasting such claims at all was in the High Court's view beyond legal reproach. The judgment's implicit conclusion that state narratives on topics of great moment should be privileged in broadcast media is unsettling. This is particularly so in the specific context of emerging and disputed scientific understandings about the spread of COVID-19 and the efficacy of public health measures designed to slow its progress through the population. When the scientific community itself is divided about how best to combat the virus, the state may well have to choose sides and follow one body of scientific opinion and reject the rival perspective of another. The concern about OFCOM's decisive favouring of the state narrative (to the point where a dutiful repeating of the account favoured by the government does not by OFCOM's rules require a broadcaster to indicate the existence of a rival scientific perspective) is that it diminishes the chances of proper debate and government accountability. When the scientists who doubt the efficacy of mask wearing or the overall public health gains of lockdowns are kept away from the broadcast media, this assumes the infallible wisdom of the current, officially preferred view. Moreover, the practical demands on broadcasters entailed in the admonition 'be strongly advised to take particular care' must only dampen the endeavours of investigative journalists to challenge state claims or, more likely still, cow their editors into refusing to broadcast such material for fear of being deemed by OFCOM not to have taken 'particular care'. The High Court's ruling thus promotes an unknowable degree of self-censorship by broadcasters in respect of critical analyses of government claims. In the longer term, it diminishes public confidence in the scientific basis of official policy for the reason given by Volokh

[102] D Sevastopolou 'How Biden Came Round to the Wuhan Lab-leak Theory' (2021) 31 May at www.ft.com/content/923e0256-7f7e-43ef-b4fe-64c066b8b70b.
[103] [2020] EWHC 3390.

cited earlier in this chapter. As non-scientists, the majority of us can have greater confidence in mainstream scientific claims when we know that dissenting scientific opinion has had the opportunity to articulate publicly the reasons and evidence for disputing the mainstream understanding.

The State as a Producer of False Statements

Amidst current anxieties about 'fake news' and democratised online speech producing a degraded public sphere, it is possible to overlook the state's role throughout history as a major and powerful producer of false and deliberately misleading statements. The distortions in public debate and weakened political accountability induced directly by state propaganda (alongside the non-disclosure of official information) has been an ever-present feature of all political systems including western liberal democratic politics. In terms of its disastrous impact on regional security and Middle East politics, the Blair Government's case for joining US forces in the Iraq conflict in 2003 must rank as one of the most consequential series of misstatements of the modern era. The Chilcot Inquiry concluded that Blair exaggerated the military threat posed by Saddam Hussein in the run-up to the conflict. Chilcot concluded that:

> The statements prepared for, and used by, the UK Government in public from late 2001 onwards conveyed more certainty than the Joint Intelligence Committee Assessments about Iraq's proscribed activities and the potential threat they posed.
>
> The tendency to refer in public statements only to Iraq's 'weapons of mass destruction' was likely to have created the impression that Iraq posed a greater threat than the detailed JIC Assessments would have supported.[104]

Chilcot further noted that this tendency to overstate the certainty of intelligence materials continued into the period immediately before military action commenced.[105] In a subsequent interview, Chilcot said that he did not believe Blair to have been 'straight with the nation' at the time of making the case for military action.[106]

More recent instances of UK public office holders acting as the source of misinformation and possibly deliberately misleading inaccurate, purportedly factual material exist. These instances arose during the state's response to the spread of the COVID-19 virus. The UK Office for Statistics Regulation criticised the presentation of data by the Government's Chief Scientific Adviser and Chief Medical Officer in November 2020, which suggested that the total of daily deaths within

[104] *The Report of the Iraq Inquiry* Executive Summary (2016) HC 264 para 806.
[105] ibid at para 808.
[106] See www.theguardian.com/politics/2017/jul/06/chilcot-tony-blair-was-not-straight-with-the-nation-over-iraq-war.

28 days of a positive COVID-19 test could reach 4,000 by December 2020. A spokesperson for the Office for Statistics Regulation was quoted as saying the data given at daily government press conferences was 'not always supported by transparent information being provided in a timely manner'.[107] The potential existed 'to confuse the public and undermine confidence in the statistics'.[108] The misleading presentation was timed to coincide with Prime Minister Johnson's announcement of the second national lockdown. Conservative MPs criticised the use of statistics by the Chief Scientific Adviser and Chief Medical Officer as 'unhelpful' to MPs and members of the public.[109] Nor was this an isolated incident. The Health Secretary was separately criticised in June 2020 by the chair of the UK Statistics Authority for exaggerating the number of daily COVID-19 tests being carried out. The figures released by the Department of Health were 'far from complete and comprehensible. The aim seems to be to show the largest possible number of tests, even at the expense of understanding'.[110] Secretary of State for Health Hancock was also culpable of a further instance of misinformation in April 2020 when he warned people thinking of sunbathing in parks and on beaches in the coming months that they risked causing a 'superspreader' event.[111] The warning naturally received prominent coverage in national media and yet, mysteriously, no such superspreading of the virus was recorded in subsequent infection rates or hospital admissions. It emerged that, at the time he gave the warning, Hancock's advice flew in the face of known facts about virus transmission outdoors. One virologist at St Andrews University commented:

> We have known for some time that only about 10% of transmission events are linked to outdoor activities. Even those events generally involve either prolonged close contact or a mixture of indoor and outdoor time. We had a lot of existing knowledge even when the pandemic began about respiratory viruses and how they transmit in general, and everything directs us to the conditions in people's homes and workplaces.[112]

Sometimes, the dissemination of false information may take the form of asserting that a true account is untrue. This is particularly disconcerting when it is

[107] J Cameron-Cheshire and G Parker, 'UK Statistics Watchdog Warns over Government use of Covid Data' (2020) *Financial Times* 5 November.

[108] ibid.

[109] ibid.

[110] L Hughes and C Giles, 'Matt Hancock Criticised by Regulator over the UK Coronavirus Testing Figures – Daily Numbers "Far from Complete and Comprehensible" says Head of Statistics Body' (2020) *Financial Times* 2 June.

[111] See www.standard.co.uk/news/uk/sunbathers-putting-lives-risk-breaking-coronavirus-lockdown-a4407291.html.

[112] Dr Müge Çevik, a lecturer in infectious diseases and medical virology at the University of St Andrews cited in A Bland, 'How the Beach "Superspreader" Myth can Inform the UK's Future Covid Response' (2020) *The Guardian* 19 February. See also cited in the same article epidemiologist Professor Mark Woolhouse, Edinburgh University who gave the following evidence to MPs: 'Over the summer we were treated to all this on the television news, pictures of crowded beaches, and there was an outcry about this. There were no outbreaks linked to public beaches. There's never been a Covid-19 outbreak linked to a beach, ever, anywhere in the world, to the best of my knowledge.'

practised by the elected representatives of the people. In January 2021, *The Yorkshire Post* published a story about government plans to switch supplies of COVID-19 vaccines away from Yorkshire to other regions of England where the vaccine roll-out was lagging behind.[113] The story was based on research and interviews with clinical commissioning groups, senior staff at local authority and Department of Health level.[114] It provoked what James Mitchinson, the editor of the *Yorkshire Post* described as a furious response from local Conservative MPs. Mitchinson wrote:

> Never in my career as a journalist have I come under such a co-ordinated attack from those in power … Those MPs – people you have put your trust and faith in – wanted you to believe that our story was 'untrue, dangerous and wrong'. It was, of course, none of those things, but they wanted you to believe them, not us. The experience has left me with a deep sense of unease.[115]

Looking beyond the UK, the French President Emmanuel Macron stated in January 2021 that the Oxford-Astra-Zeneca vaccine was 'quasi-ineffective' for people over 65 years hours after the European Medicines Agency approved the vaccine for use across all groups.[116] He later backtracked on this claim when his government approved the use of the vaccine for some of the over 65-year-old age group.[117] Across the Atlantic by contrast, a number of former US President Trump's unevidenced and/or highly questionable assertions on a range of matters have been removed or flagged by monitors at Facebook and Twitter. In January 2021, Twitter announced the permanent suspension of the @realDonaldTrump account following his tweets alleging that the outcome of the November 2020 election was 'rigged' and 'stolen'. and encouraging supporters to take to the streets outside Capitol Hill.[118] Although many who would consider themselves to be situated on the progressive side of politics have welcomed Trump's removal from the platform, I argue contrariwise below that, in the longer term, this type of censorship poses major difficulties for republican self-government. Despite self-consciously positioning themselves on the 'right side of history', supporters of the permanent ban on Trump may more accurately be said to belong among the opponents of democratic republicanism. As the Chartered Institute of Journalists has acutely observed, 'You don't have to like the outgoing President Donald Trump to

[113] G Scott 'Vaccines rationed in Yorkshire as Health Secretary says "lumpy" supply means deliveries must be diverted to worse performing regions' (2021) *Yorkshire Post* 21 January.

[114] It was later confirmed by Dr Nikita Kanani, Director of Primary Care for NHS England in an interview on *Today* Radio 4 on 22 January 2021.

[115] J Mitchinson, 'Vaccines – A National Effort in the National Interest: Letter from the Editor' (2021) *Yorkshire Post* 22 January.

[116] See www.france24.com/en/live-news/20210129-macron-astrazeneca-vaccine-quasi-ineffective-for-over-65s.

[117] H Scofield. 'What's behind France's AstraZeneca's turnaround' (2021) 2 March www.bbc.co.uk/news/world-europe-56252028.

[118] See https://blog.twitter.com/en_us/topics/company/2020/suspension.

be alarmed that a commercial entity operating in 'the public space' … can silence those with whom it disagrees'.[119]

Moreover, many members of the pro-censorship group are curiously silent on other unrestricted propagators of politically inflammatory material. Consider the online remarks of Ayatollah Khamenei, the Supreme Leader of Iran. A tweet posted by the Ayatollah in May 2020 stated 'The only remedy until the removal of the Zionist regime is firm, armed resistance.'[120] A subsequent tweet described jihadi groups as 'valuable'.[121] Is it that the Ayatollah too is on 'the right side of history'? Following an appearance before the House of Lords Communications and Digital Committee in the Spring of 2021, an internal review resulted in a decision by Twitter to remove these tweets.

Volokh considers that the control exercised by Facebook and Twitter on what citizens (including the US President) can say about disputed political questions readily morphs into broader bans on criticisms of '"concepts, institutions, ideas, practices, or beliefs associated with protected characteristics" when Facebook thinks such criticisms risk "harm" or "discrimination"'.[122] Social media giants are using their marketplace dominance to wield 'immense … political power'.[123] Some might trust Mark Zuckerberg to be publicly (republican) spirited. Others, more appropriately sceptical of the motivations behind corporate regulation of expression, would concur with Volokh when he comments that 'perhaps we should instead think that such platform power has become a danger to … democracy'.[124]

Social Media Platforms as Editors of Public Discourse

During the Covid-19 public health crisis a number of platforms have expunged from the public domain claims deemed harmful under vague and uncertain criteria. Acts of viewpoint censorship by social media platforms that were justified by reference to vague and uncertain criteria such as 'community standards' became increasingly common.[125] Though some of these acts of censorship were later

[119] Written evidence submitted to the House of Lords' Communications and Digital Select Committee and cited at *Free for All? Freedom of Expression in the Digital Age* (2021–22) HL Paper 54 at para 67.

[120] Tweet on 20 May 2020 at http://twitter.com/khamenei.ir/status/1263181288338587649 – page available in June 2021 no longer accessible in October 2021.

[121] Tweet on 21 May 2021 at http://twitter.com/khamenei.ir/status/1395801790428364802 page available in July 2021 no longer accessible in October 2021.

[122] E Volokh, 'Trump has a Point: Facebook's Policing of Speech is Ominous' (2021) *Washington Post* 15 July.

[123] ibid.

[124] ibid.

[125] There is a serious question about transparency here. How do the social media platforms define, operationalise and review the 'community standards' criterion? Specifically, how can users be assured that decisions to remove content are uninfluenced by commercial and platform shareholder considerations? The House of Lords Communication and Digital Committee commented in July 2021 that the 'market power of the largest platforms leaves them free to make content moderation decisions in their

reversed after public criticism (usually by high-profile politicians and free speech campaigners),[126] attempts to enforce political conformity plainly threaten the ability of a self-governing community of political equals to exercise effective control over the direction of public policy. It is therefore entirely appropriate that light be brought to bear on the censorship practices of these unelected for-profit gatekeepers of public speech. In this section, I detail a representative sample of both viewpoint-based acts of censorship by privately owned platforms and platform labelling of other content as 'false'. These instances are best seen in the context of complementary efforts by state agencies such as OFCOM to privilege official versions of events and to silence dissident voices. In the final analysis, we must ask whether, in a self-governing democratic community of political equals, it is fitting that platforms enjoy these powers. The House of Lords Communications and Digital Select Committee took the view in its July 2021 Report that the platforms 'should not be the arbiters of truth'.[127]

October 2021 YouTube Ban on Big Brother Watch Upload of Conservative MP David Davis Speech at the Conservative Party Conference

YouTube removed a video of David Davis MP addressing Conservative Party conference attendees in October 2021 on the basis that his comments violated its policy on medical information.[128] Specifically, the platform claimed that Davis' remarks constituted COVID-19 related content that 'explicitly contradicts expert consensus from local health authorities or the World Health Organization'.[129] Mr Davis had told his audience that he was a supporter of vaccination and had received his two doses, but criticised the idea of vaccine passports on the basis that it 'smacked of illiberal government'.[130] He went on to add that vaccination could give people a false sense of security, since such individuals could still go on to infect others. The ban was later reversed following a review. Davis himself is quoted in the BBC's account of YouTube's ban as saying:

> Throughout the pandemic, we have seen blatant attempts by Big Tech to silence opposition voices challenging the conventional wisdom. This episode serves as a further example of the worrying trend of strangling free speech. If YouTube is happy to attempt

own commercial and political interests rather than the interests of users' freedom of expression and safety'. See HL Communications and Digital Select Committee *Free for All? Freedom of Expression in the Digital Age* (2021–22) HL Paper 54 at para 70.

[126] See www.theguardian.com/technology/2021/jan/05/youtube-bans-talkradio-for-allegedly-breaching-content-policy.

[127] HL Communications and Digital Select Committee *Free for All? Freedom of Expression in the Digital Age* (2021–22) HL Paper 54 at para 81.

[128] See www.telegraph.co.uk/news/2021/10/16/big-tech-censorship-threatens-democracy/.

[129] See www.bbc.co.uk/news/uk-politics-58915092.

[130] ibid.

> to silence elected Members of Parliament, then they are also happy to censor anyone uploading content to their services.[131]

January 2021 YouTube Ban on TalkRADIO's YouTube's Channel

On 5 January 2021, YouTube suspended TalkRADIO from its platform for 12 hours after declaring that material broadcast by the radio station breached its community standards guidelines which prohibit items that 'explicitly contradict expert consensus from local authorities or the World Health Organization'. The radio station was left unclear about what content was considered problematic.[132] The ban was shortly reversed and the channel reinstated.[133] An account of the ban in *The Guardian* implied that TalkRADIO had been removed because YouTube considered that the channel had violated the platforms' three strikes in 90 days policy, noting that two of its presenters had regularly spoken out against the Government's lockdown policies.[134] If correct, it is not clear why this stance was reversed and whether OFCOM played any role in the original decision to suspend the channel or its subsequent reversal.

Facebook 'False Information' Label on Posts by Professor Carl Heneghan Commenting on Danish Study Casting Doubt on Efficacy of Face Masks

In November 2020, Professor Heneghan at the Centre for Evidence Based Medicine at Oxford University commented on the results of a large randomised controlled Danish study on the effectiveness of mask wearing for preventing the spread of the virus. This was a timely piece of research as the UK Government had made mask wearing compulsory in a number of public spaces. The study showed no significant effect on wearers' susceptibility to infection. Professor Heneghan wrote in *The Spectator*

> In the end, there was no statistically significant difference between those who wore masks and those who did not when it came to being infected by Covid-19. 1.8 per cent of those wearing masks caught Covid, compared to 2.1 per cent of the control group. As

[131] ibid.

[132] See https://techcrunch.com/2021/01/06/youtube-reverses-ban-on-uks-talkradio-for-covid-19-policy-breaches/.

[133] See www.reuters.com/business/media-telecom/uk-broadcaster-talkradio-reinstated-youtube-2021-01-05/.

[134] See www.theguardian.com/technology/2021/jan/05/youtube-bans-talkradio-for-allegedly-breaching-content-policy.

> a result, it seems that any effect masks have on preventing the spread of the disease in the community is small.[135]

When he posted links to the article on Facebook, it was labelled 'false information'. Asked by the House of Lords' Communications and Digital Select Committee about the qualifications of those entrusted with the labelling of Professor Heneghan's post, Facebook told the Committee somewhat unhelpfully that all its fact checkers were 'certified by an International Fact Checking Organisation'. It did concede, however, that these people 'may not have any scientific or medical qualifications'.[136] Interestingly in this context, Professor Simon Wood, a statistician at Edinburgh University has commented on how fact checkers have paid especial attention to the Danish study whilst being much less concerned to fact check other empirical studies that conversely endorse the wearing of face masks as a COVID mitigation strategy.[137] This ought to raise doubts about the evenhandedness of fact-checking organisations and the unadvertised political agendas that inform such fact-checking activities. A sceptical stance regarding the claimed 'independence' and 'objectivity' of fact checking would seem appropriate here. As revealed in the context of the fact checking of claims about the efficacy of face masks, when a preponderance of fact-checking activities are focused upon studies that dispute official advice as opposed to checking the empirical bases of pro-Government claims, there is a clear impact that leans towards privileging official narratives. At the very least, we should expect independent organisations to afford adequate time and resources to the careful evaluation of state claims. Where they do not and where fact checkers produce reports that tend overall to support official narratives, a sceptical onlooker must doubt the epistemic value of such contributions to public discourse.

On closer inspection, it seems that the reason for Facebook's 'false information' label was that the article did not reveal to its readers that the Danish study had not looked at whether an infected mask wearer is less able *to spread* the virus to others as compared to an infected mask-less person. So, to be clear, the specific 'misinformation' here consisted in *not* informing readers of *The Spectator* what the study had *not* looked at! How far should Facebook be able to go in deciding that a review of a scientific study is 'false' on account of the fact that the review does not list all those things about which the study did not set out to gather data? Is this a credible basis for labelling material 'false'? Fundamentally, the labelling response by Facebook raises the difficult question of contextualisation. What sorts of additional background information need the speaker provide to avoid being treated as a purveyor of falsity and, more fundamentally still, in a democracy, are we content to let Facebook determine what is and is not proper contextualisation? Is it not

[135] See www.spectator.co.uk/article/do-masks-stop-the-spread-of-covid-19- (2020) 19 November.

[136] *Free for All? Freedom of Expression in the Digital Age* (2021) HL Communications and Digital Committee 1st Report of Session 2021–22 HL Paper 54 at para 48.

[137] See www.spectator.co.uk/article/do-masks-really-halve-the-risk-of-covid-a-note-on-the-evidence (2021) 29 November.

better to let the speaker speak and then be challenged openly about the context of his/her remarks by other speakers?

Facebook Ban on Wuhan Laboratory Leak Theory

The ban on posts and blogs casting doubt on the natural 'zoonotic' or bats to humans – transmission basis of the COVID-19 virus and pointing instead to the possibility of a leak from a Wuhan laboratory of a manufactured and enhanced virus should serve as a clear warning about the extent of social media censorship on matters of legitimate public discourse. In this instance, the attempt to close down debate has been aided by academics and publishers whose conflicts of interest may not always be transparent. Initially, posts about such matters were banned under Facebook's 'harmful misinformation'. It seems that Facebook was influenced by a letter published in *The Lancet*, with the signatories of 27 leading scientists condemning the 'conspiracy' lab leak theory. The letter was drafted by scientists enjoying what one commentator has called 'extensive ties to the Wuhan Institute of Virology'.[138] One obvious worry here is that western-based scientists and publishers with research and funding ties to China would feel unable to express criticisms of Chinese authorities. Moreover, where those same scientists sit on editorial boards of journals with growing sales markets in China, they (and their publishers) might be unwilling to publish papers that offer a different narrative to the 'zoonotic' theory of transmission endorsed by the Chinese Government. In May 2021, *Science* published a letter from 18 scientists that claimed both the 'zoonotic' and 'lab leak' theories to be 'equally plausible' and criticised the World Health Organization for not giving balanced consideration to each theory.[139] In the same month, Facebook reversed its ban when President Biden ordered his intelligence agencies to investigate whether a lab leak was the real source of the virus.[140]

In the meantime, as the House of Lords' Communications and Digital Select Committee made clear in July 2021, Facebook had not fact checked or made less accessible stories published in the Chinese state news outlet *Global Times*. This publication has denied in the past that China has subjected Uyghur Muslims in Xinjiang to forced labour or the systematic elimination of the Uyghur population.[141] It is very difficult to dismiss the idea that commercial considerations lie behind Facebook's lack of evenhandedness when it comes to pro-China vs anti-China posts.

[138] I Birrell, 'Beijing's Useful Idiots – Science Journals have Encouraged and Enforced a False Covid Narrative' *UnHerd* (2021) 8 June.

[139] See www.theguardian.com/world/2021/aug/22/the-wuhan-lab-leak-theory-is-more-about-politics-than-science.

[140] See www.bbc.co.uk/news/world-us-canada-57260009.

[141] House of Lords' Communications and Digital Committee in July 2021 at *Free for All? Freedom of Expression in the Digital Age* (2021) HL Communications and Digital Committee 1st Report of Session 2021–22 HL Paper 54 at para 54.

Twitter Suspension of US Customs and Border Patrol Commissioner During US Presidential Election Campaign 2019

The Twitter account of Mark Morgan, a US Customs and Border Patrol Commissioner was suspended days before the US General Election in November 2019. Morgan had tweeted about the 'success' of the southern border wall. Subsequently before a Senate Judiciary committee hearing into the censoring practices of social media, CEO Jack Dorsey said that his company had made an error in suspending the account and that this was due to 'heightened awareness around government accounts at this time'.[142]

Twitter and Facebook Censorship of Hunter Biden Laptop Story During US Presidential Election Campaign 2019

On 14 October 2019 at a point just three weeks away from the US Presidential Election on 5 November, Twitter blocked the account of the *New York Post* (a Republican-leaning newspaper) and blocked users from re-tweeting *New York Post* articles alleging that Democratic Party candidate Joe Biden and his son Hunter were engaged in corrupt business dealings in Ukraine and China. Initially, Twitter said that the blocks had been imposed because the newspaper's reports had been based upon 'hacked materials'.[143] In fact, Biden Jr had abandoned a water-damaged laptop at a Delaware repair shop whose proprietor thereby came into lawful possession of the device. On 30 October 2019, Twitter unblocked the account of the *New York Post* and allowed posts from the unblocked newspaper to be retweeted. Before a Senate Judiciary Committee hearing, CEO Dorsey later admitted to a 'total mistake' in blocking the story.[144]

YouTube Ban on Roundtable Discussion on Public Health Strategy for Combating Coronavirus

In April 2021, a discussion between Ron DeSantis, the Governor of Florida, and Professors Kulldorff (Harvard), Gupta (University of Oxford) and Bhattacharya

[142] See https://m.washingtontimes.com/news/2020/nov/17/jack-dorsey-twitter-ceo-admits-pre-election-errors/.

[143] Of course, even if the hacking allegation had been true, it is not an absolute legal bar to public dissemination as a number of lawful whistleblowing acts in the public sector such as *New York Times v US* 403 US 713 (1971) amply support.

[144] See www.youtube.com/watch?v=tWayExRuaYk and see also www.washingtonpost.com/technology/2020/11/17/tech-hearing-dorsey-zuckerberg/.

(Stanford) was removed from YouTube on account of an infringement of the platform's rule that prohibits viewpoints at odds with those held by the World Health Organization.[145]

The Use of AI Systems to Monitor and Remove Online Content

As referred to in earlier sections of this chapter, the House of Lords Communications and Digital Select Committee considered the free speech impact of the draft Online Safety Bill in 2021. In an appropriately critical approach to online censoring, the Committee expressed concern that the current use of artificial intelligence systems by platforms to meet increasing pressures to monitor and remove content was already leading to improper removals and proportionately higher numbers of removed content.[146] The Committee noted that in the period between April and June 2020, YouTube used fewer numbers of staff to moderate content by deploying AI systems in their place. The result was that twice as many videos (11 million) were removed over these three months than would have been expected under human moderators. On appeal, some 116,000 videos were 're-instated' since these did not infringe any of YouTube's content prohibitions.[147] This suggests that AI algorithms as currently configured are frighteningly more restrictive of free expression than their human counterparts. As one copyright law expert witness to the HL Select Committee observed, 'an algorithm is never going to develop a sense of humour and be able to distinguish between a copyright infringement and a legal parody, because algorithms look for patterns that are the same and do comparisons'.[148]

Stjernfelt and Lauritzen observe that AI software is 'not semantically savvy'. It is likely to produce both false positives and false negatives. They argue that whilst it can detect proxies for problematic content (eg large areas of skin surface tone as a proxy for nudity; sexual slang and swearwords as proxies for pornographic material and 'hate speech'), this is likely to capture beach holiday/hotel poolside promotional materials aimed at families. As for false negatives, this will occur

[145] See www.bbc.co.uk/news/technology-52388586 and cited by the House of Lords' Communications and Digital Committee in July 2021 at *Free for All? Freedom of Expression in the Digital Age* (2021) HL Communications and Digital Committee 1st Report of Session 2021–22 HL Paper 54 at para 49.

[146] A Barker and H Murphy 'Youtube reverts to human moderators in fight against misinformation' (2020) *Financial Times* September 20 www.ft.com/content/e54737c5-8488-4e66-b087-d1ad426ac9fa. In 2016, it was claimed that the artificial intelligence software used by Facebook 'discovered' more photos in breach of its community standards policy than its human moderators, J Constine, 'Facebook Spares Humans by Fighting Offensive Photos with AI' (2016) *TechCrunch* 31 May.

[147] Representing a 50 per cent success rate on appeal to an appellate human moderator.

[148] J Reda, Society for Civil Rights evidence cited at HL Communications and Digital Select Committee *Free for All? Freedom of Expression in the Digital Age* (2021–22) HL Paper 54 at para 40.

when a writer creatively writes text as 'fokking migr@nts' instead of 'fucking migrants'.[149]

AI deployment on social media platforms is likely to increase in the future, however, as governments require instant responses to problematic content and advertisers signal their intention to boycott platforms that disseminate viewpoints that advertisers perceive as commercially damaging. The threat of income stream losses will incentivise platforms to speed up removal processes by moving more firmly to automated systems, with the added bonus of lowering staffing costs. The House of Lords Select Committee concluded that online content posed real challenges for algorithmic *and* human moderators. The evidence seen by the committee led it to conclude that 'platform moderation decisions are often unreasonably inconsistent and opaque, and sometimes seem to be influenced by commercial and political considerations'.[150]

The Free Speech Implications of the Online Safety Bill

At the time of writing, clause 11 of the draft Online Safety Bill requires social media platforms to identify and assess risks of harm to adults posed by lawful content that is available on their service. Platforms need to inform service users of how harmful materials will be dealt with in accordance with their terms and conditions. The latter are to be formulated after consultation with civil society and other 'expert' groups. There are two main mechanisms by which content can be deemed harmful. The first is where a risk assessment identifies that material poses a material risk of adverse physical or psychological harm (the latter not requiring adherence to a clinical definition) to an adult of ordinary sensibilities (but curiously not a 'reasonable adult of ordinary sensibilities'). The second is where the Secretary of State considers that material falls within a 'priority category' of material deemed harmful to adults.

The House of Lords Select Committee was forthright in its criticism of clause 11. It stated that it was

> not convinced that (the duties on social media companies) … are workable or could be implemented without unjustifiable and unprecedented interference in freedom of expression. *If a type of content is seriously harmful, it should be defined and criminalised through primary legislation.*[151]

The Bill would thus render material which is lawful and permitted in the offline world vulnerable to removal in the online world on account of the standards of an

[149] F Stjernfelt and A Lauritzen, *Your Post has been Removed – Tech Giants and Freedom of Speech* (Berlin, Springer, 2020) at 100.

[150] *Free for All? Freedom of Expression in the Digital Age* (2021–22) at para 78. See for an interesting analysis F Stjernfelt and A Lauritzen, *Your Post has been Removed – Tech Giants and Freedom of Speech*, see ch 10 'Nipples and the Digital Community'.

[151] *Free for All? Freedom of Expression in the Digital Age* (2021–22) at para 182.

unreasonable adult with extraordinary sensibilities. This is incoherent. It disproportionately impedes access to content by people of ordinary sensibility. The House of Lords Select Committee concluded that the Bill should instead adopt the standard of the 'reasonable person of ordinary sensibilities'.[152] Even this enhanced degree of protection for online expression might be thought to fall short of the desired level of protection for instances of political expression. For reasons developed throughout this book, the sensibilities of 'ordinary people should not be the touchstone by which political speech forms are permitted/shut down by the state or private corporations. It is pertinent in this context to recall US academic Burt Neuborne's observation that

> (v)irtually every attempt at censorship is premised on an assertion that speech causes serious harm. A social science theory can be generated on demand. One of Justice Holmes' great legacies to us was his warning that an alleged bad tendency to cause harm can ever be enough to warrant censorship.[153]

To enshrine *simpliciter* a standard such as serious harm in law is to facilitate the closing down by majoritarian sentiment of speech that unsettles and discomforts. Speech, in other words, that is extremely valuable to both the individual and society.

Defenders of the Bill point to clause 13 'Duties to protect content of democratic importance'. This imposes a duty on service providers to:

> ensure that the importance of the free expression of content of democratic importance is taken into account when making decisions about – (a) how to treat such content (especially decisions about whether to take it down or restrict users' access to it), and (b) whether to take action against a user generating, uploading or sharing such content.

Can social media companies be entrusted to 'take account of expression of democratic importance' when fulfilling their content moderation duties when the bottom line for private sector platforms is growing shareholder value? The respective track records of YouTube, Facebook, Twitter etc so far in shutting down specific instances of dissenting expression do not augur well here. Does the '*take account* of expression of democratic importance' standard come anywhere close to attaching the appropriate level of importance to political speech in a vibrant, conflictual democracy? Or, conversely, do the accompanying fine levels attaching to duty breaches incentivise a platform to shut down speech that has the potential to 'trigger' a vulnerable individual on that individual's say so or on the prompting of speech-hostile others claiming to represent the individual? Then there is the question of what sort of content is of 'democratic importance'? The explanatory notes accompanying the Bill offer illustrative examples that include 'content promoting or opposing government policy and content promoting or opposing

[152] ibid at para 183.

[153] B Neuborne, 'Ghosts in the Attic: Idealized Pluralism, Community and Hate Speech' (1992) 27 *Harv. C.R. – C.L.L. Rev.* 371 at 394.

a political party'.[154] As the House of Lords Select Committee remarked, 'this definition privileges debates initiated by elected representatives and political parties over those initiated by members of the public as well as excluding those campaigning for social rather than policy change'.[155]

The Bill makes a token gesture towards recognising the importance of citizen journalism and something it calls 'journalistic content' in clause 14. When taking decisions about removing or restricting access to such content, platforms must show (once more in that underwhelming phrase) that they have 'taken into account' the importance of free expression. Platforms will be required to make a 'dedicated and expedited complaints procedure' available to a person who considers the content to be journalistic content. There is little guidance on how, if at all, this clause is intended to dovetail with content that is of 'democratic importance'.[156] There is additionally a very real danger that the practices of professional journalism will be used as a yardstick to assess whether non-professionally produced material is properly 'journalistic' and thus deserving of having its free expression 'taken into account'.

Conclusion

The increasing reliance of the UK Government on private providers of media platforms to police the contours of acceptable expression online is likely to throw up further instances of democratically unaccountable censorship. The flawed design of the Online Safety Bill shifts the UK regulatory position far away from the republican design of an active, regularly engaged citizenry, to one in which the commercial interests of multinational corporations will de facto set the limits on political expression. Adapting James Madison's famous admonition to present circumstances it might be said that the true nature of self-government requires that the 'censorial power is in the people over the Government (and corporate media platforms), and not in the Government/Jack Dorsey/Mark Zuckerberg over the people'.[157]

[154] ibid at para 73.
[155] ibid at para 74.
[156] E Harbinja, 'UK's Online Safety Bill: Not That Safe, After All?' www.lawfareblog.com/uks-online-safety-bill-not-safe-after-all.
[157] Letter to James Monroe (1794) 4 December available at US Library of Congress website www.loc.gov/resource/mjm.05_0799_0804/?sp=2&st=text.

7

Restoring the Agon: Re-opening the Channels of Political Change

Introduction – Swimming against the Liberal Tide

The present defence of sovereign, pluralist, popular participation in political decision-making is confessedly contrarian. It goes against the tide of intellectual opinion and the prevailing legal culture in the UK and elsewhere. For example in the US, Larry Kramer has pointed out how an '(a)nti-populist sensibility presumes that ordinary people are emotional, ignorant, fuzzy-headed, and simple-minded in contrast to a thoughtful, informed and clear-headed elite'.[1]

Mark Tushnet has similarly written of intellectuals with a 'deep-seated fear of voting' who were 'more enthusiastic about judicial review than recent experience justifies, because they are afraid of what the people will do'.[2] Roberto Unger has offered a particularly scathing indictment of this intellectual 'discomfort with democracy'.[3] In *What Should Legal Analysis Become?* Unger noted the broader tendency of legal culture to obsess over the need for restraints on majority rule rather than identifying means of reining in dominant minorities.[4] He observed lawyers' opposition to institutional reforms that would enhance popular participation in politics on the basis of the putative threat posed to a regime of rights. The idealisation of deliberative democracy as the desire to promote a style of political discourse approximated in Unger's eyes to 'a polite conversation among gentlemen in an eighteenth century drawing room'.[5] He helpfully reminds us that liberals' distrust of popular participation harks back to the Enlightenment.[6] Fast forward to the era of universal franchise and mass democracy and the destabilising spectre of the ordinary citizen which once haunted the parlours of the Enlightenment

[1] *The People Themselves – Popular Constitutionalism and Judicial Review* (New York, OUP, 2004) at 242.

[2] *Taking the Constitution Away from the Courts* (New Jersey, Princeton University Press, 1999) at 177.

[3] *The People Themselves* at n 1.

[4] London, Verso, 1996.

[5] ibid at 73.

[6] I am including liberal elitist and deliberative democratic accounts of democracy here and outlined earlier in ch 2.

continues to cast its shadow over elite accounts of the law and institutions of the liberal democratic state:

> Fear and loathing of the people always threatens to become the ruling passions of this legal culture. Far from being confined to conservative variants of contemporary legal doctrine, these passions have left their mark upon centrist and progressive legal thought.[7]

The untutored ordinary citizen cannot be relied upon to discern clearly the path towards the rationally derived societal institutions and norms. This is best left to those who perceive with extraordinary insight the essential sameness of people through time and across continents. Progress towards the perfected constitution must be guided by the knowledgeable few. Take 'fake news' off our electronic devices. Demand that speakers reveal their true identities. Insist that legislatures and courts outlaw 'irresponsible' and factually unverified contributions to public discourse. Require all online speakers more generally to adhere to standards of professional journalism and civility. Then allow Facebook and Google and their 'fact checkers' to be the arbiter of truth in the public square and the journey towards our elevated end of history can be resumed. After all, who would cavil if the next time we logged on we encountered fewer Trumpian rednecks (and the former President himself) and their wilfully ignorant takes on the big issues of modern life? A return to Enlightenment values and rational public discourse is the cure-all that we ignore at our peril.

The dominance of this type of thinking today can lead us to overlook the fact that value pluralism with its disruptive implications for an ultimate convergence upon the good society arrived in European political thought well in advance of Kant and Voltaire. Greek tragedy, Machiavelli and Montesquieu all point us away from the Enlightenment's promised unitary destination. Machiavelli, for example, raised a permanent question for posterity when the author of *Discourses on Livy* pointed out that the Christian life and the politically virtuous life were irreconcilable, alternative choices open to people. Isaiah Berlin argued that the Florentine had successfully shown that 'ends equally sacred may contradict each other'.[8] That is to say entire value systems may on a daily basis stand in opposition to one another without there being the possibility of any 'rational' overcoming or resolution of their fundamental quarrel.

Montesquieu, in *L'Esprit des Lois*, famously maintained that the climate of a society and, more crucially, its distinct moral forces (or 'general spirit' that was reflected in its specific history, religion, laws and customs) all combined to produce individuated societies.[9] Richter comments how Montesquieu's approach to the

[7] ibid.

[8] I Berlin, 'The Originality of Machiavelli' in *Against the Grain – Essays in the History of Ideas* (London, Hogarth Press, 1979) at 74.

[9] *The Spirit of the Laws* (Cambridge Texts in the History of Political Thought) (ed A Cohler et al) see especially Part 3, Bks 14–19.

comparative study of human culture leads to a disturbing conclusion for adherents of ultimate convergence upon the good society. If we take Montesquieu seriously, he argues, it is 'difficult to reconcile with the project of arriving at a science based on a few laws applicable to all societies'.[10] Stuart Hampshire similarly observed that the Enlightenment's anticipated gradual convergence at a global level upon on 'our values'[11] has simply not occurred and does not look like occurring any time soon. The failure of humankind after two hundred years to have landed upon ideal, logically constructed institutions and rationally derived norms is undoubtedly the elephant in the room that modern defenders of the Enlightenment would rather you did not mention or discuss.

At the level of each individual's perception of the world, Iain McGilchrist's magisterial study of the hemispheric structure of the human brain, *The Master and His Emissary*, vividly shows how Enlightenment thinking is heavily centred upon and reflective of left hemisphere activity. The left side of our brains sees only a version or representation of the world around us however. To this partially observed world, the left hemisphere applies rational and logical systems of enquiry to generate knowledge claims. The left hemisphere is convinced, as McGilchrist puts it, 'of its own self-sufficiency'.[12] The entire world is a closed system, one that is knowable and fixed. Its finite complexities can be mastered. All that remains is for the application of rational systems of thought. By contrast, right-sided hemispheric activity is 'grappling with experience, in principle unknowable in its totality, changing, infinite, full of individual differences …'[13] The logical left hemisphere confronts sensory experiences seeking order and rational explanations that advance objective knowledge and truth. The weakness in an exclusively left-hemisphere approach to gaining complete knowledge about the world is that reason itself is able to appreciate that there are limits to what reason can uncover. For the Romantic (or counter-Enlightenment) movement, the limits of rational enquiry were all too apparent. Individuals differed in character and outlook in ways that did not conform to a single representative type of human being. People were not all alike across time and place. Their passions, imaginations, sense of humour, metaphoric and symbolic understandings of the world all lie beyond the left sphere's abstracting, rationalising modus operandi. The Romantics' assault on rational thought recalls Montaigne's earlier pre-Enlightenment claim about the provisional and refutable nature of what we think about the world:

> philosophy never seems to me to have a better hand to play than when she battles against our presumption and vanity; when in good faith she acknowledges her weakness, her ignorance and her inability to reach conclusions.[14]

[10] M Richter, 'Comparative Political Analysis in Montesquieu and Tocqueville' (1969) 1 *Comparative Politics* 129 at 140.

[11] S Hampshire, *Presidential Address to the American Philosophical Association* in 1991 *Proceedings and Addresses of the American Philosophical Association* (1991) Vol 65 at 25.

[12] I McGilchrist, *The Master and His Emissary – The Divided Brain and the Making of the Western World* (New Haven, Yale University Press, 2009) at 209.

[13] ibid at 352–53.

[14] Montaigne, 'On Presumption', *Essais*, Bk II:17 and cited in McGilchrist, ibid at 354.

Thus stated, the overreach by modern proponents of a return to Enlightenment thinking is disclosed. From the daring assertion of fixed, knowable and complete truths about 'human rights' and the desired end goals of all societies on the surface of the Earth, it is but a few short steps to denounce all dissenting opinion and to identify it as 'irresponsible' and then censor 'fake news'. The infallible Enlightenment mind can confidently set out 'right' answers for the benefit of the un/misinformed that might forgivably be understood to circumvent the need for any form of intervening democratic agency. The state and private owners of social media platforms can reinforce the prevailing consensus by removing inconvenient, dissonant and, most importantly of all, incorrect thinking from the public square. This very approach in respect of scientific truths is to be found in current official and social media platform approaches to emerging data about the spread of COVID-19 and the most efficacious means of halting the spread of the virus. Critics would contend that this stance loses sight of the provisional and incomplete nature of advances in scientific understanding. The absolute conviction with which platforms have shut down dissenting scientific viewpoints to advance official narratives betrays a fundamental failure to understand the scientific method of evaluating evidence. It is also self defeating. Public confidence in health policy is likely to be heightened when the non-expert majority rightly perceive that the critics and dissenting viewpoints have been able to communicate their concerns and disagreements. Conversely, the banning or removal of critical viewpoints from scientists and professionals not co-opted by the government is likely to fuel speculation that official accounts are unable to withstand serious scrutiny. Additionally, the dangers of 'groupthink' in this type of scenario ought to be obvious.

In the UK, the idea that popular participation in politics propels us towards irrationally self-harming outcomes is an established and core feature of anti-populist discourse in general circulation. The contributions of public intellectuals/members of the media commentariat (including Anthony Grayling, Matthew D'Ancona and Will Self – mentioned in passing in chapters four and six) were seen to highlight an urgent crisis for liberal democracy at home. In the case of D'Ancona's post-truth politics thesis for example, there is a pressing need to return to an earlier era of truthful and honest politics by eliminating 'fake news'. Leaving aside the highly problematic assumption of there being an earlier era of 'truthful' political discourse, D'Ancona's argument fails to engage with the important observation made by the European Commission's High Level Group on Fake News and Online Disinformation that the regulation of online speech can 'rarely be neatly categorised as simply false or true'. Instead we should recognise both that 'no authority has a monopoly on knowledge, and the belief that free societies benefit from – and are defined by the acceptance of – free confrontation of diverse and sometimes uncomfortable ideas and information'.[15]

[15] *A Multi-dimensional Approach to Disinformation* (European Commission, DG for Communication Networks, Content and Technology, 2018) at 20.

On the anti-populist view of these commentators on the other hand, what is needed is fewer, not more, opportunities for popular participation in everyday politics. This particular instantiation of liberals' fear and loathing of the people is shared in elements of domestic legal culture. Foremost among the tasks of liberal constitutionalist lawyers today is the shoring up of counter majoritarian institutions and taming the destabilising influence of popular opinion whether as expressed in and mediated by representative assemblies or, more problematically still, as directly in referenda. Encouraged by court judgments such as *Miller 2* and *Cherry*[16] and dicta in cases such as *Jackson v AG*[17] – where members of the senior judiciary arrogated to themselves entirely novel powers to review the adequacy of the political part of the constitution – emboldened adherents of liberal (legal) constitutionalism encourage a re-configuring of the relationship between the representative element of the Constitution and its judicial component that tilts sovereign power away from former and towards the latter. The immodest avowed aim is to ensure for all time hereafter that 'Parliament is not sovereign in the sense of being the sole holder of constitutive power'.[18] The people (who on this view are not and never were the constitutive power) are not entirely passed over however. Some liberal constitutionalists, for example, summon the non-sovereign citizens to help the liberal project reimagine the new sorts of enhanced judicially policed checks and balances to which the citizens and their democratically elected representatives will be made permanently subject in a redesigned constitution. That is to say the citizens find themselves occasionally enjoined to contribute to the design of new structures that will affirm liberalism's eternal victory over popular sovereignty.

These accounts share a common anti-republican objective: namely to place the constituted authorities and overarching constructs of the liberal state beyond the amendatory reach of the constitutive power. Popularly held opinion is valued only in so far as it affirms and elaborates liberal ideals. In *We the People*, for example, Ackerman's 'people' make rare and fleeting appearances to confer democratic legitimacy on progressive proposals to amend the constitution when the normal daily politics is unable to rise to the challenge of constitutional reform. Popularly based corrective action functions in these extraordinary moments to jolt the liberal enlightenment project back on track. Thus jolted, the project can head on towards its more perfectly envisioned final form. The people return to their passive onlooker role where they resume their ordinary, non-political lives. There they wait in the political shadows to be summoned episodically once every four years to signify approval of the policies and actions of incumbent office holders or their rivals. The business of daily politics returns to the professionals and those socio-economic elites with privileged access to public office holders. Indeed, it is difficult to detect much of a difference between Ackerman's episodic account

[16] [2019] UKSC 41.
[17] [2005] UKHL 56.
[18] A Young, 'Populism and the UK Constitution' (2018) *C.L.P.* 17, 52.

of popular participation and that advanced 200 years previously by Benjamin Rush, one of the signatories to the US Declaration of Independence. Rush spoke of the 'sovereign power' as a possession, usually held by the constituted authorities but handed over to the electorate on Election Day, thereafter to be returned to the constituted authorities. The people, he stated in 1777, 'possess [their sovereignty] only on the days of their elections. After this, it is the property of their rulers.'[19] In Ackerman's 'extraordinary moments', the initiator of a constitutional amendment is never the people or a section of the people at the grassroots level. The 'moment' is identified and seized upon by political elites who then proceed to formulate and refine the proposal that is needed to switch constitutional direction. It is critical to note that the revising energies set loose in Ackerman's constitutional moments work within the boundaries of existing institutional constraints.[20] They are locked into pre-existing constitutional structures and legal mechanisms for change. The 'dead hand' of the Founders works to prevent this being an authentically republican moment when the people get, in Thomas Paine's words, to 'begin the world again'. For Ackerman we need to resist the move outside existing constitutional structures since this signals the end of law and the beginning of something truly dreadful, viz politics.

In *We the People*, popular involvement at the ballot box functions to give democratic legitimacy to the amending proposition. In Ackerman's thesis, outside of the rare moments when called upon to endorse elite-initiated reform, the citizens are to all intents and purposes as politically inert in their daily lives as they are patronisingly depicted in Rush's defence of representative politics.[21] These structural exclusions of ordinary citizens from daily governance activities in the versions of minimalist democracy proffered respectively by Ackerman and Rush produce in turn a stultification of popular interest in politics. The former's annual 'Deliberation Day' offers at best a modest pivot away from regimes of minimalist democracy.[22] There is little reason to believe that such rarely held events can generate sufficient levels of antagonist oversight for elites to believe that they act under the watchful and constant scrutiny of the citizenry. And yet, as McCormick maintains, powerful political and social elites 'can only be checked by a populace with a disposition toward distrust, suspicion, and even resentment of them'.[23]

[19] B Rush, *On the Defects of the Confederation* in D Runes (ed) *The Selected Writings of Benjamin Rush* (New York, Philosophical Library, 1947) 26 at 28. And see also B Rush, 'Order' *Columbian Centinel* 1 (3 September 1794).

[20] A point made by J Colón-Ríos, *Weak Constitutionalism – Democratic Legitimacy and the Question of Constituent Power* (Abingdon, Routledge, 2012) at 110.

[21] For discussion of the problems of popular participation in Ackerman's account from a republican perspective see J Pope, 'Republican Moments: The Role of Direct Popular Power in the American Constitutional Order' (1990) 139 *U. Pa. L. Rev.* 287.

[22] B Ackerman and J Fishkin, 'Deliberation Day' (2002) 10 *Jo. Pol. Phil.* 129.

[23] J McCormick, 'Machiavellian Democracy: Controlling Elites with Ferocious Populism' (2001) 95 *Am.Pol.Sci.Rev.* 297, at 310.

Dealing with the Problem of the 'Ins' and the Role of Plural Political Expression in Preserving Open and Fractious Republican Liberty

The various legal and extra-legal devices used by office holders to block off the channels of political change to outsiders was a particular concern of the US constitutional scholar John Hart Ely. In *A Theory of Judicial Review* Hart Ely argued that a democratic state had to be alive to the threat that the 'ins' – existing power holders in democratic regimes – would seek self-interestedly to narrow and diminish opportunities for their challengers (the 'outs') to compete for office with a view to holding onto public power. Beyond limits on the direct expression of dissenting, non-centrist opinion which is the central focus of this book, a number of tools in the armoury of incumbents may be deployed to retain political office. These include partisan gerrymandering of electoral districts when the 'ins' can shape and re-shape constituency boundaries in ways that favour themselves. The requirement for election candidates in the UK and elsewhere to lodge a deposit with the state plainly also impacts adversely on the ability of less well-financed outsiders to challenge for political office. Candidates in UK General Elections must deposit £500 – a sum that is forfeited upon failure to secure 5 per cent of the actual votes cast. To stand for London Mayor, a deposit of £10,000 is required. In 2015 the UK Electoral Commission produced a report which reviewed the existing rules. It noted that the larger parties had been mainly in favour of keeping deposits. Conversely, smaller parties and independent candidates gave evidence that the £500 sum was in some instances 'unaffordable' and limited their ability to participate in electoral contests. The Commission concluded that making the ability to contest elected office dependent upon a person's financial means was not an appropriate means of demonstrating the requisite serious intent to hold public office.[24]

In contrast to the prevailing ochlophobic narratives in much contemporary legal and political culture, I have set out an account of freedom of online expression that is located within a self-governing republican polity characterised by intense and fractious disagreements between elite office holders and ordinary, non-office holding citizens. I have argued that freedom of expression needs to be seen as belonging more fundamentally still to a tragic world in the sense understood in ancient Greek plays where the various flawed protagonists find themselves locked in conflicts with other flawed individuals over ideas of the just society and the right way to live. In the time allotted to them, individuals may be able to come together to secure transient resolutions of particular conflicts via compromises with their political opponents. These accommodations are temporary however. They do not conclude in any definitive sense disputes over the best way to live with each other.

[24] *Standing for election in the United Kingdom: Report and Recommendations* (2015) www.electoralcommission.org.uk/who-we-are-and-what-we-do/our-views-and-research/our-consultations/standing-election-united-kingdom-report-and-recommendations.

Further disputes are ineliminable. Further political acts aimed at temporary stabilisation and establishing concord among hitherto discordant voices will be needed. On an Aristotelian view such as that elaborated by Arendt, political activity points up the human drive to act and be politically creative. That future conflicts will require further acts of creativity and compromise highlights the reality of an open agon where no one idea or norm can ever seal off all future contestation.

I have relied upon a Machiavellian account of the value of ongoing, discordant and antagonistic popular participation. This state of perpetual political conflict can never be satisfied by voting at regular intervals to choose from among competing, politically centrist elites. As the recent body of work by John McCormick has impressively detailed,[25] Machiavelli's prescription for maintaining a state of republican liberty in modern, large-scale liberal democracies requires significant institutional reforms. McCormick usefully reminds us that Machiavelli would have viewed the present-day institutions of a liberal democratic polity as amounting to an elective oligarchy.[26] An account of the institutional reforms needed to secure the regular ongoing participation of ordinary citizens in the making of the laws is, however, well beyond the scope of the present work. My narrower project has been to set out the principled case for political pluralism that facilitates an ongoing popular contestation and authorship of laws and policies. I have then highlighted the various ways in which laws and regulatory policy in the UK and in other liberal democracies close down forms of popular contestation. The argument made in the preceding pages for regular and ongoing authorship of the laws has not been grounded in an Aristotelian notion of the perfectability of people of the sort that is present in Arendt and Jefferson. Such a grounding is problematic for agonist and republican accounts for the reason that it is liable to be captured by elite conceptions of civilised discourse among empathetic individuals seeking the common good. The 'ferocious populism'[27] defended in democratic republican thought of the sort traced back to Machiavelli is not a perfectionist project intended to reflect and develop an innate drive of humans to create with others. It aims instead at instituting and preserving a state of liberty for all wherein non-elites are constitutionally empowered to resist the self-aggrandising schemes of elites and render the latter politically accountable. This cannot be done by elections alone. Additional institutional mechanisms are needed to allow for non-elite voices to be given a formal stake in the business of government. Combined with the fostering of a disputatious culture on social media, some measure of popular control of elite office

[25] See inter alia *Machiavellian Democracy* (Cambridge, CUP, 2012); J McCormick, 'The New Ochlophobia? Populism, Majority Rule and Prospects for Democratic-Republicanism' in (ed) Y Elazar and G Rousseliere, *Republicanism and the Future of Democracy* (New York, CUP, 2019); J McCormick, 'Machiavellian Democracy: Controlling Elites with Ferocious Populism' (2001) 95 *Am. Pol. Sci. Rev.* 297.

[26] Machiavellian Democracy: Controlling Elites with Ferocious Populism', ibid at 303.

[27] The phrase is taken from McCormick 'Machiavellian Democracy: Controlling Elites with Ferocious Populism'.

holders may thereby be secured. Unlike deliberative democratic/civic republican approaches, there need be no convergence on the 'common good'. For agonists, the pluralism and inherent dissents of political discourse are the pre-eminent values worth preserving. Conflict between classes and discrete interest groups is accepted as an immutable ontological fact. Resolutions of political disputes are necessarily revisable by the sovereign citizens. For both democratic/agonistic republicans therefore a broad measure of freedom to participate in political argument is a pre-requisite of a functioning democratic state. It follows that, among the biggest threats to democratic republican and agonist projects today, are viewpoint-based regulatory approaches of the state and social media platforms to online expression.

Common Carriers Not Editors – Public Forums and Banning Viewpoint Discrimination by Social Media Platforms

> We can have intellectual individualism and the rich cultural diversities that we owe to exceptional minds only at the price of occasional eccentricity and abnormal attitudes. When they are so harmless to others or to the State as those we deal with here, the price is not too great. But freedom to differ is not limited to things that do not matter much. That would be a mere shadow of freedom. The test of its substance is the right to differ as to things that touch the heart of the existing order.
>
> *West Virginia Board of Education v Barnette* 319 US 624 (1943) Justice Jackson at para 33.

Chapter six established beyond any doubt that social media platforms act now as the editors and censors of particular viewpoints and opinions. Sometimes this occurs when platforms are in active collusion with/under legal coercion from state bodies (see for example Germany's woefully over-inclusive Network Enforcement Act 2017, which sanctions inter alia 'disturbing the exercise of religion' and 'insulting expression'). On other occasions editorialising occurs on the platforms' own initiative to promote values dear to shareholders. At the level of users' daily experiences, we can say that online public spaces are increasingly curated by democratically unaccountable, privately owned for profit entities. Recall too that the undisclosed algorithms used to rank search engine results push certain sorts of content our way and relegate other content well away from the first few pages of the search results. 'Shadow banning' of certain speakers thus constitutes another, albeit more subtle, facet of the private manipulation of public discourse.[28] Despite

[28] K Ranttila, 'Social Media and Monopoly' (2020) 46 *Ohio N.U.L. Rev.* 161.

repeated public denials by platforms, a number of individual speakers and groups have testified before US Congressional committees that their content is made much harder for others to find in their search results.[29] It would be unsurprising if unpopular speakers in other jurisdictions likewise struggled to be heard in virtual public spaces.

The aim of these value-based interventions is at least openly acknowledged by the various platforms in their mission statements. Initially conceived as digital means of advancing the common good via open dialogue and free exchange of ideas and opinions, Facebook, Twitter and YouTube now explicitly offer individuals the opportunity to correct their false consciousness via devices such as 'community standards'.[30] If online speakers are unwilling to participate in this common venture towards the better society as defined by the platforms, they will be removed from the platform. Unsurprisingly, there is scant evidence to support the claim that such coercive tactics convert individuals and groups who enter the digital arena in various states of political conflict into empathetic and mutually regarding people who come to adopt shared values and outlooks.[31] If anything, the data on platform exclusions suggests that intense political disagreement remains an ongoing feature of the digital landscape as perceived by platform users.[32] The excluded – including those that incite hateful attitudes – are able to present themselves as martyrs. Moreover, resentment towards the supposed beneficiary communities may not unreasonably be supposed to be increased by such exclusions. Any serious commitment to political pluralism must in contrast rule out the digital equivalent of compulsory prayer or enforced saluting of the flag. Conscripting speakers to refrain from statements that have a 'bad tendency' to cause speculative, non-physical harms to others ought therefore to be a non-starter. Neuborne, one of the most thoughtful critics of the use of law to create a community of shared values, puts it thus:

> Sociological theories, even passionately held ones, about the adverse impact of unpopular speech on a category of hearers cannot justify censorship. The precise harm must be specified and proven, not merely alleged and assumed. The causal nexus between the speech and the proven harm must be virtually certain … The assertion that hate speech should be uniquely targeted because it 'silences' vulnerable targets is emotionally appealing but empirically empty.[33]

[29] ibid at 163–64.

[30] See https://transparency.fb.com/en-gb/policies/community-standards/ see section on 'Objectionable Content'; https://help.twitter.com/en/rules-and-policies/twitter-rules; www.youtube.com/intl/ALL_uk/howyoutubeworks/policies/community-guidelines/.

[31] See further B Neuborne, 'Ghosts in the Attic: Idealized Pluralism, Community and Hate Speech' (1992) 27 *Harv. C.R.-C.L.L. Rev.* 371, 378–79: 'Coerced communities neither deliver their participants from atomism into the joys of sharing, nor foster empathy and mutual regard. Instead they often perpetuate hatred, fear and mistrust. Coerced communities use force often to impose a false facade of unity, a process that has very often resulted in procrustean abuse and tyranny, without materially advancing the values of caring and humanity that make true community worth striving for.'

[32] M Barnidge, 'Social Affect and Political Disagreement on Social Media' (2018) 4 *Social Media & Society* 1.

[33] ibid at 393–94.

It is plainly mistaken to equate all speech that criticises others and may consequently cause psychological hurt and bruised feelings with speech that is hateful of its targets.[34] For republicans, the latter becomes problematic only when its effect on reasonably robust people is so severe as to prevent them entirely from entering the public domain and participating in political discourse. Neither can a republican polity function if the boundaries of permitted republican discourse are set by the frailties of the least psychologically strong. In *Miller v College of Policing* which concerned alleged transphobic tweets, a unanimous Court of Appeal ruled that a perception-based system of recording and storing on databases by police forces of 'non-crime hate incidents' risked chilling legitimate expression on matters of public controversy.[35] Aside from the practical difficulties of enforcement, the very wide definition of a 'non-crime hate incident' in the College of Policing's Guidance to include unevidenced and non-targeted assertions of hostility, meant that speakers' Article 10 freedom of expression rights were impermissibly interfered with by the Guidance.

The republican state therefore has a very powerful incentive to develop the mental robustness of citizens (primarily through schooling and the flourishing of civic society institutions) that enables current and future participants in political disagreements and policymaking to accept, and endure the fact of, often heated and occasionally intractable disagreement in political discussion. Deeply irreconcilable accounts of the good life and the just society characterise the political world we are born into and die out of. Personal courage in the face of this authentically tragic account of human existence is required of citizens.

Misguided efforts via legally enforceable terms and conditions to create and sustain a community of shared substantive values must be distinguished from the essential importance of ensuring that all citizens are free at the outset to participate in political expression. No service provider should be at liberty to use its contractual standards of service to exclude potential speakers on matters of public discourse on account of class, race, gender etc. But neither, outside of the most exceptional and compelling circumstances involving immediate and unlawful threats of violence, should platforms be able to exclude political expression on the basis of viewpoint. Justice Robert Jackson's admonition in *West Virginia Board of Education v Barnette* remains to this day one of the clearest and most attractive statements of plural, participatory republican government. To paraphrase Justice Jackson, it signifies little in a democratic society to possess a freedom to differ from others on the more trivial aspects of human existence. What is of vital importance to self-government is that we have the freedom to differ among ourselves on

[34] For a slightly more hopeful note on this point see the Law Commission of England and Wales *Hate Crime Laws Final Report* (2021) HC 942 Law Com 402 which explicitly rejects the view that discussion and criticism of gender reassignment per se amounts to vilification and hatred of transgender people, at para 10.509.

[35] Decided 20 December 2021 www.judiciary.uk/wp-content/uploads/2021/12/Miller-v-College-of-Policing-judgment-201221.pdf.

the matters that go to the heart of the existing societal order. That freedom to differ extends, it is suggested, to forceful criticisms of liberalism's cherished institutions and doctrines.

The situation in respect of online speech has now become far removed from the initial idea of mere common carriers of others' expression that animated federal immunity in the US and took shape in section 230 of the Communications Decency Act 1996.[36] This provision replicated the carrier immunity that had long existed in respect of the conventional mail and landline telephone services. AT&T which was the successor to the Bell Telephone Company founded by Alexander Graham Bell was not at liberty, for example, to refuse to allow its phone lines to be used by the Communists or Anarchists or Black Panther movement on the basis that the shareholders disagreed with the political message being communicated. Package delivery services run by UPS and FedEx may not to this day refuse to deliver parcels with books and pamphlets praising the activities of the Westboro Baptist Church or the Ku Klux Klan. By contrast, the owners of platforms treat online speech as subject to their editorial control, much as newspaper proprietors have always done. Volokh argues that we need to debate whether Facebook and YouTube et al are to be treated as closer to newspapers and thus subject to the same overall regulatory regime as print media, or whether these and other platforms are akin to common carriers of conventional mail and parcels.[37] If the former, then they should be denied section 230 immunity (or its equivalent in other jurisdictions) and treated like any other newspaper and face liability in defamation, contempt, copyright etc when they make these kinds of material available online.[38] Platforms could then editorialise without the false pretence that they offer an open viewpoint neutral space for unhindered public debate.

This, however, is an unattractive approach for democratic republicans. Far from acknowledging the critical democratic function that might be played by platforms in modern political discourse in contesting elite power, such a move would entrench yet further corporate control of the virtual public square and thereby incentivise greater cooperation between office holders (the 'ins') and established platform providers. The 'outs' who exist at the margins of political power would then face an even more intense struggle to grab digital audiences for their dissenting critiques of modern society.

Although this book does not engage at the level of technically detailed structural reforms to the practice of digital communications, the normative commitment

[36] For the UK's considerably narrower degree of ISP immunity position, see Defamation Act 1996, s 1 and the High Court ruling incentivising ISP removal of potentially defamatory material in *Godfrey v Demon Internet* [1999] EWHC 240.

[37] E Volokh, 'Trump Has a Point: Facebook's Policing of Speech is Ominous' (2021) *Washington Post* 15 July.

[38] For such an approach see the majority of the Grand Chamber of the European Court of Human Rights in *Delfi AS v Estonia* (2013) App No 64569/09 Judgment of 10 October.

to active republican citizenship requires urgent consideration be given to certain issues of political principle that might in turn inform regulatory policy. Chief among these is whether social media platforms should be treated as public forums with carrier immunity from liability in respect of the material capable of being described as pertaining to public discourse. This is a solution that is urged by free marketeers as well as by democratic republicans. It is only the latter, however, that want additionally to prohibit platform regulation by viewpoint.

For free marketeers, political expression is a commodity like any other form of expressive activity such as advertising. Left to themselves, platforms can be left to devise algorithms that match providers and seekers of specific content. They will need to be able do so in an efficient (profit-generating) manner or else face loss of digital traffic to rival platforms and ultimate revenue collapse/business failure.[39] The private property claims of platform owners ought to continue to enjoy primacy over any competing considerations. Provided market entry for other would-be platform providers is not obstructed, the type of content that users encounter online should be left to service providers to determine as they see fit via non-negotiable contractual terms of service.

The democratic republican standpoint by contrast rests explicitly upon a quid pro quo for carrier immunity; namely that platforms and intermediaries should be obliged to host the political speech of others without engaging in viewpoint discrimination. It would not of course imply that the platform approved the content and there would be content categories (such as child pornography or false statements in relation to commercial products and services) that would remain excludable by platforms. In proposing this radical shift towards a legal/constitutional duty on private individuals/companies to observe viewpoint neutrality, it is only right to anticipate and consider the types of objection that might be made. For example, the analogue equivalent of requiring private owners of physical space to host someone else's speech is either unknown or under-protected in many liberal democracies.[40] In the UK, for example, the rights of property owners to control access to shopping centres has tended to be given primacy.[41] The European Court of Human Rights ruled somewhat technically in *Appleby v UK* that there was nothing in Article 10 of the Convention that bestowed a right to access a privately owned forum for the purpose of exercising Article 10 freedoms.[42] In the US, the

[39] See M Mueller, Challenging the Social Media Moral Panic' (2019) *Policy Analysis* Cato Institute 876.

[40] For an interesting overview see T Perroud, 'Privately-Owned Public Spaces: A Comparative Study of the Legal Responses to Their Development and A Proposal for Reform', www.law.ox.ac.uk/research-and-subject-groups/property-law/blog/2020/03/privately-owned-public-spaces-comparative (22 March 2020).

[41] See, for example, the Court of Appeal decision in *CIN Properties v Rawlins* [1995] 2 EGLR 130.

[42] *Appleby & others v UK* App No 44306/98 (2003) 24 September. The Court did, however, recognise a possible exception to its ruling where, in a corporately owned town, 'the entire municipality is controlled by a private body'. As the Court acknowledged, this was the factual situation in the US case of *Marsh v Alabama* 326 US 501 (1946) where the US Supreme Court did prioritise the right to freedom of expression over the right of the property owner.

current position under federal law is to accord a degree of discretion to state legislatures. The First Amendment does not require the owner of private shopping malls to allow entry to protestors who wish to communicate their grievance to mall shoppers.[43] That said, it is open to state legislatures to carve out greater free speech protections for protestors on privately owned land such as shopping malls where members of the public are lawful visitors without infringing the constitutional rights of mall owners.[44] Perroud found in 2020 that five states offered forms of statutory protection to speakers in privately owned malls.[45]

What is clear in practical terms is that, for the republican virtual public square to flourish, the primacy of the right to speak online over countervailing interests in private property will need to be enshrined in law. Reform of current rules should be inspired by the Democratic Republican societies of 1790s the post-revolutionary US and the task seen in terms of facilitating popular scrutiny and control over elected office holders. Chapter five drew attention to some of the writings that emerged in this period. Emphasising a contestatory and pluralist form of public discourse, the pamphleteers and their anti-Federalist allies among the owners of printing presses gave powerful meaning to grassroots political expression that was, at times, openly and robustly sceptical of office holders. Theirs was a conception of active citizenship and free enquiry that rejected Madison's wish to avoid factious disagreement. It held out no guarantees of eventual convergence and consensus on the matters of topical dispute. The Democratic Republicans deserve credit for their Machiavellian insight that elites will always be tempted to prefer broad readings of executive powers for self-interested reasons. Tunis Wortman's *Treatise Concerning Political Enquiry and the Liberty of the Press* appropriately took aim at both Federalist and anti-Federalist office holders who sought to use seditious libels to silence their critics. The 'licentiousness' of the pamphleteers was a far less significant evil than the act of censoring disrespectful expression concerning the conduct of elected officials. In Wortman's view, 'society should constitute a University of Politics open to the instruction of each of its members'.[46] The writings of Numa, one of the pseudonymous political commentators to surface in the 1790s, also repay close attention. Numa made the case for a broad expressive freedom on the part of the citizens to discuss the characters putting themselves forward for public office. Where such speech was criminalised on account of its purported falseness, there would inevitably be a loss of public confidence in the electoral process and the elected class. Numa is presciently sceptical of ideas of truth in political discourse when they are advanced by one set of 'fallible men' to determine

[43] *Lloyd Corporation v Tanner* 47 US 551 (1972).

[44] *Pruneyard Shopping Center v Robins* 447 US 74 (1980).

[45] California, Colorado, Massachusetts, New Jersey and Washington. See T Perroud, 'Privately-Owned Public Spaces: A Comparative Study of the Legal Responses to their Development and a Proposal for Reform' at n 40 above.

[46] Cited in R Martin, *Government by Dissent: Protest, Resistance and Radical Democratic Thought* (New York, NYU Press, 2013) at 166.

the political liberties of other citizens. In a piece published in November 1796, he condemned the use of sedition laws as amounting to yet another Inquisition that would 'suppress enquiry and … subject public opinion to the direction of single or multivarious despotism'.[47]

Though carrier immunity and the prohibition of viewpoint censorship by platforms and intermediaries undoubtedly represent some necessary steps in the right direction, these reforms will not be sufficient in themselves to safeguard the democratic functioning of the virtual public square. Today, Numa's 'fallible men (and women)' are to be found in both private and public settings. They comprise in part the shareholders, directors and employees of the social media platforms, alongside in-house and external 'fact check' organisations and, increasingly, clumsy and clunky AI systems. Specifically, in respect of fact-checking organisations, greater transparency is plainly needed in respect of the qualifications and political affiliations of 'independent fact checkers'. Occasionally, when powerful organised groups are the victims of a questionable fact-checking exercise that prevents the sharing of a news story, appropriate public attention can be brought to bear on the fact-checking process. Thus, in November 2021 the editors of the *British Medical Journal* published an open letter to Facebook in which they criticised the platform's treatment of a peer (and lawyer-reviewed article published in early November 2021 about poor clinical trial practices at a contract research company working on a COVID-19 vaccine trial for a major vaccine manufacturer.[48] Readers of the article reported difficulties in sharing it on Facebook. Other readers stated that their posts were flagged with the following warning: 'Missing context … Independent fact-checkers say this information could mislead people.' Readers were then warned that users who tried repeatedly to share 'false information' might have their posts removed. Criticisms of the conduct of Facebook (and, by implication, their contracted fact checker) has fortunately been given considerable publicity by sole virtue of the fact that the victim of the fact checking is a powerful national voice in the UK scientific community. Clearly an equivalent degree of scrutiny over platforms' fact checking does not occur routinely. Other, less influential speakers on the receiving end of such decisions will be less able to publicise acts of platform censorship.

Statistical data disclosing the range of groups and individuals fact checked (and the frequency with which they have been fact checked) should also be made publicly available. If it transpires that notionally independent fact-checking organisations rarely or infrequently fact check governmental claims or disproportionately target particular sections of public opinion, this fact should be easily ascertainable via a URL link on the webpage and Twitter/Facebook accounts of the fact-checker organisation. This could be a statement along the lines of 'Last year/month/week, we fact checked 60 statements reported on the Government's

[47] Numa, 'A Culture of Democratic Dissent' (1796) republished in S Smith, *Freedom of Expression – Foundational Documents and Historical Arguments* (Oxford, Oxbridge Research Associates, 2018).

[48] See www.bmj.com/content/375/bmj.n2635/rr-80.

websites; 35 on BBC news web pages; 25 on Sky News; 95 on *The Times*; 15 on the *Anarchist's Guide to Dystopia* website etc. We found factual errors in respect of the following statements … The justification for the finding of a factual error in each instance is as follows …'

Fallibility also exists in governmental circles as revealed by self-serving acts of censorship practised by ministers and regulatory agencies. It is wholly antithetical to a system of self-authoring of laws to privilege (as the operationalisation of the OFCOM Code patently does) government narratives on matters of public interest and legitimate debate. We should be very concerned when a government minister or government agency justifies their actions on the basis that they are seeking to rid the public arena of misinformation and disinformation. Official claims that certain types of speech pose potential harms to the public interest need particularly exacting scrutiny in public discourse. It should be a given that official accounts of 'harmful material' are openly and routinely queried in the public sphere. Instead the conferral of 'trusted flagger' status on civil servants facilitates the rapid removal of content considered problematic by office holders.

Other matters of political principle include a commitment to transparency in respect of the nature and frequency of government requests to social media platforms to remove particular content. Some platforms do issue transparency reports that reveal which states around the world have requested removal of material that is alleged to concern terrorism in breach of the platform's terms of service conditions.[49] Much greater parliamentary scrutiny is needed of the daily activities of behind-the-scenes censorship practised by low-visibility bodies such as the Coronavirus Disinformation Unit. Disappointingly, the House of Commons Digital Media Culture and Sport Select Committee has shown no appetite to date to hold ministers or Unit officials to account. This is quite simply a dereliction of the Committee's parliamentary duty to the rest of us.

More fundamentally still, search engines which provide the gateways many of us use to discover online materials need to be reconfigured and placed on much more republic-friendly footing. The biases that search engines display towards specific content and away from other content must be revealed to users. If Google tends to push news consumers with search requests towards *The Guardian* and relegate same subject matter stories from *The Daily Mail* down to page 4 of the search results (or vice versa), should Google not be compelled to disclose this fact to its users?[50] Just as we know that *The Guardian* is a centre left-leaning publication

[49] For example, in the period July to December 2020, Twitter states that it received 38,524 'legal demands' to remove material from 131,933 accounts. The demands were made by 53 different countries with Japan being the country that most frequently asks for the removal of materials followed by India, Russia and Turkey, see https://transparency.twitter.com/en/reports/removal-requests.html#2020-jul-dec. For commentary, see D Citron, (2017) *Policy Analysis* 828.

[50] C Tobbit, 'Left-wing Bias or SEO Supremacy? Inside Mail Online's Struggle with The Guardian on Google' (2021) 2 December and see thttps://pressgazette.co.uk/inside-mail-onlines-struggle-to-compete-with-guardian-on-google/.

and *The Telegraph* a Conservative supporting newspaper, so too we ought to know that Google, Twitter, Facebook, YouTube etc will steer us towards certain news and opinion content and away from others. It is, of course, a logical impossibility for all viewpoints be given equal prominence on page 1 of a platform's search results and therefore some degree of prioritisation will inevitably occur. Users should, however, have some reassurance that what they are seeing is not the result of viewpoint-based ranking by the platform. The pressing challenge then falls upon speakers to grab and hold onto the attention of their audiences.

Final Thoughts: The Threat to Self-government

Addressing the sorts of abuses that had occurred in the US political sphere, Hart Ely argued for a judicial role in keeping channels of political representation open. A jurisprudence was needed that buttresses the openness of representative democracy through generous rights of political participation. Although Hart Ely was careful not to attribute special wisdom to the federal US judiciary, he nonetheless recognised that our elected representatives in the legislature were the least appropriate people to whom we should turn when attempting to prevent the blocking of channels of political change. Hart Ely maintained that 'Courts must police inhibitions on expression and other political activity because we cannot trust our elected officials to do so: ins have a way of wanting to make sure that outs stay out.'[51]

In the final analysis, Ely seems to be saying the courts can function legitimately *only where* they safeguard a self-governing community by upholding broad freedoms to participate in political discourse. Ely recognised at the same time that the actual record of the US courts is not impressive. They have been 'swept along' by similar sorts of anxieties to those which have impelled politicians to curtail speech freedoms. That history 'mocks our constitutional commitment to an open political process'.[52] Ad hoc assessments of current threats to the national interest could thus never afford a firm basis for constitutional protection of speech interests. As free speech scholars in other jurisdictions know all too well, the US Supreme Court is not alone in this regard. Constitutional and supreme courts elsewhere in the world have patchy records defending expressive freedoms in the face of executive claims of irreparable damage to public order and the national interest. So, whilst the courts could in theory play a valuable role in buttressing the democratic republican state, it would be deeply unwise to assume an unswerving and principled devotion on the part of the judicial branch to the practice of participatory and pluralist republican government. It is more likely that we should expect a degree of judicial ambivalence or even hostility to broad rights of political

[51] *Democracy and Distrust – A Theory of Judicial Review* (Mass. Harvard University Press, 1980) at 106.

[52] ibid at 109.

participation that underpin authentically republican forms of popular sovereignty. After all, the judge-developed common law stands for restraints on the powers of transient political majorities. It demands that the political energies of the people be contained within an overall commitment to the norms and institutions of the existing constitutional order. The obverse – an invocation of the constituent power via the most extensive sets of freedoms to engage in political expression and association – risks, as the liberal constitutionalist envisions it, a descent into anarchy and arbitrariness. Out of that anarchy bounds the charismatic leader who claims to speak for 'the people', but quickly establishes a form of despotic rule in which free political expression is a prominent and early casualty.

For democratic republicans committed to restoring the agon where ongoing, robust contestations of elite governance occur, a dependence upon the courts to shore up the vibrancy of democracy is fundamentally misplaced. Kalyvas' account of popular sovereignty reminds us that the constituent power is not the normative void of despotic rule that liberal constitutionalists would have us believe.[53] The very statement of republican freedom – the ability of politically equal citizens to participate in the design and redesign of the state and to co-author the laws under which all live – suggests something far removed from the condition of arbitrary rule charged by its liberal critics. The people must at all times enjoy the freedom to come together to remake and to constitute the society in which they live. There must at all times be a wholly unlimited power for all citizens to act as the constituent power. This means, of course, that any single exercise of the constituent power cannot close off future exercises of the same power. Colón-Ríos' remarks that:

> Since constituent power is closely related to the democratic ideal … it requires that a constitution created in a manner consistent with the principles of democratic openness and popular participation. In fact, it can be said that the principles of democratic openness and popular participation are contained in the very concept of constituent power.[54]

To let the constituted authorities (elected officials) or, today, the CEO of Twitter determine the boundaries of acceptable expression threatens republican self-government by closing down the system of political contestation between incumbents and their rivals. Jack Dorsey's successor as CEO of Twitter is Parag Agrawal. In 2010 he tweeted 'I am not sure what is more troubling: death of free speech or that "peace in society" is threatened if a book is not banned'. Recently he commented,

> Our role is not to be bound by the First Amendment, but our role is to serve a healthy public conversation, and our moves are reflective of things that we believe lead to a healthier public conversation … The kinds of things that we do about this is: Focus

[53] A Kalyvas, 'Popular Sovereignty, Democracy and the Constituent Power' (2005) 12 *Constellations* 233.

[54] J Colón-Ríos, *Weak Constitutionalism – Democratic Legitimacy and the Question of Constituent Power* (London, Routledge, 2013) at 111.

> less on thinking about free speech, but thinking about how the times have changed … Most people can speak. Where our role is particularly emphasized is who can be heard. The scarce commodity today is attention. There's a lot of content out there. A lot of tweets out there, not all of it gets attention, some subset of it gets attention. And so increasingly our role is moving towards how we recommend content.[55]

Agrawal's power to skew online expression towards his version of a 'healthy public conversation' should cause alarm. In the regrettable instance that his organisation is allowed to continue to editorialise, then it is difficult to see how Twitter can retain its federal immunity in respect of materials allowed to remain on the platform. Removal of the immunity would, however, likely incentivise more regular and more extensive acts of platform censorship 'to be on the safe side'. To invoke the spirit of Machiavelli and his insights into oligarchic threats to liberty, democratic republicans would do well to value and constantly affirm broad freedoms of online expression as a vital means of vigorously contesting all forms of elite rule.

[55] See www.technologyreview.com/2020/11/18/1012066/emtech-stage-twitters-cto-on-misinformation/.

BIBLIOGRAPHY

Ackerman, B, *We the People, Vol 1: Foundations* (Massachusetts, Harvard University Press, 1991)

Ackerman, B, *We the People Vol II: Transformations* (Massachusetts, Harvard University Press, 1998)

Ackerman, B, and Fishkin, J, 'Deliberation Day' (2002) 10 *Jo. Pol. Phil.* 129

Aitchison, G, 'Three Models of Republican Rights: Juridical, Parliamentary and Populist' (2017) 65 *Pol. Sts.* 33

Albini, J, 'Crisis or Reconstruction: Mannheim's Alternatives for Western Democracies' (1970) 3 *Sociological Focus* 63

Anderson, D, 'The Promises of New York Times v Sullivan' (2015) 20 *Roger Williams University L. Rev.* 1

Arendt, H, 'The Concept of History: Ancient and Modern' in *Between Past and Future* (New York, Penguin, 1977)

Arendt, H, *The Life of the Mind* (Boston, Harcourt, 1978)

Arendt, H, *The Human Condition* (Chicago, University of Chicago Press, 1998)

Arendt, H, *On Revolution* (London, Penguin Classics, 2009)

Aswad, E, 'In a World of "Fake News," What's a Social Media Platform to Do?' (2020) 4 *Utah L. Rev.*1009

Baker, CE, *Media, Markets and Democracy* (New York, CUP, 2002)

Barendt, E, *Broadcasting Law – A Comparative Study* (Oxford, Clarendon Press, 1995)

Barendt, E, 'Balancing Freedom of Expression and the Right to Reputation: Reflections on Reynolds and Reportage' (2012) 63 *N.I.Q.R.* 59

Barendt, E, *Anonymous Speech* (Oxford, Hart, 2016)

Barker, E, *Entering the Agon: Dissent and Authority in Homer, Historiography and Tragedy* (New York, OUP, 2009)

Barnidge, M, 'Social Affect and Political Disagreement on Social Media' (2018) 4 *Social Media & Society* 1

Barnett, A and Carty, P, *The Athenian Option – Radical Reform for the House of Lords* (London, Demos, 1998)

Barrett, W, *Irrational Man – A Study in Existential Philosophy* (New York, Anchor Books, 1990)

Bartlett, J, *The People vs Tech – How the Internet is Killing Democracy (and How we Save it)* (London, Ebury Press, 2018)

Bates, S, *An Aristocracy of Critics – Luce, Hutchins, Niebuhr and the Committee that Redefined Freedom of the Press* (New Haven, Yale University Press 2020)

Bellamy, R, *Political Constitutionalism – A Republican Defence of the Constitutionality of Democracy* (Cambridge, CUP, 2007)

Bellamy, R, 'Rights as Democracy' (2012) 15 *Crit. Rev. of Int. Soc. & Pol. Phil.* 449

Benckler, Y, *The Wealth of Networks – How Social Production Transforms Markets and Freedom* (New Haven, Yale University Press, 2006)

Benjamin, W, 'Theses on the Philosophy of History' in *Illuminations: Essays and Reflections Theses on the Philosophy of History* (Boston, Mariner Books, 2019)

Berlin, I, *Against the Grain – Essays in the History of Ideas* (London, Hogarth Press, 1979)

Berlin, I, *The Roots of Romanticism* (New Jersey, Princeton University Press, 1999)

Bingham, T, 'The Rule of Law' (2007) 66 *C.L.J.* 67

Blumberg, P, *Repressive Jurisprudence in the Early American Republic* (New York, CUP, 2010)

Bodin, J, *Les six livres de la Rèpublique* (Paris, Librairie Generale Francaise, 1993)

Bon, G, Le, *The Crowd – A Study of the Popular Mind* (New York, Dover Publications, 2002)

Bradford, R, *Orwell – A Man of Our Time* (London, Bloomsbury, 2020)
Brennan, J, *Against Democracy* (New Jersey, Princeton University Press, 2016)
Buchstein, H, 'Countering the "Democracy Thesis" – Sortition in Ancient Greek Political Theory' (2015) 18 *Redescriptions* 126
Buren, MV, *Inquiry into the Origin and Course of Political Parties in the United States* (New York, Hurd & Houghton, 1867)
Burnham, P, 'New Labour and the Politics of Depoliticisation' (2001) 3 *Brit. Jo. of Politics and Int. Rels.* 127
Canovan, M, 'Taking Politics to the People: Populism as the Ideology of Democracy' in Meny, Y, and Surel, Y (eds) *Democracies and the Populist Challenge* (London, Palgrave MacMillan, 2002)
Canovan, M, *The People* (Cambridge, Polity Press, 2005)
Carey, J, *The Intellectual and the Masses – Pride and Prejudice among the Literary Intelligentsia 1880–1939* (London, Faber & Faber, 1992)
Carolan, E, 'Ireland's Constitutional Convention: Behind the Hype about Citizen-led Constitutional Change' (2015) 13 *Int. Jo. Const. Law* 733
Clarke, H, Goodwin, M and Whiteley, P, *Brexit: Why Britain Voted to Leave the European Union* (Cambridge, CUP, 2017)
Clarke, H, and Stewart, M, 'The Decline of Parties in the Minds of Citizens' (1998) 1 *Am. Pol. Sci. Rev.* 35
Coe, P, '(Re)embracing Social Responsibility Theory as a Basis for Media Speech: Shifting the Normal Paradigm for a Modern Media' (2018) 69 *NILQ* 403
Cohen, S, *Folk Devils and Moral Panics* (Abingdon, Routledge, 2011)
Colón-Ríos, J, *Weak Constitutionalism – Democratic Legitimacy and the Question of Constituent Power* (Abingdon, Routledge, 2012)
Conant, J, *Thomas Jefferson and the Development of American Public Education* (California, University of California, Berkeley and Los Angeles, 1962)
Cooper, L, 'Hannah Arendt's Political Philosophy: An Interpretation' (1976) 38 *The Review of Politics* 145
Cram, I, 'Keeping the Demos out of Liberal Democracy? Participatory Politics, "Fake News" and the Online Speaker' (2019) 11 *Journal of Media Law* 113
Crouch, C, *Post Democracy* (Cambridge, Polity, 2004)
Crouch, C, 'The March Towards Post-Democracy, Ten Years On' (2016) 87 *Pol. Quarterly* 71
Crozier, M, Huntington, S and Watanuki, J, *The Crisis of Democracy: Report on the Governability of Democracies to the Trilateral Commission* (New York, NYU Press, 1975)
Cutts, D, Goodwin, M, Heath, O, and Surridge, P, 'Brexit, the 2019 General Election and the Realignment of British Politics' (2020) 91 *Pol. Quarterly* 7
D'Ancona, M, *Post-Truth: The New War on Truth and How to Fight Back* (London, Ebury Press, 2017)
Deibert, R, 'The Road to Digital Unfreedom: Three Painful Truths about Social Media' (2019) 30 *Jo. of Democracy* 25
Dostoevsky, F, *Notes from the Underground* and *The Double* (London, Penguin, 2009)
Dotts, B, 'The Democratic-Republican Societies: An Educational Dream Deferred' (2010) 88 *Educational Horizons* 179
Dowlen, O, 'Sorting out Sortition: A Perspective on the Random Selection of Political Officers' (2009) 57 *Pol. Sts.* 298
Dunn, J, *Setting the People Free – The Story of Democracy* (London, Atlantic Books, 2006)
Dunn, J (ed) *Democracy: The Unfinished Journey 508 BC to AD 1993* (Oxford, OUP, 1992)
Dworkin, R, *Law's Empire* (Massachusetts, Harvard University Press, 1986)
Dworkin, R, *A Bill of Rights for Britain* (London, Chatto & Windus, 1990)
Eatwell, R and Goodwin, M, *National Populism – The Revolt Against Liberal Democracy* (UK, Pelican Books, 2018)
Ekins, R, and Gee, G, 'Putting Judicial Power in its Place' (2017) 36 *Uni. Queensland Law Journal* 375
Embery, P, *Despised – Why the Modern Left Loathes the Working Class* (Cambridge, Polity, 2021)

Estlund, D, *Democratic Authority: A Philosophical Framework* (New Jersey, Princeton University Press 2008)
Estlund, D and Landemore, H, 'The Epistemic Value of Democratic Deliberation' in Bachtiger, A, Dryzek, J, Mansbridge, J, and Warren, M (eds), *The Oxford Handbook of Deliberative Democracy* (Oxford, OUP, 2018)
Etxabe, J, *The Experience of Tragic Judgment* (Abingdon, Routledge, 2014)
European Commission for Democracy through Law: Compilation of Venice Commission Opinions and Reports Concerning Freedom of Expression and Media (Strasbourg, Council of Europe Publishing, 2016)
Everson, M, 'Beyond the Bundesverfassungsgericht: On the Necessary Cunning of Constitutional Reasoning' in Bankowski, Z, and Scott, A (eds) *The European Union and its Order: The Legal Theory of European Integration* (Oxford, Blackwell, 2000)
Farrell, D, Suiter, J, and Harris, C, '"Systematizing" Constitutional Deliberation: The 2016–18 Citizens' Assembly in Ireland' (2018) 34 *Irish Pol. Sts.* 113
Farrell, M, and Cupito, M, *Newspapers: A Complete Guide to the Industry* (New York, Peter Lang, 2010)
Fenton, N, *Digital, Political and Radical* (Cambridge, Polity Press, 2016)
Feynman, R, *The Pleasure of Finding Things Out* (New York, Basic Books, 1999)
Foner, P (ed), *Thomas Jefferson – Selections from his Writings* (New York, International Publishers Co 1943)
Forsdyke, S, 'Athenian Democratic Ideology and Herodotus' "Histories"' (2001) 122 *Am. Jo. Philology* 329
Frank, T, *People Without Power – The War on Populism and the Fight for Democracy* (London, Scribe, 2020)
Fukuyama, F, *The End of History and the Last Man* (London, Penguin, 1992)
Fuller, J, *What is Happening to News* (Chicago, University of Chicago Press, 2010)
Furedi, F, *Populism and the European Culture Wars* (Abingdon, Routledge, 2018)
Furedi, F, *Democracy under Siege* (Winchester, Zero Books, 2021)
Galston, W, *Anti-Pluralism the Populist Threat to Liberal Democracy* (New Haven, Yale University Press, 2020)
Gey, S, 'The First Amendment and the Dissemination of Socially Worthless Untruths' (2008) 36 *Fla. St. U. L. Rev.* 1
Giddens, A, *The Global Third Way Debate* (Cambridge, Polity Press, 2001)
Gleason, T, 'Saving Journalism from Itself (and From us): The Hutchins Commission was Right then, so What About Now?' (1998) 3 *Comm. L & Poly.* 409
Goodhart, D, *The Road to Somewhere* (2017, Penguin, London)
Gray, J, *Enlightenment's Wake* (Abingdon, Routledge Classics, 2007)
Gray, J, 'The Strange Death of Liberal Politics' *New Statesman* (2016) 5 July
Grayling, A, *Democracy and its Crisis* (London, Oneworld Publications, 2017)
Gunaratne, S, and Safar Hasim, M, 'Social Responsibility Theory Revisited a Comparative Study of Public Journalism and Developmental Journalism' (2014) 3 *Javnost: The Public Journal of the European Institute for Communication and Culture* 97
Guttman, A, 'The Challenge of Multiculturalism in Political Ethics' (1993) 22 *Philosophy and Public Affairs* 171
Habermas, J, *Between Facts and Norms* (Massachusetts, MIT Press, 1996)
Habermas, J, 'The Inclusion of the Other' in Cronin, C, and Greiff, P, *Studies in Political Theory* (Massachusetts, MIT Press, 1998)
Habermas, J, 'Constitutional Democracy: A Paradoxical Union of Contradictory Principles?' (2001) 29 *Pol. Theory* 766
Hamilton, A, *The Papers of Alexander Hamilton*, Vol 17, *August 1794–December 1794*, Syrett, HC (ed) (New York: Columbia University Press, 1972)
Hampshire, S, 'Presidential Address to the American Philosophical Association' *Proceedings and Addresses of the American Philosophical Association* (1991) Vol 65

Hardt, M, and Negri, A, *Empire* (Massachusetts, Howard University Press, 2001

Hart-Ely, J, *Democracy and Distrust – A Theory of Judicial Review* (Massachusetts, Harvard University Press, 1980)

Hausheer, R, 'Introduction' in I Berlin, 'The Counter-Enlightenment' in *Against the Current – Essays in the History of Ideas* (London, Hogarth Press, 1979)

Hayek, F, *The Constitution of Liberty* (Abingdon, Routledge Classics, 2006)

Heinze, E, *Hate Speech and Democratic Citizenship* (Oxford, OUP, 2016)

Hempel, S, *The Medical Detective: John Snow, Cholera and the Mystery of the Broad Street Pump* (London, Granta, 2007)

Herodotus, *The Histories* Book Five (Oxford, OUP, 1998)

Hirschl, R, *Towards Juristocracy – The Origins and Consequences of the New Constitutionalism* (Massachusetts, Harvard University Press, 2004)

Holmes, S, 'Precommitment and the Paradox of Democracy' in Elster, J, and Slagstad, R (eds) *Constitutionalism and Democracy* (Cambridge, CUP, 2018)

Holst, C, and Molander, A, 'Epistemic Democracy and the Role of Experts' (2019) 18 *Contemp. Pol. Theory* 541

Holznagel, B, and Hemmert-Halswick, M, 'Securing Rational Discourse Surrounding Referenda in Germany' in Baume, S, Boillet, V, and Martenet, V (eds) *Misinformation in Referenda* (Abingdon, Routledge, 2021)

Honig, B, 'Another Cosmopolitanism? Law and Politics in the New Europe' in R Post (ed) *Another Cosmopolitanism* (New York, OUP, 2006)

Honig, H, 'Dead Rights, Live Futures: A Reply to Habermas' "Constitutional Democracy"' (2001) 29 *Pol. Theory* 792

Horder, J, 'Criminal Law at the Limit: Countering False Claims in Elections and Referendums' (2021) 84 *M.L.R.* 429

Horwith, M, 'Tocqueville and the Tyranny of the Majority' (1966) 28 *The Review of Politics* 293

House of Commons *The Report of the Iraq Inquiry* (2016) HC 264 (Chilcot Report)

House of Commons Treasury Select Committee Report *Lessons from Greensill Capital* at https://publications.parliament.uk/pa/cm5802/cmselect/cmtreasy/151/15102.htm (July 2021)

House of Lords Communications and Digital Select Committee *Free for All? Freedom of Expression in the Digital Age* (2021–22) HL Paper 54

Hutchins Commission *A Free and Responsible Press, A General Report on Mass Communication: Newspapers, Radio, Motion Pictures, Magazines and Books* (Chicago, University of Chicago Press, 1947)

Jefferson, T, *Thomas Jefferson: Selections from His Writings* Foner, P (ed) (US, International Publishers, 1943)

Johnson, S, *The Ghost Map: The Story of London's Most Terrifying Epidemic* (US, Riverhead Books, 2006)

Kalyvas, A, 'Popular Sovereignty, Democracy and the Constituent Power' (2005) 12 *Constellations* 223

Kant, I, 'An Answer to the Question: What is Enlightenment' in Reiss, H (ed) *Political Writings* (Cambridge, CUP, 1991)

Kant, I, Second Proposition' in 'Idea for a Universal History with a Cosmopolitan Purpose' in Brown, G and Held, D (eds) *The Cosmopolitan Reader* (Cambridge, Polity Press, 2010)

Kaufmann, W, *Nietzsche: Philosopher, Psychologist and Antichrist* (New Jersey, Princeton Classics, 2013)

Keller, D, 'Internet Platforms: Observations on Speech, Danger and Money' (2018) Hoover Institution Aegis Paper Series at https://papers.ssrn.com/sol3/papers.cfm?abstract_id=3262936

Ketcham, K, *The Anti-Federalist Papers and the Constitutional Convention Debates* (New York, Signet, 1986)

Kramer, L, *The People Themselves – Popular Constitutionalism and Judicial Review* (New York, OUP, 2004)

Kratsev, I, and Holmes, S, *The Light that Failed – A Reckoning* (London, Penguin, 2020)

Landemore, H, *Democratic Reason: Politics, Collective Intelligence and the Rule of Many* (New Jersey, Princeton University Press, 2011)

Landemore, H, 'Deliberation, Cognitive Diversity, and Democratic Inclusiveness: An Epistemic Argument for the Random Selection of Representatives' (2013) 190 *Synthese* 1209

Landemore, H, *Open Democracy – Reinventing Popular Rule in the Twenty-First Century* (New Jersey, Princeton University Press, 2020)

Lane, M, *Greek and Roman Political Ideas* (London, Pelican, 2014)

Larmore, C, *Morals of Modernity* (Cambridge, CUP, 1996)

Lasch, C, *The Revolt of the Elites and the Betrayal of Democracy* (New York, WW Norton, 1995

Law Commission of England and Wales *Hate Crime Laws Final Report* (2021) HC 942 Law Com 402

Leipold, B, Nabulsi, K, and White, S (eds), *Radical Republicanism: Recovering the Tradition's Popular Heritage* (Oxford, OUP, 2020)

Levy, L, 'On the Origins of the Free Speech Clause' (1984–85) 32 *UCLA L Rev* 177

Lind, M, *The New Class War – Saving Democracy from the Metropolitan Elite* (London, Atlantic Books, 2020)

Link, E, *Democratic-Republican Societies, 1790–1800 – Number 9 of the Columbia Studies in American Culture* (New York, Octagon Books)

Lintott, A, *The Constitution of the Roman Republic* (Oxford, OUP, 1999)

Lippman, W, *Public Opinion* (New York, Free Press, 1922)

Lippman, W, *The Phantom Public* (New York, Harcourt, Brace and Co, 1925)

Loughlin, M, 'Rights, Democracy and Law' in Campbell, T, Ewing, K, and Tomkins, A, (eds) *Sceptical Essays on Human Rights* (Oxford, OUP, 2001)

McCormick, J, 'Machiavellian Democracy: Controlling Elites with Ferocious Populism' (2001) 95 *Am. Pol. Sci. Rev.* 297

McCormick, J, *Machiavellian Democracy* (New York, CUP, 2011)

McCormick, J, 'Of Tribunes and Tyrants: Machiavelli's Legal and Extra-Legal Modes for Controlling Elites' (2015) 28 *Ratio Juris* 252

McCormick, J, 'The New Ochlophobia? Populism, Majority Rule and Prospects for Democratic-Republicanism' in Elazar, Y, and Rousseliere, G (eds) *Republicanism and the Future of Democracy* (New York, CUP, 2019)

McElligott, J, *Royalism, Print and Censorship in Revolutionary England* (Woodbridge, Boybell Press, 2007)

McGilchrist, I, *The Master and his Emissary – The Divided Brain and the Making of the Western World* (New Haven, Yale University Press, 2009)

Machiavelli, N, *The Prince* (London, Penguin Classics, 2003)

Machiavelli, N, *Discourses on First Ten Books of Titus Livy* (Oxford, OUP, 2008)

Machiavelli, N, *Letter to Zenobius* in Burnham, J, *The Machiavellians – Defenders of Freedom* (London, Lume Books, 2020)

Madison, J, *The Papers of James Madison* Hutchinson, W (ed) (Chicago and Charlottesville, University of Chicago and University Press of Virginia, 1962)

Madison, J, Hamilton, A, and Jay, J, *The Federalist Papers* (London, Penguin, 1987)

Mair, P, *Ruling the Void: The Hollowing of Western Democracy* (London, Verso, 2013)

Mair, P, Muller, W, and Plasser F (eds), *Political Parties and Electoral Change: Party Responses to Electoral Markets* (London, Sage, 2004)

Manin, B, *The Principles of Representative Government* (Cambridge, CUP, 1997)

Mannheim, K, 'The Democratization of Culture' in Wolff, K (ed) *From Karl Mannheim* (London, Transaction Publishing, 1993)

Mannheim, K, 'Present Trends in the Building of Society' in Cattrell, R, Cohen, J and Travers, R (eds) *Human Affairs* (London, Macmillan, 1938)

Mannheim, K, 'Democratic Planning and New Science of Society' in Brumwell, J (ed) *This Changing World* (London, Routledge, 1944)

Mannheim, K, *Diagnosis of Our Time* (New York, OUP, 1944)

Marcus, M, *Documentary History of the United States Supreme Court 1789–1800* (New York, Columbia University Press, 1990)

Martin, R, *Government by Dissent: Protest, Resistance and Radical Democratic Thought* (New York, NYU Press, 2013)

Matthews, R, 'The Radical Political Philosophy of Thomas Jefferson: An Essay in Retrieval' (2004) *Midwest Studies in Philosophy* XXVIII

Matthews, R, 'James Madison's Political Theory: Hostage to Democratic Fortune' (2005) 67 *The Review of Politics* 49

Maynor, J, *Republicanism in the Modern World* (Cambridge, Polity Press, 2003)

Meacham, J, *Thomas Jefferson – The Art of Power* (New York, Random House, 2013)

Mill, JS, *Utilitarianism, Liberty and Representative Government* (London, Everyman's Library, 1910)

Miller, D, 'The Place of Plural Voting in Mill's Conception of Representative Government' (2015) 77 *The Review of Politics* 399

Miller, J, *The Federalist Era 1789–1801* (London, Hamish Hamilton, 1960)

Montaigne, M, *The Complete Essays* (London, Penguin, 1993)

Montesquieu, CL, *The Spirit of the Laws* (Cambridge Texts in the History of Political Thought) Cohler, A (ed) (Cambridge, CUP, 1989)

Monti, M, 'The EU Code of Practice on Disinformation and the Risk of the Privatisation of Censorship' in Giusti, S and Piras, E (eds) *Democracy and Fake News* (London, Routledge, 2020)

Mouffe, C, 'Democracy and Pluralism: A Critique of the Rationalist Approach' (1995) 16 *Cardozo Law Rev* 1358

Mouffe, C, *The Democratic Paradox* (London, Verso, 2005)

Mouffe, C, 'Democracy, Power and the "Political"' in Benhabib, S (ed) *Democracy and Difference: Contesting the Boundaries of the Political* (New Jersey, Princeton University Press, 1996)

Mudde, C and Kaltwasser, C, *Populism: A Very Short Introduction* (Oxford, OUP, 2017)

Mueller, M, 'Challenging the Social Media Moral Panic' (2019) 876 *Policy Analysis* (Cato Institute)

Müller, J-W, *What is Populism?* (London, Penguin, 2017)

Mumford, L, *The City in History* (Harcourt, Brace & World, 1961)

Nasaw, D, *The Chief: The Life of William Randolph Hearst – The Rise and Fall of the Real Citizen Kane* (London, Gibson Square Books, 2003)

Neuborne, B, 'Ghosts in the Attic: Idealized Pluralism, Community and Hate Speech' (1992) 27 *Harv. C.R.-C.L.L. Rev.* 371

Nicol, D, *The Constitutional Protection of Capitalism* (Oxford, Hart Publishing, 2010)

Nietzsche, F, *The Birth of Tragedy and the Genealogy of Morals* (New York, Anchor Books, 1956)

Numa, 'A Culture of Democratic Dissent' (1796) in Smith, S, *Freedom of Expression – Foundational Documents and Historical Arguments* (Oxford, Oxbridge Research Associates, 2018)

Nyhan, B and Reifler, J, 'When Corrections Fail: The Persistence of Political Misperceptions' (2010) 32 *Pol. Behaviour* 303

Ober, J, *Demopolis: Democracy Before Liberalism in Theory and Practice* (Cambridge, CUP, 2017)

O'Connell, R, *The Ghosts of Cannae: Hannibal and the Darkest Hour of the Roman Republic* (New York, Random House, 2011)

O'Leary, K, 'Machiavellian Democracy: An Engine for Reform' (2011) *The Good Society* 141

O'Neill, J, 'The Rhetoric of Deliberation: Some Problems in Kantian Theories of Deliberative Democracy' (2002) 8 *Res Publica* 249

Ortega y Gasset, J, *The Revolt of the Masses* (New York, WW Norton, 1993)

Orwell, G, *The Road to Wigan Pier* (London, Penguin Modern Classics, 2001)

Oster, J, *European and International Media Law* (Cambridge, CUP, 2016)

Paine, T, *Rights of Man, Common Sense and Other Political Writings* (Oxford, OUP, 2016)

Pettit, P, 'Republican Theory and Political Trust' in Braithwaite, V and Levi, M (eds) *Trust and Governance* (New York, Russell Sage Foundation, 1998)

Pettit, P, *Republicanism: A Theory of Freedom and Government* (Oxford, OUP, 2001)

Pettit, P, 'Depoliticizing Democracy' (2004) 17 *Ratio Juris* 52

Pettit, P, *On the People's Terms – A Republican Theory and Model of Democracy* (Cambridge, CUP, 2012)

Perroud, T, 'Privately-Owned Public Spaces: A Comparative Study of the Legal Responses to Their Development and A Proposal for Reform' at www.law.ox.ac.uk/research-and-subject-groups/property-law/blog/2020/03/privately-owned-public-spaces-comparative

Plato, *Gorgias* (London, Penguin Classics, 1973)

Pope, J, 'Republican Moments: The Role of Direct Popular Power in the American Constitutional Order' (1990) 139 *U. Pa. L. Rev.* 287

Post, R, *Democracy, Expertise, Academic Freedom – A First Amendment Jurisprudence for the Modern State* (New Haven, Yale University Press, 2012)

Ranttila, K, 'Social Media and Monopoly' (2020) 46 *Ohio N.U.L. Rev.* 161

Rawls, J, *Political Liberalism* (New York, Columbia University Press, 1993

Raz, J, *The Morality of Freedom* (Oxford, OUP, 1986)

Redish, M, and Lippman, G, 'Freedom of Expression and the Civic Republican Revival in Constitutional Theory – The Ominous Implications' (1991) 79 *Cal. L. Rev.* 267

Renner, R, 'The Historical Development of Norms of Journalism' in *Journalism and Media Privilege* IRIS *Special* European Audiovisual Observatory (Strasbourg, Council of Europe, 2017)

Renwick, A and Palese, M, *Doing Democracy Better: How Can Information and Discourse in Election and Referendum Campaigns in the UK be Improved* (London, UCL Constitution Unit, 2019)

Renwick, A, Palese, M and Sargeant, J, 'Information in Referendum Campaigns: How Can It be Improved?' (2020) 56 *Representation* 521

Richter, M, 'Comparative Political Analysis in Montesquieu and Tocqueville' (1969) 1 *Comparative Politics* 129

Robertson, C, Mourao, R, and Thorson E, 'Who Uses Fact-Checking Sites? The Impact of Demographics, Political Antecedents, and Media Use on Fact-Checking Site Awareness, Attitudes and Behaviour' (2020) 5 *Int. Jo. of Press Politics* 217

Robertson, R, *The Case for the Enlightenment – Scotland and Naples 1680–1760* (Cambridge, CUP, 2005)

Robertson, R, *The Enlightenment: The Pursuit of Happiness* (London, Allen Lane, 2020)

Rowbottom, J, 'To Rant, Vent and Converse: Protecting Low Level Digital Speech' (2012) 71 *CLJ* 355

Rowbottom, J, 'Lies, Manipulation and Elections – Controlling False Campaign Statements' (2012) 32 *O.J.L.S.* 507

Rush, B, 'On the Defects of the Confederation' in Runes, D (ed) *The Selected Writings of Benjamin Rush* (New York, Philosophical Library, 1947)

Rush, B, 'Order' *Columbian Centinel* 1 (1794) 3 September

Ryan, A, *On Politics* (London, Penguin, 2012)

Sanders, L, 'Against Deliberation' (1997) 25 *Pol. Theory* 347

Schaap, A, 'Agonism in Divided Societies' (2006) 32 *Phil. & Soc. Crit.* 255

Schumpeter, J, *Capitalism, Socialism and Democracy* (New York, Harper & Row, 1942)

Schwartzberg, M, 'Epistemic Democracy and its Challenges' (2015) 18 *Am. Rev. Pol. Sci.* 187

Schwiddessen, S, et al 'Germany's Network Enforcement Act – Closing the Net on Fake News?' (2018) 40 *European Intellectual Property Review* 539

Shapiro, I, 'Enough of Deliberation: Politics is about Interests and Power' in Macedo, S (ed) *Deliberative Politics: Essays on Democracy and Disagreement* (New York, OUP, 1999)

Sheehan, C, *James Madison and the Spirit of Republicanism* (New York, CUP, 2009)

Siebert, F, 'The Role of Mass Communication in American Society' in Henry, N (ed) *The Fifty-Third Yearbook of the National Society for Study of Education* (Chicago, National Society for the Study of Education, 1954)

Sintomer, Y, 'From Deliberative to Radical Democracy? Sortition and Politics in the Twenty-first Century' (2018) 46 *Pol. & Soc.* 337

Skinner, Q, *Liberty before Liberalism* (Cambridge, Canto Classics, 2012)

Sola, J, and Rendueles, C, 'Podemos, the Upheaval of Spanish Politics and the Challenge of Populism' (2018) 26 *Jo. of Contemporary European Studies* 99

Staloff, D, *Hamilton, Adams and Jefferson: The Politics of Enlightenment and the American Founding* (New York, Hill and Wang, 2007)

Steinfeld, R, 'Property and Suffrage in the Early American Republic' (1989) 41 *Stan. L. Rev.* 335

Stjernfelt, F, and Lauritzen, A, *Your Post has been Removed – Tech Giants and Freedom of Speech* (Berlin, Springer, 2020)

Stokes, S, 'Perverse Accountability: A Formal Model of Machine Politics with Evidence from Argentina' (2005) 99 *Am. Pol. Sci. Rev* 315

Stone, G, *Perilous Times – Free Speech in Wartime* (New York, WW Norton, 2004)

Suiter, J, Farrell, D, and Harris, C, 'The Irish Constitutional Convention: A Case of "High Legitimacy"?' in Reuchamps, M, and Suiter, J (eds) *Constitutional Deliberative Democracy in Europe* (Colchester, ECPR, 2016)

Sumption, J, *Trials of the State – Law and the Decline of Politics* (London, Profile Books, 2019)

Sunstein, C, *#Republic* (New Jersey, Princeton University Press, 2018)

Sunstein, C, 'Beyond the Republican Tradition' (1988) 97 *Yale L.J.* 1539

Thomson, J, *An Enquiry Concerning the Liberty and Licentiousness of the Press* (New York, Da Capo Press, 1970)

Tocqueville, A, *Democracy on America* (ed I Kramnick) (London, Penguin New Classics, 2003)

Tushnet, M, 'Policy Distortion and Democratic Debilitation: Comparative Illumination of the Countermajoritarian Difficulty' (1995) 94 *Mich. L. Rev.* 245

Tushnet, M, *Taking the Constitution Away from the Courts* (New Jersey, Princeton University Press, 1999)

Ullrich, V, *Hitler: Ascent 1889–1939* (New York, Vintage, 2017)

Unger, RM, *What Should Legal Analysis Become?* (London, Verso, 1996)

UN *Freedom of Expression and the Elections in the Digital Age* UN Research Paper 1/2019 (June 2019)

Upham, CW, *Life of Timothy Pickering* Vol 3 (France, Ulan Press, 2012)

Urbinati, N, *Democracy Disfigured: Opinion, Truth and the People* (Massachusetts, Harvard University Press, 2014)

Villari, P, *The Life and Times of Niccolò Machiavelli* (London, T Fisher Unwin, 1878)

Volokh, E, 'Trump has a Point: Facebook's Policing of Speech is Ominous' (2021) *Washington Post* 15 July

Voorhoof, D, 'Same Standards, Different Tools: The ECtHR and the Protection and Limitations of Freedom of Expression in the Digital Environment' in Bratza, N, et al *Human Rights Challenges in the Digital Age: Judicial Perspectives* (Strasbourg, European Court of Human Rights & Council of Europe, 2020)

Waldron, J, *Law and Disagreement* (New York, OUP, 1999)

Waldron, J, 'The Core of the Case against Judicial Review' (2006) 115 *Yale L.J.* 1346

Walker, J, 'The Censorship of the Press during the Reign of Charles II' (1950) 35 *History* 219

Wenman, M, *Agonistic Democracy – Constituent Power in the Era of Globalisation* (Cambridge, CUP, 2013)

Wharton, F, *State Trials of Washington and Adams* (Philadelphia, Carey & Hart, 1849)

Wilentz, S, *Chants Democratic: New York City and the Rise of the American Working Class* (New York, OUP, 2004)

Wilentz, S, *The Rise of American Democracy* (New York, WW Norton & Co 2006)

White, S, 'Citizens' Assemblies and Republican Democracy' in Leipold, B, Nabulsi, K, and White, S (eds) *Radical Republicanism – Recovering the Tradition's Popular Heritage* (Oxford, OUP, 2020)

Wolin, S, 'The Liberal/Democratic Divide: On Rawls's Political Liberalism' (1996) 24 *Pol. Theory* 97

Wood, G, *The Radicalism of the American Revolution* (New York, Vintage Books, 1993)

Yarrow, D, 'From Fact-checking to Value-checking: Normative Reasoning in the New Public Sphere' (2021) *Pol. Quarterly* at https://doi.org/10.1111/1467-923X.12999

Young, A, 'Populism and the UK Constitution' (2018) *C.L.P.* 17

INDEX

CPSIA information can be obtained
at www.ICGtesting.com
Printed in the USA
LVHW080212120922
728136LV00003B/26

9 781509 945825